Community Co

D0273952

Community Cohesion

A New Framework for Race and Diversity

Revised and Updated Edition

Ted Cantle
Institute of Community Cohesion, UK

LIS - LIBRARY

Date	Fund
8/7/09	Cwr

Order No.

2031747

University of Chester

palgrave
macmillan

© Ted Cantle 2005, 2008

All rights reserved. No reproduction, copy or transmission of this publication may be made without written permission.

No portion of this publication may be reproduced, copied or transmitted save with written permission or in accordance with the provisions of the Copyright, Designs and Patents Act 1988, or under the terms of any licence permitting limited copying issued by the Copyright Licensing Agency, Saffron House, 6-10 Kirby Street, London EC1N 8TS.

Any person who does any unauthorized act in relation to this publication may be liable to criminal prosecution and civil claims for damages.

The author has asserted his right to be identified as the author of this work in accordance with the Copyright, Designs and Patents Act 1988.

First published in hardback 2005

First published in paperback 2008 by
PALGRAVE MACMILLAN

Palgrave Macmillan in the UK is an imprint of Macmillan Publishers Limited, registered in England, company number 785998, of Houndmills, Basingstoke, Hampshire RG21 6XS.

Palgrave Macmillan in the US is a division of St Martin's Press LLC, 175 Fifth Avenue, New York, NY 10010.

Palgrave Macmillan is the global academic imprint of the above companies and has companies and representatives throughout the world.

Palgrave® and Macmillan® are registered trademarks in the United States, the United Kingdom, Europe and other countries.

ISBN-13: 978–1–4039–4114–5 hardback
ISBN-10: 1–4039–4114–9 hardback
ISBN-13: 978–0–230–21673–0 paperback
ISBN-10: 0–230–21673–0 paperback

This book is printed on paper suitable for recycling and made from fully managed and sustained forest sources. Logging, pulping and manufacturing processes are expected to conform to the environmental regulations of the country of origin.

A catalogue record for this book is available from the British Library.

Library of Congress Cataloging-in-Publication Data

Cantle, Ted, 1950–
    Community cohesion : a new framework for race and diversity / Ted Cantle.
        p. cm.
    Includes bibliographical references and index.
        ISBN 1–4039–4114–9 (cloth)   ISBN 0–230–21673–0 (pbk)
        1. Pluralism (Social sciences). 2. Multiculturalism. 3. Intergroup relations.
    4. Race relations. 5. Group identity. 6. Community. 7. Prejudices. I. Title.
HM1271.C36 2005
305.80091722—dc22   2005049673

10   9   8   7   6   5   4   3   2   1
17 16 15 14 13 12 11 10 09 08

Printed and bound in Great Britain by
CPI Antony Rowe, Chippenham and Eastbourne

Contents

List of Tables and Figure

Tables

Figure

Acknowledgements

I am grateful to all my friends and colleagues for their ideas and views which have greatly aided both the emergence of community cohesion and the development of this book.

1
Coming to Terms with Change

Anyone could be forgiven for believing that problems of racism, inter-ethnic conflict and prejudice and intolerance are simply intractable and that the idea of peace and harmony between different communities is just a naive pipe dream. After all, these problems seem to have been with us for all time, they also have been the cause of some of the most appalling atrocities and injustices and are present in some form or another in every part of the world. And what could be more understandable than wanting to favour our own kind? Surely it is natural to be suspicious about people who appear not to be 'like us' and with whom we are asked to believe that we have little in common? Is the 'fear of difference' then, simply a natural phenomenon with which we have to live?

However, any study of race and diversity tends to focus on the problems of multiculturalism and ignore the fact that many mixed ethnic and faith communities do live in harmony and that they are generally more successful in creative and entrepreneurial terms. In addition, we tend to forget that our ideas about who is 'different', about who we have some affinity to and understand and trust, change profoundly over time. Further, many of the people that are familiar with diverse communities, would not even agree that 'difference' is something we should fear, as it expands our knowledge and learning and provides additional and more interesting life experiences.

There is little choice in any event, for there is no turning the clock back to the days of rigid national borders built around homogeneous populations and where the vast majority of people had virtually no knowledge of, let alone affinity to, whoever lived beyond them. Migration is a fact of life and though it is often turned into a political issue, the march of global communications, international trade, business and tourism means that dynamic community relations are now the norm. Even greater diversity is inevitable – it is simply the way in which our world is moving – becoming 'smaller' in every way. The challenge for us, then, is to make multi-faith, multi-ethnic and multicultural communities work.

This chapter provides an overview of the development of our present state of race and community relations and the present debate about the nature of 'multiculturalism'. It also begins to develop the more fundamental question of, how 'difference' has been conceptualised and dealt with in the past and how and why we have also failed to tackle underlying societal attitudes and values. A new framework based on community cohesion is proposed.

The world on the move

The composition of many industrialised societies is changing. In little short of 50 years many, predominantly, white nation states have become multicultural, with the influx and growth of ethnic minorities on a significant scale. For the most part, ethnic minorities were encouraged to emigrate from their own countries, with the expectation of a higher standard of living and a welcome place – at least in the labour markets – of their new countries.

Hundreds of thousands of people moved from the West Indies and the Indian sub-continent to Britain to work in the textile factories, or the new National Health Service; from North Africa to France, Germany and other European countries, to boost production in the burgeoning car assembly plants and the manufacturing sector generally; from South America to North America to fill a wide range of labour market gaps; and from South Asia and across the globe to create a labour market of sufficient size to build the new nations of Australia and Canada. Migration also impacted on many other countries and, significantly, became aligned with clear racial or ethnic differences.

The increasing mobility of the world's population has been very marked. The number of people living outside their country of birth has doubled since the mid-1970s and now stands at about 175 million (UNDP, 2004, p. 30). The number is continuing to grow and at an accelerating rate. Globalisation of the economy, more accessible travel, the ease of communications and the expanded horizons of tourists, all combine to ensure that we really do live in a small world. However, it is ironic that whilst migration patterns have created tensions between ethnic groups, much of the present movement of population is attributable to inter-ethnic conflict, persecution and war in the originating countries. Over 70 per cent of the world's conflicts have an ethnic or religious dimension (Baldwin *et al.*, 2007) and the consequent flow of people fleeing from them, has increased in recent years and shows no sign of slowing down.

Tourism is adding to the world movement of population, particularly since the advent of cheaper air travel with, for example, some 60 million British tourists now leaving the country each year, and travelling to more far-flung places than ever before. In the other direction, over 26 million tourists travel to Britain and as many as 25,000 people even commute in to the country to work. Students now think little of studying abroad, with the western universities courting students from the Far East and even establishing campuses in countries like China and Malaysia. Global businesses, with global brands, also extend their operations and international trade knows virtually no boundaries as the movement of goods becomes relatively easy and low cost. From these, largely short-term movements of people, it is not surprising that an increasing number develop into permanent re-locations and migration patterns.

Perhaps, the most surprising migration trend has been 'tourism to residency', in which the middle classes of the more affluent countries gradually make the transition from the occasional visitor to second home owner and eventually buying a property for their permanent use, often settling into retirement in a new country. The exercise of choice in the housing market has now crossed national boundaries. It is estimated, for example, that 300,000 British citizens have moved permanently to Spain and many more live and work in other European countries, such as France, Greece, Cyprus and Italy (Blair, 2004). These out-migration figures are destined to rise, with 180,000 second homes being built in Spain alone (40 per cent of which are being purchased by Britons) and as new destinations such as Turkey, Bulgaria and Slovakia, become more popular due to price differentials.

The net result is that, in the nearly 200 countries of the world, there are some 5,000 ethnic groups and in two-thirds of these nations there is at least one substantial minority – an ethnic or religious group – that makes up at least 10 per cent of the population (UNDP, 2004, p. 2). However, the number of foreign citizens in developed nations is often exaggerated and is still quite small, with most of the European countries remaining under five per cent of population and virtually all under ten per cent in 1998. Countries with the largest programmes of 'nation-building', of course, have larger proportions, (of foreign-born) with the United States at 9.8 per cent, Canada at 17.4 per cent and Australia at 23.4 per cent (Stalker, 2001, p. 15).

Many developed nations have experienced both outward migration as well as inward migration over many years. Over the past two centuries, millions of Britons have left the United Kingdom to seek work in all parts of the world, especially America, Canada and Australia. There are 200,000 UK passport holders living in New Zealand alone and applicants from the UK account for almost a quarter of employment visas issued each year by the New Zealand government. The United Kingdom remains the largest source country for skilled migrants to Australia. Nationals from the UK form the third most important group of immigrant workers to Canada – behind only the United States and Mexico in 2002 (Blair, 2004). Many British people, it seems, take the opportunity to live in other countries and see it as their right to do so, whilst their former compatriots often remain hostile to the reverse trend – inward migration. In a recent radio interview, one unnamed migrant from Britain to Spain, for example, claimed that she had left Britain to live in Spain because 'there were too many foreigners in Britain'. But, a number of factors could lead to further, more dramatic and sudden population movement. Catastrophic change through the impact of global warming could create millions of 'eco-refugees'. Flooding is likely to have the most immediate and devastating impact, but changes in the world's climate could make huge areas of the world uninhabitable within relatively short periods. This could include parts of the developed world, such as the American mid-west, as well as those countries and continents already regularly ravaged by climate extremes, desertification and soil erosion. The Head of the European Environment Agency recently predicted 'climate refugees, probably within ten years' from the southern part of Europe due to increasing temperatures (McGlade, 2007). Some climate models also predict much colder climates for countries like the UK and Ireland, because of the potential breakdown of the Gulf Stream. Sea levels are rising and are forecast to rise another 88 cm by 2100 threatening 100 million people globally who currently live below this level. The number of people affected by floods worldwide has already risen from seven million in the 1960s to 150 million today (Blair, 2004a). Bangladesh is perhaps one of the countries at most immediate risk from flooding with tens of millions of people potentially affected, even on the mid-range scenarios that have been developed. Violent storms and hurricanes now regularly ravage the Caribbean and the United States, destroying the infrastructure upon which normal life depends and necessitating millions of people to move away on a temporary basis. What once seemed far-fetched and distant possibilities are now very real threats, not just for future generations but for the present one too.

In the even shorter term, the process of EU enlargement is enabling many thousands of people from the poorer sections of Eastern Europe to move unhindered across European boundaries, though the potential impact of this was used to raise the political temperature. For example, in early 2004 the British press worked itself into a frenzy about the tens of thousands of Roma people or 'Gypsies', then only mobile within a limited number of eastern European states but apparently poised to move in great numbers to Britain (Ouseley, 2004). This proved to be scaremongering of the worst sort, and the focus has more recently shifted to the prospect of Turkey joining the EU with the 'clash of cultures' being the source of new consternation.

The continuing process of migration remains a political and social challenge, largely because the attempts at managing it were limited to the economic sphere, with little investment in the management of settlement of people into communities. The necessary support to migrants, to help them to integrate, along with the necessary support to assist the host community to come to terms with change and to provide additional resources to prevent conflicts over facilities and services, have all been lacking, or simply too little too late. Only now, under the banner of community cohesion, are guides and support processes beginning to be developed.

Migration has, more than any other factor, been responsible for the growth in support for far right parties across Europe, where they regularly attract around 20 per cent of the popular vote.

However, more generally, globalisation is changing our perceptions of race and culture, making some boundaries redundant and yet, creating new divisions and threats. We need new paradigms to help us to conceptualise this change and to develop policy and practical responses to it. These are more urgent than ever before.

Learning the lessons of the past

The position and status of foreigners in the nation state has changed very quickly. Prior to the Second World War, most foreigners were simply seen as 'aliens', people who would seldom be invited to become part of the host nation. Their rights were limited and they did not expect equal treatment. As most European nations are the products of centuries of successive waves of immigrants, often the result of conflict, war and persecution, aliens were eventually assimilated over the generations, becoming almost indistinguishable from the host community. Nevertheless, the pace of change was slow with, perhaps, only the Jewish community managing to remain a significant and visible international minority over hundreds of years, with a diaspora identity and culture that transcended the many nations in which they were to be found. Small black communities were also resident in a number of European cities in the early part of the twentieth century (and earlier), often settling in major ports that had had some connection with the slave trade, but without the means to maintain an international conception of themselves and often surviving as a beleaguered minority. A very different picture is evident today, with modern communications allowing transnational identities to be much more easily supported and even reinforced.

As the twentieth century unfolded, nations were still grappling with the development of the concept of equal rights for their own citizens. Political power was only beginning to slip from the hands of the landed class and the right to vote was still related to property rights. These were societies in which everyone 'knew their place', in which rigid class divisions and deference defined social relations. Women did not enjoy a number of basic entitlements, let alone equality; universal suffrage was not yet established. In these circumstances, the promotion of foreigners' rights to equality before the law was unlikely to be a priority. The pace of social and political change was, however, quickening. The growth of mass political movements, the real possibility of revolution and the rights of the common people moved inexorably up the political agenda. By the Second World War, the political landscape had changed forever and the days of empires and colonialism were coming to an end (at least in a political, if not economic, sense). The colonies of European nations were gaining independence, just at a time when more labour was required to fuel post-war reconstruction and economic expansion. Mass production of consumer goods, fashion items and clothing, the rapid expansion of the automotive industry and the development of service industries required to look after the new 'affluent workers', meant that many nations looked beyond their borders for extra labour. Where better than their former colonies and dependencies – people with an understanding of the cultural and linguistic requirements of the host countries?

But just as earlier immigrants had found, the new arrivals were soon the subject of racism and discrimination and conflicts developed in the newly settled neighbourhoods. The host community, which was almost entirely white and overwhelmingly Christian was, at best, ambivalent towards their new fellow workers and, in some cases, implacably hostile. Attempts were made in Britain to stem the tide of immigration almost as soon as it had started, but this had to be balanced with the evident continuing need for labour and the need to keep faith with the people from the colonies who had always been afforded special status as British subjects with the right to enter and live in Britain. Similar debates were held in many other European countries and especially those, like Holland, that had also had a number of former colonies and dependencies. The first response of the British Government, again in parallel with developments in other European countries, was to, by degrees, to try to institute controls on the numbers of immigrants, from the early 1960s. In Britain the number of immigrants from the Commonwealth had nevertheless reached 336,000 by 1951 and 942,300 by 1966. Crucially, however, the number of black and Asian people had grown from 74,500 in 1951 to 595,100 in 1966. The number of immigrants from Ireland, Cyprus and Malta had also grown significantly (Rose *et al.*, 1969, p. 97).

The 'immigration problem' was now, more evidently than ever before, a matter of 'race'. To the people of Britain and the many other white European nations that had for so many generations dominated the world, maintained empires and controlled international trade, their evident military and economic superiority was synonymous with their whiteness. Their 'pecking order' had been constructed over many years, reinforced by their history and by lifelong socialisation processes. Black and Asian people, migrants from southern European states – and most foreigners – were by definition inferior 'races'. Yet, they were now suddenly to be welcomed in to the nation state and to be regarded as equals. This change had come upon these countries in dramatic fashion; empires were fast disappearing, and people from those empires and elsewhere were moving into their communities, appearing amongst them as doctors and nurses, or working alongside them in factories and serving them in the corner shop – and in Britain at least it was increasingly recognised that migrants were here to stay.

Whilst governments again turned to the use of immigration controls to assuage the concern of the host white communities, they also had to respond to the immigrant communities that were demanding an end to the discrimination and, in particular, to the unfair treatment in housing and employment. Governments were forced to recognise that the disaffection of both the host white community and the immigrant communities would lead to even greater potential for conflict. Immigration controls were no longer an adequate response. They therefore developed two further approaches (which are dealt with in more detail in Chapter 2). First, anti-discrimination measures were introduced. In Britain, these did not appear until the mid 1960s, with the Race Relations Acts of 1965 and 1968, following many years of wrangling and heart searching about the rights and wrongs of immigration (see for example, Pannell and Brockway, 1965).

Second, there were some very limited attempts to 'promote good race relations' by working with the white community to improve their understanding of the black and minority ethnic communities and by promoting more effective support for immigrants to help them settle and integrate. In Britain, this approach has been enshrined in legislation since the 1968 Act in some form or other, though it has never been more than a marginal activity with very little energy and resources behind it. By contrast, the 'equalities agenda' burgeoned, with an increasing weight of legislative programmes, which were also extended to other disadvantaged groups. The failure to invest in promoting good race relations and helping people, especially from the host community, to come to terms with change is of great significance and very relevant to the present day community cohesion agenda. Many lessons can be learnt from this period, especially the need to attend to the social and psychological needs of communities; to develop a clear awareness of and commitment to, the need for change; to provide a realistic level of local resources to reduce competing demands upon them and; the need for clear leadership, in which programmes are mainstreamed, rather than left to poorly resourced voluntary organisations.

The developments in Britain were, nevertheless, relatively progressive compared to other European countries and represented a more coherent, albeit limited, national strategy than attempts elsewhere, which were even more piecemeal and localised. However, they had been preceded by anti-discrimination measures in the United States in the 1940s and 50s and by more radical 'affirmative action' in the early 1960s, culminating in the 'monumental piece of social legislation' – the Civil Rights Act of 1964 (Micklethwait and Wooldrige, 2004, p. 54). The enlistment of hundreds of thousands of black servicemen in the Second World War (and in subsequent conflicts, most notably Vietnam), could only enhance the demands for equal rights. The Civil Rights movement in the United States grew and developed with the enactment of further significant civil rights legislation in the 1960s, including the 1965 Voting Rights Act and a further Civil Rights Act in 1968, as well as a range of social programmes to tackle education and health inequalities. The period of non-violent and peaceful protest under the civil rights movement, however, seemed to pass with the death of its most powerful advocate, Martin Luther King in 1968. It gave way to a more radical approach, epitomised by 'black power' (Ratcliffe, 2004, p. 130) the ripples from which soon spread across the Atlantic. Many European countries were experiencing similar tensions by the 1970s; the black and Asian communities in developed countries had grown in confidence, would no longer accept either second-class citizenship, nor take kindly to being patronised with attempts at initiatives designed 'to understand them'. Young second generation black men were beginning to take to the streets.

Primary migration into Europe was ended, or all but ended, in the early 1970s. Britain acted first in 1971, followed by Germany and Denmark in 1973 and France and a number of other countries in 1974 (MacMaster, 2001, p. 188). But by then countries were having to re-define themselves as 'multicultural', including countries like Germany, where their 'guest-worker' schemes had enabled them to harbour an illusion that the migration was temporary. Further, most of the European states had little option but to allow family dependents to join the existing migrants, which consolidated their positions as de facto citizens.

Gradually the anti-discrimination legislation was extended, for example, in Britain it covered 'indirect' forms, through the 1976 Race Relations Act. However, this has only had a limited effect with black and minority ethnic households remaining at the bottom end of virtually every social and economic indicator and with limited attitudinal change amongst the host community. In 1980 and 1981 there were riots in Bristol, Liverpool, Brixton in London and elsewhere bringing with them a recognition of the impact of poverty and social disadvantage, through the recommendations of the Scarman Report in 1981. Another wave of riots nevertheless took place in other cities with substantial black and minority populations, such as Birmingham and Nottingham, in the mid-1980s. The Macpherson Report in 1999 following the murder of black teenager, Stephen Lawrence, moved the equalities agenda on still further by focussing on 'institutional racism'. It was followed by the Race Relations (Amendment) Act in 2000, which ensured that all public bodies had further race relations measures imposed upon them. But 'disturbances' again took place in 2001, this time in the northern cities Bradford, Burnley and Oldham and, on this occasion, they involved the Asian community of Pakistani and Bangladeshi heritage.

Over this period, the focus of legislation had gradually shifted from the individual and from individual acts of discrimination, to tackling social and organisational forms, but was still based on controlling behaviour and making good the deficits faced by Black and Minority Ethnic (BME) communities. Progress had, nevertheless, been made though not yet had the desired effect of either delivering equal opportunities, nor of convincing BME communities that they were accepted and could attain an equal stake in their society (Modood *et al.*, 1994, p. 184). Relatively little attention had also been given to tackling the underlying causes of prejudice and discrimination.

The limitations of this approach soon became apparent. First, as the agenda was almost entirely focussed on people from black and minority backgrounds to enable them to compete on a more equal basis, it tended to perpetuate the very myths that the agenda sought to address, namely that disadvantaged individuals need special treatment to overcome their apparent inadequacies. The backlash against the 'affirmative action' programmes in the United States, which relies on positive discrimination, is a more obvious expression of this, reinforcing claims of preferential treatment and 'problematising' the black community. It can also be argued that affirmative action, or positive discrimination, makes people more conscious of group differences and more resentful of them (Kymlicka, 1995, p. 4). The same argument could be applied to the British approach of 'positive action' (see Chapter 6), which stops short of discrimination in favour of a particular group and generally only provides development opportunities, but is also seen in the same light. However, without some form of intervention it is difficult to see how minority groups are ever going to be empowered to catch up. Legislation to prevent direct discriminatory rules and behaviours has, of course, been directed at the white community, but little attempt was made to influence the underlying attitudes and values upon which they were based. These measures did have some success, but the justification for them had not been universally accepted and more covert and discriminatory behaviours began to emerge and the opportunity for a more open – and more difficult – debate was rarely encouraged. Anti-discrimination measures also depended upon quite invasive procedures to check and monitor potentially discriminatory actions, such as the use of employment targets by ethnic origin. This process does allow organisational blockages to be identified and addressed, but also tends to create a focus on the black and minority communities as the 'problem'.

Second, remedial measures were also focussed upon disadvantaged communities as a whole, providing resources to build their capacity and confidence, ensuring that they were consulted and involved, translating communications into minority languages, developing their understanding and providing 'access pathways' to social and economic goals. This again created the perception of preferential treatment – even though equality of opportunity had not yet even begun to be approached – and also largely ignored the white community who were experiencing as much, if not more, difficulty in coming to terms with the change and were often seeking to protect their own interests. 'Separateness' was also reinforced by the focus on identifiable communities; many social programmes being based upon distinct residential areas or separate educational and employment initiatives.

Very little thought was given as to how the host community and the new minorities might actually relate to each other and how mutual respect and understanding might develop, let alone how the host community might begin to welcome the new diversity in their midst. This lack of attention to relationships was despite a statutory duty on both central and local agencies to 'promote good race relations' over several decades (this is also discussed further in Chapter 2). Consequently, though multicultural societies now have substantial minority communities, many of the predominantly white communities still do not accept the idea – let alone the reality – of multiculturalism and see it as a threat, rather than as an enrichment of their lives. The very terms 'multicultural' or 'diversity' do not necessarily resonate with them. And many of the ethnic minority youngsters that took part in the British riots in Bradford, Burnley and Oldham in the summer of 2001, as second and third generation British Asians, did not feel that they had an equal stake in their own land, nor did they believe that their ethnicity, faith and culture was accepted within the multicultural framework.

The 2001 riots, and the subsequent reports (Cantle, 2001; Clarke, 2001; Denham, 2001; Ritchie, 2001), together with a report into Bradford commissioned prior to the riots (Ouseley, 2001) brought about a major re-think of Government policy on race and community relations. The concept of 'community cohesion' was quickly developed to tackle the 'parallel lives' (Cantle, 2001) experienced by white and black communities and the resulting ignorance and lack of understanding and trust that pervaded so many of the relationships between communities. This did not in any way imply the abandonment of the 'equality agenda'. Equality of opportunity and tackling racial discrimination are a central part of the community cohesion approach and the lack of any real sense of fairness in community relations would, in itself, threaten the 'common vision and sense of belonging' and undermine the idea that 'different backgrounds are appreciated and valued', set out in the definition of community cohesion (see Figure 2.1). It would also be difficult to imagine a successful and cohesive society where substantial differences between the rich and poor communities are juxtaposed. Severely disadvantaged communities will inevitably develop into disaffected communities if they believe that they have no real opportunities to grow and develop.

Black and minority ethnic communities, who believe that they are routinely discriminated against on the arbitrary basis of visible differences, may well choose to build a common bond of disaffection both within nation states and across national borders, embracing a transnational identity, rather than with their fellow citizens. This is of course in contrast to expectations that minorities will 'integrate' and see themselves as citizens of their host countries. But identity is not automatically defined by the nation state in which one happens to live, even where citizenship is given by birth, let alone subsequently granted through naturalisation. This association will inevitably be more difficult for minorities that believe they are discriminated against, denied equal opportunities and made to feel generally unwelcome and especially if they have the option of retaining and reinforcing a diaspora affinity. In a modern world with advanced communications, cultural reinforcement through contact with people of the same heritage is relatively easy and those bonds will be all the stronger if the national common sense of belonging is limited. In such circumstances, minorities are likely to cling to their cultural, linguistic and religious symbols, rather than feel an affinity with, let alone integrate into, a society that appears hostile to them.

However, the notion of 'difference' is generally ill-defined in many of the debates about multiculturalism. What constitutes 'difference' may be visible, though often many of the differences that we regard as being significant have few if any such obvious distinctions. The significance of difference is socially constructed around a wide range of variables in both the private and public realms including social, economic and cultural factors. Multiculturalists have tended to regard all of these differences as being of equal value, to be defended as a means of protecting the heritage of each culture and as a means of avoiding any tendency towards assimilation. Given the history of racism, such a defence has been understandable.

The usefulness of the concept of 'multiculturalism' is now beginning to be questioned, however, in part because of the way in which it encompasses such a wide spectrum of difference and fails to reconcile them within a societal framework. Further, it has, for some commentators at least, actually become the vehicle by which divisions and inequalities are reinforced:

> Multiculturalism ... has not simply entrenched the divisions created by racism, but made cross-cultural interaction more difficult by encouraging people to assert their cultural differences. And in areas where there was both a sharp division between Asian and white communities, and where both communities suffered disproportionately from unemployment and social deprivation, the two groups began to view these problems through the lens of cultural and racial differences, blaming each other for their problems. The inevitable result was the riots. (Malik, 2002)

Community cohesion, then, became established on the basis of trying to create shared experiences and values, rather than continuing to entrench separation and to reinforce differences. Concern was, in particular, expressed about the role of the statutory agencies involved in regeneration and housing, but with increasing recognition of the role played by the voluntary sector in 'capacity building' differences rather than reinforcing similarities. This is explored in greater detail in Chapters 2 and 6.

Multiculturalism and difference

Most advanced industrialised nations are now 'multicultural' – if only in the sense that they have significant black and minority ethnic populations who have established themselves over several decades, with second and third generation descendants. The extent to which minority groups see themselves as full members of that society and whether they are accepted by the majority population as permanent and equal citizens is another matter. Progress, in multicultural terms, is generally only measured numerically, such as by the number of black and minority ethnic recruits into the higher echelons of public service, a reduction in the number of racial attacks, or complaints regarding employment discrimination. Little has been done to provide a deeper understanding of the social processes involved, nor to clearly establish and promote the terms upon which minorities relate to society as a whole. There has also been a failure to clearly establish where each nation stands on the multicultural axis: from the 'assimilation' model, in which the identity and characteristics of minorities are simply merged into the prevailing culture, to the 'co-existence' model, in which different groups and the host community retain a high degree of separateness, and in which each community maintains distinct values and lifestyles.

However, even this 'axis of multiculturalism', provides only a limited approach to what, in reality, is a much more complex issue. Many aspects of difference have little or no impact upon societal cohesiveness and could be maintained as a means of supporting distinct cultures. Some differences are structural, like those in the economic sphere, and can have a profound impact upon the success of individuals and their communities; others are generally confined to the private realm rather than in the public sphere. The 'degree of difference' set out in Chapter 3, therefore attempts to separate some of the components of 'cultural' difference. It is recognised that each of these domains are entwined with the others and, therefore, a perfect model is not possible. It is also recognised that the present discussion about 'multiculturalism' soon becomes entangled with wider political debates in which immigration and multiculturalism are defended, or opposed, because of the way in which they have become linked to racist and anti-racist theology.

Multicultural societies now need to come to terms with the domains of difference and to develop a greater consensus, not only to agree upon the areas which should be rigorously defended, but also where the bonds between fellow citizens require a greater sense of commonality. Further, more agreement about how to achieve such a consensus will also be required and it is suggested that this will depend upon breaking down the separateness between the minority and majority community and between the different minority communities themselves. Mutual trust and a common sense of belonging will only be created through constant interaction and shared experiences.

Whilst much of the pseudo science that underpinned racist ideology has been debunked (discussed in Chapter 4) there is a danger that the same robust approach has not yet been shown to new theories which have developed the idea of 'people like us' as a primordial, or 'natural' affinity. Ethnic and faith divisions have now begun to replace those based upon ideas about 'race' but are also often presented as fixed and immutable, rather than socially and politically constructed. This allows the idea that solidarity is undermined by cultural diversity – people who are 'not like us' – to flourish and seems to be a new and particularly dangerous line of argument in support of a deterministic definition of 'culture'. This view also unfortunately appears to be shared by those who promote minority cultures, but do so as rigid conceptions, with unchanging values and behaviours.

Ethnic identities are also constantly changing (Cornell and Hartmann, 1998), even diasporic boundaries are not fixed (Soysal, 2000) and a homogeneous representation of minority cultures is no more justifiable than a selective and rigid idea of 'Britishness', or any other national culture. The idea of 'natural' affinity is also discussed further in Chapter 4 and is rejected, along with the view that ethnic differences and divisions (and those based on faith, class and other 'cultural' affinity) ever have any more significance than the social and political meaning that we ascribe to them.

This theme is taken up again in Chapter 5 where 'difference' is related to ideas about identity and citizenship and in which it is suggested that political unity, generally encompassed under the principles of nationality and citizenship, should provide the key requirements of societal cohesiveness, rather than any attempt to agree on a national identity which embraces so many different subjective views in both the public and private realms. Establishing a clearer sense of political unity is, nevertheless, no easy option, especially as mainstream politicians have been reluctant to enter into such debate because of fears that it may either provide extremists with a platform, or create uncertainties within the minority communities upon whose vote they may depend. It may however, also reflect the same ambivalence of political leaders on this issue, as is evident in the community as a whole.

In a multicultural country there must be a clear political will to reach a consensus on what level of 'difference' is accepted and which differences are acceptable. The practical arrangements also threaten to confound many of the theories, largely because 'multiculturalism' does not exist in any meaningful way in many of the communities that make up the so-called multicultural nations, with the same physical separation of minority communities established at the point of initial migration, continuing to a greater or lesser extent thereafter. This has helped to maintain the pretence in the eyes of the majority, that the minorities are separate and distinct, unwilling or unable to develop an affinity to a different culture and simply not part of the same society. It may also create a feeling, from the perspective of the minorities, that they are being denied access to the host society and must cling to their former identities and affinities. Whilst the initial separation often arises from a simple development of the historic divisions linked to the settlement patterns of successive waves of immigrants moving in to the most affordable – and worst – housing areas, it is closely linked to economic circumstances and social class. Nevertheless, from the majority population's point of view these enclaves represent almost separate states, limited to the margins and which do not change the overall nature of *their* society – except for the poorer white communities, who often compete for the same territory and who become the most fertile breeding ground for racism.

In Britain, the ethnic minority population remains surprisingly concentrated, with London accounting for around 50 per cent of the entire BME population and with most of the remainder heavily concentrated in a small number of urban areas. This also means that the white population is similarly 'concentrated' in other areas and that many youngsters attend either all-white schools or all-black schools and that they grow up in monocultural areas, with little or no real experience of multiculturalism. Whilst the BME population has grown significantly in recent years, most of that growth has been within those areas that already had an above average proportion of the BME population. A number of English regions, such as in the North East, the East, the South West and Wales have also seen an increase – and even a doubling in percentage terms – but from a very low base and still remain almost exclusively white, with the exception of a few urban enclaves (though the recent influx of largely white Europeans from the A8 accession states has created a new population dynamic). The geographic concentration of the BME community has therefore changed little over the last 40 years or so and has actually been reinforced by the recent trends. This clearly has an impact on many areas of daily life, particularly schooling, employment and leisure patterns.

There is a very similar pattern in other multicultural countries; almost half the inhabitants of Toronto and Los Angeles are foreign born (UNDP, 2004) and immigrants to France, the Netherlands and other European countries still gravitate towards the major cities like Paris and Amsterdam where the BME community remains heavily concentrated.

Even within the multicultural cities, there is evidence of considerable levels of separation, to the extent that the relationship between communities might also be characterised as one of 'parallel lives' (see for example, Hussain *et al.*, 2007 and Johnson *et al.*, 2006). The inner city 'ghettoes', mono-cultural schools, separate employment patterns and distinct faith and cultural associations, are simply seen as part of the natural fabric of many cities. But whilst it is the case that some of the segregation is due to purely economic factors (which, in itself is problematic), settlement patterns also reflect preferences of both a positive nature, such as people choosing to live in an area which is supportive of their culture and also, for negative reasons, for example, because people feel unsafe and insecure in different areas.

The experience of multiculturalism will therefore be very varied within what are essentially multicultural countries. A Commission for Racial Equality Report indicated that 94 per cent of whites in Britain had no friends from other ethnic groups (CRE, 2004b) and many people will have no experience of, nor meaningful contact with, other ethnic groups. For many people, interaction will therefore be limited to 'visible contact' through the shared experience of travelling, shopping or other mundane activities and will not amount to an activity in which the barriers might be expected to be broken down – some studies have actually shown a correlation between proximity and anti-black sentiment (Brown, 1995, p. 237) with differences being observed, but neither understood, nor tolerated and accepted. Again, this points to the need to reinforce the equalities agenda, so that equal opportunities can underpin integration in the working environment and other structural processes.

Settlement patterns are therefore important on a number of levels and the paucity of Government statistics has been the subject of heated debate. The Independent Panel on Community Cohesion recommended that the deficiency be rectified by routine monitoring by the Office of National Statistics (ONS), which could then be used to inform policy (Cantle, 2004). The population estimates at a local level prepared by ONS have been contested by a number of local government agencies, especially as funding is dependent upon resident numbers (iCoCo, 2007). In Britain, there have also been relatively few attempts to map and understand the segregation and integration of communities. Patterns are not routinely examined, let alone monitored and the Census and other records have failed to keep pace with the new categories of migrant communities. Settlement patterns can, however, indicate the nature of discrimination, the extent to which different groups feel able to move to other areas, either for reasons of safety and security, or because in a cultural sense, they are perceived as 'not for them'. This also applies to the white community where, again, movement is neither properly mapped, nor understood – and is also ill-defined, especially in relation to new migrant communities.

In Britain there have been a few studies of the phenomenon of 'white flight', where white families leave areas because of the perceived negative impact of a growing number of black and ethnic minority people on the area. It has been difficult to determine whether white households leave because of these negative views or simply because white families tend to be more affluent and move to more expensive residential areas as part of ongoing social mobility. However, a number of studies, particularly those that record the expressed preferences of white households themselves clearly indicate a degree of white flight (see, for example, Simpson *et al.*, 2007). The anticipation of a fall in house prices, which is of course an embodiment of the same negative views and a component of white flight, has also been one of the recorded drivers, sometimes encouraged by local estate agents hoping to profit from the increased activity. The desire to exercise parental choice and to move into different catchment areas for schools, which are seen as more desirable and where the white intake is still predominant, is also an increasing consideration.

It is essential to develop a clearer understanding of the nature of 'segregation' and how the term is used. The literal meaning suggests a separation of particular groups, which is decreed by law and enforced by the state, or created by the presence of such significant barriers that the ability to move to other areas cannot be freely exercised and is 'involuntary'. However, 'segregation' has become more generally used to denote an area, which is dominated by one group and effectively mono-cultural. The term 'self-segregation' has also been employed to describe this process, where it is assumed that particular communities have preferred to live in separate areas – in other words, the segregation is 'voluntary' (although such assumptions often overstate the real constraints upon free choice). However, whatever the cause of 'segregation' the impact on inter-community relations is profound and the lack of contact between communities can lead to ignorance and irrational fears of each other, especially where extremists seek to capitalise upon that ignorance and to demonise one or more communities.

At one extreme, segregation has been described as 'parallel lives' a concept first established by the Independent Review Team which considered the significance of the disturbances in a number of British towns and cities in 2001 (Cantle, 2001). This demonstrated that the physical separation of BME households in distinct housing areas had become underpinned by a complete lack of contact between people from different communities. Social and economic ties had lessened, or ceased altogether and there was little or no contact of any sort between different groups, such that

> separate educational arrangements, community and voluntary bodies, employment, places of worship, language, social and cultural networks, means that many communities operate on the basis of a series of parallel lives, (which) often do not seem to touch at any point, let alone promote any meaningful interchanges. (Ibid., p. 9)

However, it is possible to distinguish this 'exclusive' pattern of segregation from a more open 'critical mass' model, in which a given community is clustered in a particular area, but do not occupy it exclusively. Their concentration is sufficient to support a range of distinct cultural facilities and a support network that helps to preserve cultural identity whilst the presence of other groups within the same area means that contact and interaction can still be facilitated through shared local activities and by mixed intake schools and integrated employment and entrepreneurial arrangements. In these circumstances, the 'layers of separation' will not be cumulative and interaction will be able to take place at some level.

It is suggested, therefore, that in order to provide a better understanding of the dynamics of community relations and particularly the interaction between communities, the 'layers of separation' should be explored in each case (discussed in Chapter 3) to distinguish many different patterns of 'segregation' and to develop subsequent policy responses.

The causes of racism

Social policy has generally been framed on the basis that racism is a regrettable, but inevitable, part of multicultural life. The focus has been very much one of trying to prevent discrimination and to provide equal opportunities, with little by way of the examination of the root causes of tensions and conflicts. Strategies to reduce inter-ethnic tension and conflict, and the 'fear of difference', have been notable by their absence. The causes of most tensions are simply seen as 'historical', with the divisions between communities lost in the mists of time. In so far as the causes of racism have been addressed, it has generally been on the basis of controlling the actions and behaviours of individuals, rather than considering the social and psychological processes involved in inter-ethnic divisions and hostility. In the 1960s a small attempt was made in Britain to 'promote good race relations', but these measures were very limited, left largely to under-resourced voluntary agencies and not taken seriously and, in any event they only lasted for less than a decade, after which they were largely forgotten (even though both the CRE and local authorities retained a statutory duty in this respect).

The relations between ethnic and faith communities have been shaped of course, by historic patterns of development. The legacy of colonialism is still very evident and follows on from centuries dominated by a European view of the world, in which the white nations were regarded as 'civilisation' and other 'races' seen as genetically inferior. But whilst in general, the white nations had seen themselves as superior to black and Asian people, many complex divisions between nations, ethnicities and faiths have led to mistrust, prejudice and discrimination. All nations and ethnic groups, have their own 'pecking order', it seems, which puts themselves at the top and others below them – an order which is generally reversed and re-ordered by the 'others' involved. In this sense 'racism' is a relatively simple concept. It is based upon a shared belief that one group is congenitally inferior and that the other is congenitally superior. The same dogma, however, is now beginning to be used by people who believe in superiority of their faith, their ethnicity or some other identifiable group characteristic.

In fact, these ethnocentric ideas are so prevalent that we sometimes lose sight of the fact that they are also part of the same unfounded and irrational belief systems. We can only look back with incredulity at some of the past ideas, for example, the Nazi belief in a superior Aryan 'race', or that South Africans could be divided by whether a pencil could be retained in their hair – though none of this prevents us from holding similarly irrational views today. At least the eugenicist theories and the debates linking intelligence to 'race' are now largely seen as being in the past and the proof against them, whether in the form of debunked pseudo-scientific research, or the evidence from our own eyes from working with people who were once condemned as inferior and are now performing at the highest levels, has clearly demonstrated that everyone, irrespective of ethnicity, faith and gender is capable of all levels of attainment.

The 'science of racism' conveniently provided justification to those individuals who might otherwise be accused of unjust and irrational behaviour. Racism and discrimination perpetrated by individuals, or by one community against another, however, may well have a rational, if unacceptable, basis. The denial of equal rights and opportunities by one community – generally the host or majority community – in order to safeguard their privileged and advantageous position is not unusual, particularly where they themselves feel insecure in social and economic terms. As such a position is clearly socially and morally unjust and indefensible, the dominant group will often seek to justify their privileged position by the creation and perpetuation of prejudicial views and myths – possibly backed by spurious scientific theory – about the subordinate community. The need to implement corrective socio-economic and structural measures to tackle the very real conflicts over resources is therefore clearly necessary.

Much of the legislation over the last 50 years or so has been founded on the principle of controlling the behaviour of individuals and is aimed at either ensuring equal opportunities, or preventing discrimination, in a wide range of social, economic and political activities, rather than changing attitudes and values. Of course, the introduction of legislation and the debate that surrounds it, can in itself, assist the process of change by drawing upon the respect for the force of the law. Conditioning behaviour over a period of time, will also begin to instil a renewed sense of right and wrong and the values inherent in the legislation may well be internalised. However, such legislation can also reinforce the idea that those apparently benefiting from the protection of the law are in need of it because of an innate inferiority. In any event, years of such legislation have also proved to be of limited effect in many areas, with racism and religious bigotry remaining evident, simply rising or falling depending on a range of political, economic and social factors.

The establishment of a fair and cohesive society will need to underpin any development of the 'rights agenda' with a much more effective approach to attitudinal change, ensuring that the 'fear of difference' is constantly assuaged by regular and positive interaction between different communities. Many of the social psychological theories now support the view that whilst we categorise 'others' and create groups based on stereotypes and a perception of difference, regular and positive contact between communities can create a shared understanding and remove much of the anxiety that such differences represent any real threat. This is discussed further in Chapter 4.

Modern multicultural societies are also characterised by segregation, with historic patterns of settlement being reinforced by separate schooling, social, cultural and other economic spheres. Cross cultural contact, based upon a growing scientific body of knowledge in 'contact theory' has demonstrated that prejudice can be broken down effectively where out-group relationships are facilitated. A range of special programmes are now being developed (discussed in Chapter 6) but are perhaps only necessary as a means of compensating for the structural divisions and separation which militate against natural inter-group contact in the course of daily life.

We also need to look beyond the immediate confines of the race debate and the 'fear of difference' is by no means confined to ethnic and faith divisions. Gays and lesbians, travellers and people characterised as 'disabled' face issues which are similar, with pre-conceived notions and stereotypes creating barriers and allowing discriminatory behaviour to be justified on the basis of an imagined inequality. There is much good practice in other fields that is now enshrined in social policy. For example, children with special needs are increasingly being taught within mainstream schools, and mentally ill people are now often cared for in community settings. These developments have not been without controversy and proposals to move people out of institutional care still meet with concern, and even hostility, in many areas. However, once provision has been established in the community, everyday contact generally results in the removal of fears and allows the differences that people have to be seen in a more rational and reasoned way. Interaction allows people to be appreciated for what they are, rather than what the popular misconceptions might suggest. This interaction will not be successful, however, if it is superficial and simply allows the myths and prejudices to be reinforced. A number of pre-conditions for contact are therefore necessary. (The theory and practice of interaction and cross-cultural contact is discussed in Chapters 4 and 6.)

In Britain community cohesion work has been developing over the last five or six years and whilst the practice is still continuing, there is increasing evidence that the new approaches have had some success. The recent national review of community cohesion conducted by a government appointed Commission produced a welter of evidence in support of the cohesion agenda (Commission on Integration and Cohesion (CIC), 2007). This is further discussed in Chapter 6, where links are made to the work in other countries which appear to be developing programmes based on similar principles, such as the work in Frankfurt to reduce the host community's fear of the 'other' by developing shared experiences and mutual trust (Sandercock, 2004, p. 259). In other cases the circumstances may be very different, for example, the work on inter-ethnic conflict in India, the reconciliation of ethnic groups in Rwanda and the bringing together of Jews and Arabs in parts of Israel, where the experiences are no less relevant. Also, at a much more mundane level, work has been undertaken in several countries, to settle asylum seekers in hostile environments, by working with the host community to 'buddy' new arrivals, such as in the Canadian 'host programme', which enables cross-cultural contact to be established in the first instance. Similarly the work in schools to explain why asylum seekers have come to live in their area and to make sure their culture and background is understood, has also had some success in ensuring greater understanding and reducing the ignorance about different groups.

Further, the South African approach to 'truth and reconciliation', following the ending of apartheid, was a testament to a much more radical approach of building bridges between communities. Given that this has not yet been fully supported by work to close the social and economic gaps between the communities, it remains to be seen whether cohesion is possible with such differences in lifestyle and life opportunities reinforcing ethnic or religious boundaries, but there are a growing number of reconciliation programmes in different parts of the world.

The impact of immigration

Modern democracies have failed as yet, to create truly harmonious and just societies in which opportunities are equal and majority and minority communities tolerate and respect each other's differences. As multiculturalism continues – and accelerates – so the need to respond to what is already a difficult and challenging agenda will require new impetus. Community cohesion cannot claim to be the complete answer to this challenge but does represent an attempt to both understand the basis of prejudice and the resulting discriminatory behaviour and to confront their causes. Past attempts to tackle discrimination and promote equalities has had some success, but this has relied upon the introduction of systems and processes to control behaviour rather than tackle underlying attitudes and values.

Most controversy still revolves around the subject of immigration, which appears to constantly renew the idea of 'difference' and continually re-open the basis upon which longer standing migrants are settled. Immigration is, therefore, rarely debated in relation to the real practical and present issues and inevitably draws upon preconceived ideas based upon past controversies. Moreover, the debate has become polarised: to support inward migration is to be a supporter of multiculturalism, and a liberal anti-racist; to oppose migration, is to be racist and illiberal. With debate constrained in such limited terms, however, it is not possible to address more significant and real questions about the sort of multicultural country that we want to become and the nature and extent of 'multiculturalism' that we wish to see. Political leaders have also attempted to avoid debate altogether – preferring to tiptoe around issues which are seen as simply too sensitive. Indeed, very often it is only the extreme right wing groups that are willing to talk about race issues. And they have had some success. In a number of European countries, they continue to make substantial inroads into mainstream politics. Jean-Marie Le Pen's National Front party achieved nearly 18 per cent of the vote in the French Presidential elections in 2003 and in Belgium the far right Vlaams Blok party achieved 11.6 per cent of the vote in general elections in the same year. More recently, similar parties in Austria have topped 20 per cent and in Italy the extreme right have gained places in ruling coalitions. Meanwhile in Britain, the British National Party has proved to be the most successful extreme right party for many years, although it commands much lower support than for similar parties in other parts of Europe.

The CRE took heart from a survey which found that 86 per cent of Britons disagree with the suggestion that 'you have to be white to be British' (CRE, 2002) and there are some features of the British 'model', which appear to have had greater success. However, race and immigration remain very volatile and with the rise in international tensions and the concerns about asylum seekers in the press and media, opinion polls suggested that the proportion of British people seeing it as a major issue rose to 30 per cent in 2004 – at the top of the list of 'most important issues facing the country', alongside the health service and education. More recently, the debate about the number of EU migrants has meant that race and immigration remain at the top of the agenda. Between May 2004, when the EU was enlarged with the accession of eight countries (known as the A8) and September 2006, over 500,000 new workers were registered under the British scheme to manage migration from these countries (Spencer *et al.*, 2007) (though the actual number of migrants was higher as the figures excluded self-employed persons and other categories of entrants), many of whom were absorbed into areas of the UK, which had not experienced significant migration in the past to undertake work in many rural industries which had struggled to attract labour, like food picking, packing and processing.

Economic considerations have largely driven immigration, although the more general effects of globalisation and the rise in inter-ethnic conflicts are now also significant factors. Relatively little thought was given to the impact that population movement will have, either on the host community, or how the new migrant minority populations will themselves cope with the change in their new social and economic circumstances. There has also been little appreciation that migrants would quickly begin to put down roots and that the subsequent generations of migrant families would come to see the host country as their home – indeed, their only home. Further, it was not anticipated that new generations would aspire, not only to have an equal stake in their homeland, but that they would be less willing than their parents to accept anything other than equal treatment. It is a little difficult to understand why these apparently predictable responses were not anticipated at the time, with little done by way of planning and preparation for the inevitable demands for citizenship and equal rights. But this is not a matter of past history – the same tensions are apparent in the approach to the present wave of immigration, whether in respect of refugees or economic migrants. They are generally 'accommodated' in much the same way as migrants were before them, often with the same pattern of geographical, social and economic separation, with little thought about the social and psychological needs of host and migrant communities.

Even the physical needs of the migrant and host communities have taken time to address and conflicts have often arisen as a result of pressure on hard-pressed local services. In Britain, for example, it has been suggested, though hopefully not too seriously, that in order for a particular community, or area, to attract additional resources to alleviate the pressure on housing, health and educational facilities 'you have to have a riot'. Those countries which set out to build a nation from a majority immigrant population, such as Canada, have been more willing to properly plan resources and create a strategy which promotes a sense of belonging for all. More generally, however, nations where immigrants form minorities, often visible by their race, ethnicity and culture, have muddled along with a mixture of pragmatism and special programmes to respond to conflict and discrimination. The need for a more pro-active and purposeful approach was stressed by the Community Cohesion Panel (Cantle, 2004), which proposed a programme of 'managing settlement' so that at least as much attention would be paid to addressing the social and psychological needs of communities, as to the economic considerations of 'managed migration'. The CIC proposed that a new national body be set up to be 'responsible for the integration of new migrants', which would include working with settled communities (CIC, 2007, p. 68).

Clear leadership has often also been lacking, reflecting the uncertainties and ambivalence of the political mood at the time. Black and ethnic minorities have often found that, for them, the continuing reality has been one of racism and discrimination, as evidenced by disadvantage on just about every social and economic indicator. But, also, at a basic and human level there has also been a failure to make immigrants feel truly valued and to give them an equal social standing. Race and community relations have always been vulnerable to the routine 'playing of the race card' by those, usually on the extreme right of the political spectrum, to whip up fear and hatred of minorities and to secure the support of the majority voting population. There is, however, a more collective national hypocrisy in which the indigenous population (or their governments) encourage immigration whenever it suits their economic circumstances and at the same time, do little or nothing to create an equal place for those immigrants that inevitably become, or aspire to become, longer-term residents and citizens. This is not in any way confined to the host white population and there is increasing recognition that established BME people are also beginning to express opposition to new migrants, despite their communities having experienced a similar level of prejudice just a generation or so ago. Racism is certainly not limited to the relationship between the, predominantly, host white communities and the, mainly, black minority communities and there is now also recognition that conflicts between BME groups are growing, despite having in some ways,

shared a common bond within an inherently 'racist' society. I
of the minor conflicts between ethnic groups are between diffe
of the ethnic minority community and in some cases, such as th
Lozells area of Birmingham in October 2005, have resulted in loss of life.

Deriding the concerns about migration of the host community (both black
and white citizens) is not sufficient. True, such concerns have often been
used to underpin racist sentiment, but if change is to occur, difficult areas
need to be tackled, rather than simply avoided. The liberal response has been
to maintain the idea of 'cultural pluralism' or a 'community of communities',
and this has certainly been helpful in the past as a means of emphasising the
need to respect differences and avoid assimilation. However, these models
are no longer adequate and have become a justification for a continual
separation and coexistence, which has militated against the development of
mutual trust and co-development. These models also do not address the
multicultural variation now emerging and which are re-shaping our towns
and cities. For example, in London there are now over 300 languages spoken
and in many of the larger and principal cities of Europe and North America,
we now see the development of an 'international culture'. These cities may
ultimately have more in common with each other than with the country in
which they are situated. In this sense they may become homogenising, in
the way that global brands like McDonalds and Coca Cola have become (and
are generally disparaged as a result). In the meantime, many of the smaller
towns, suburbs and rural areas that surround these cities have remained
largely mono-cultural.

Such changes are largely driven by economic requirements rather than the
result of any planned policy, which is a response to a particular conception
of cultural identity. However, 'planning cultural change' immediately smacks
of Soviet style centralism and, in any case, could any fixed conception of culture really survive in such a dynamic situation? But the alternative seems
equally unattractive, with a tacit acceptance that the pattern of migration
will simply continue to be driven by economic and market considerations
(especially as there is the prospect of even greater levels of immigration to
restore a more favourable balance of a working population to retired people)
rather than by the desire to build a mixed and vibrant community, which is
based on values and a behavioural consensus.

The future of multiculturalism is inevitably entwined in the much bigger
issue of population strategy, which is seldom part of any formal government
policy, in the West at least, as it again would create overtones of central
planning and be at odds with all liberal and libertarian principles. However,
such strategies are now being seriously discussed in the context of environmental sustainability, which, as Sir David King, the Government's Chief
Scientist suggests, presents a greater threat to the world than international
terrorism. The Western world's consumption of resources is presently hugely
disproportionate to their population and continuously depends upon the

consumption of resources originating in other countries. Britain, alongside the Netherlands, is one of the most densely populated countries in the world and yet has one of the highest projected levels of population growth in Europe, most of which is because of the predicted level of inward migration. Genuine concerns about environmental sustainability are profound and some authoritative commentators suggest that major *reductions* in population will be necessary. The Optimum Population Trust (OPT, 2004), for example, whose patrons include Jonathon Porritt, Chairman of the UK Sustainable Development Commission and Sir Crispin Tickell, a Government advisor on the environment, believe that the United Kingdom's sustainable population level may have to be as low as 30 million in the twenty-second century, compared to a present Government projection of nearly 67 million by 2050. Malthusian projections of sustainable population levels are now being taken more seriously as food production begins to compete with energy crops for land, and the loss of fertile areas caused by climate change, as the world population continues to grow. Given the nature of debates to date, however, it is difficult enough to de-couple race issues from immigration, let alone from wider population and sustainable development strategies. The origin of such questions is often, in itself, enough to determine the character of the ensuing debate. For example, when Michael Howard, the leader of the Conservative Opposition, raised the possibility of an annual target for immigration in 2004 (which was incorporated into the Conservative Manifesto for the 2005 general election) it was attacked as a racist agenda, whereas when a very similar proposal was made, almost coincidentally, in *Prospect* Magazine (Sriskandarajah, 2004) it barely drew any adverse comment. Context therefore matters and, given the history of immigration debates, raising generalised concerns about migration means that motivation for doing so will inevitably be questioned and is almost certain to invite charges of racism. Raising genuine concerns is of course essential, but will only be seen as genuine if they are part of a process of identifying and solving the problems, rather than heightening concerns and casting doubts on the value of immigration – and, thereby, on past and present migrants. The failure to discuss such issues is potentially equally problematic and will mean that a consensus, or shared 'vision', will be difficult to achieve and that misgivings will continue to be harboured and constantly open to exploitation.

The migration debate must be put into a broader context of economic and demographic change. But this is only likely to be an open and honest debate and relatively free from racist overtones, if it follows on from a much clearer acceptance of difference and diversity and a positive vision of a future multicultural society. If our starting point is that we are now, and for all time, multicultural and that our diversity is valued and celebrated, then perhaps the balance and relationship between different cultures can not only be discussed in a more mature way, but also in the context of even wider social, economic and environmental concerns.

Citizenship in a multicultural society

The terms 'citizenship', 'nationality' and 'national identity' are not well defined and they have often been conflated. There is also a lack of clarity about the way in which these concepts are underpinned by 'values' and whether other forms of identity are likely to reinforce or undermine national solidarity and allegiance. Chapter 5 attempts to establish a few common principles, but also recognises that societies are dynamic and constantly changing and adapting.

'Nationality' does little more than express, in contractual terms, the relationship between an individual and the state in which they were born or of which they have become a member. 'Citizenship' is increasingly being using to describe that relationship and has developed into a more value-laden concept, and assumes a level of allegiance to the state, which creates some semblance of national identity. For those people who view it in its most limited and contractual form, nationality will nevertheless have a considerable impact on our identity over time, if only because of the subtle and continuous processes of socialisation, which are hardly apparent but nevertheless constantly 'flag' our daily lives (Billig, 2002). Some people will, of course, wish to see their identity defined by their nationality, however homogenising this may appear. For others, the picture is more complex, with national identity supplemented, or even supplanted, by other identities. For example, people may describe themselves as British and Catholic, Irish and gay, or Black and American. Such loyalties and affinities may well transcend national boundaries and mean that, whilst they respect the contract with their nation state, they have other allegiances which can be at odds with the prevailing norms of that state, for some or all of the time. There is no general coincidence of nationality and national identity as they express two quite different concepts, one based on an objective relationship and the other, on a wide variety of subjective and emotional views about the public and private dimensions of identity.

There is also every likelihood that faith will play an increasingly important role in determining identity and has been something of a political obsession since 9/11 and the London and Madrid bombings. Samuel Huntingdon's *The Clash of Civilisations* (2002) first published in 1997, set out his theory that the rivalry of superpowers would be replaced by the clash of civilisations, including the division between the West and 'the Muslim world'. This has been given real credence by the so-called 'war on terror' which has sharpened faith divisions within Western nations, as much as between the West and other nations. The intensity of identification with the *ummah* – the worldwide Muslim community – by Muslims in Britain has clearly risen as a result of the perception that foreign policy is a threat to Muslims in many different countries and generally anti-Muslim in nature. Certainly the world is no longer defined by past political and national identities and has become more fluid as population movement accelerates, with cultural and diaspora identities becoming easier to develop and sustain, as a result of both negative reaction and positive attraction. And faith divisions now appear to be just as pertinent to identity as much longer-standing ethnic divisions, and making for a more complex picture which will inevitably require new and more sophisticated responses.

Some commentators suggest that the requirements of nationality – and the membership of a *political* entity, which being a citizen entails – are sometimes at odds with the membership of an identifiable *cultural* (whether defined by ethnicity, by faith, or other difference) group and it becomes the 'acid test' of the tolerance of diversity. However, such differences are inherent within a democratic society and are in no way confined to minority ethnic and faith groups. For example political groups, on either the extreme left or right of the spectrum, will generally hold views which are not part of the comfortable majority consensus and, so too, will special interest groups, such as militant animal welfare activists. However, the views of minority ethnic and faith groups are often presented as an alternative set of 'values', which underpin and define a way of life which has sufficient coherence to be recognised as an entity.

Leaving aside the question of whether either, the majority group or minority group, really does have a level of internal coherence to counter-pose them as groups, it is claimed that a 'clash of cultures' can be avoided by assuming that each nation has a core set of values, which all must share, and that each group – whether defined by ethnicity, culture, faith, or other form of identity – adopts a sub-set of values which nests within the core. The Communitarians, for example, talk about 'over-arching' values (The Communitarian Network, 2002) and the British Government now demands that fundamental democratic values be upheld (Crick, 2003). The Parekh Report (2000), on the other hand, illustrated the real difficulty of such an approach and whilst supporting the Communitarian concept of 'diversity within unity' and arguing that cohesion depends upon a set of common values, it also asserted that each community should be allowed to live by their separate values. Parekh's model of multiculturalism, is presented as a 'community of communities', a form of liberal pluralism which is regarded by others as one in which the common bonds envisaged are far too elastic (Wolfe, 2002).

Alibhai-Brown (2000) has also cast doubt on the usefulness of the whole concept of multiculturalism and this view has gained support from Trevor Phillips, the then Chairman of the CRE, who dramatically called for the 'scrapping of multiculturalism' and its replacement by 'integration' (Phillips, 2004a). (The Commission for Racial Equality was merged into the Equality and Human Rights Commission (EHRC) in 2007 and Trevor Phillips was appointed its first chairman.) Both Parekh and Phillips, however, have argued against 'assimilation' and both support some form of cultural distinctiveness, but the question of how much and in what form, is still open. The term multiculturalism certainly has a limited usefulness in this context as it embraces all forms of interface between minorities and between minorities and majority groups.

Whilst it seems that most advocates of some form of multiculturalism can agree that diversity is something that should be protected, there has been little attempt to codify these 'common values' nor to agree upon the limits of separate values and how to reconcile any conflicts between the two. A theoretical debate, conducted by a range of groups, at a distance from each other, may only succeed in reinforcing stereotypes and compounding ignorance. Diversity is not an end in itself; it allows us to expand our own horizons by contrasting our beliefs and values with those of others. We come to define our own identity by reference to that of others. Mutual understanding and a shared set of values are much more likely to result from a real interchange and from shared experiences at all levels (Malik, 2002a).

This not only lends support to 'community cohesion' but also to the approach in Britain which is beginning to turn the theoretical conception of 'citizenship' into more practical action, echoing some of the developments in Canada, Australia and the United States. These include the new programme of citizenship education in schools and the Government's new 'civil renewal' agenda, which aims to encourage more active forms of engagement, the introduction of citizenship ceremonies and a new citizenship 'handbook', although these are still very much in their infancy and have not been without their problems. This is discussed in Chapter 5.

The practice of community cohesion

The practice of community cohesion is set out in Chapter 6 and includes the emerging work to 'create a vision and sense of belonging', 'value diversity', 'ensure equality of opportunity' and 'develop cross-cultural interaction' (for full definition of community cohesion, see Figure 2.1). In the last few years, much more guidance has been made available at both the strategic level and at the practitioner level. Central and local government collaborated on the first guide in 2002 (LGA *et al.*, 2002) and this has been updated and expanded (LGA *et al*., 2004) with 'strategic guidance' in 2005 (LGA and IDeA, 2005). The CRE also published their somewhat belated guidance on 'promoting good race relations' in the same year (CRE, 2005). Further, the Government published their new Community Cohesion and Race Equality Strategy in 2005 (Home Office, 2005) following up on a consultation paper entitled 'Strength in Diversity' (Home Office, 2004). This has since been updated by the Department of Communities and Local Government on two separate occasions (DCLG, 2006 and DCLG, 2007). The CIC also gave a considerable impetus to the development of community cohesion with the publication of its Final Report (CIC, 2007) and a range of other publications including, *'What Works' in Community Cohesion* (CIC, 2007a) and *Integration and Cohesion Case Studies* (CIC, 2007b). Many local authorities, national agencies and voluntary and community organisations have now also developed cohesion programmes in a wide variety of settings and these are gradually being evaluated and published. Fortunately, a considerable amount of good practice on equal opportunities already exists (and is described in Chapter 6); having been established and documented over the years and this can easily be integrated with the community cohesion programme.

The Commission on Integration and Cohesion (CIC, 2007) report is much more than the sum of its parts and clearly establishes the concept of community cohesion and, despite a somewhat cautious and occasionally critical reaction to the initial debate about the emerging concept, it is now widely seen as offering a new framework for race and diversity.

The CRE, in their final report, which reviewed the 30 years or so since the establishment of the CRE had sufficient confidence in the concept of community cohesion to able to recommend a:

> Focus on improving community cohesion and integration, recognising the ways in which these concepts are closely intertwined with equality. (CRE, 2007, p. 60)

Community cohesion, however, is fundamentally concerned with changing underlying attitudes and values and represents a very different approach to the work presently done under the equal opportunities banner, which emphasises the use of systems and processes to constrain and change behaviour as a means of delivering equality and fairness. A different set of skills will therefore be required, as well as the development of new techniques and approaches. The Institute of Community Cohesion (iCoCo) was established in 2005 to build capacity and develop both the theoretical and practical basis for community cohesion and has produced a wide range of guides and case study material and is to become a 'one-stop shop on cohesion' (Blears, 2007). More action research, to robustly test 'what works' is also still necessary and both the theoretical framework and the skills of practitioners will require more investment. It is also not yet clear which agencies will be accountable, at both national and local levels, for taking forward the community cohesion programme, especially in the light of the demise of the CRE and its replacement with a much more wide-ranging agency including human rights and other equality issues. Further, the process of 'mainstreaming' the programme is only just beginning, with many governmental agencies appearing to prefer that under-resourced voluntary agencies and community organisations remain responsible for delivery, rather than change their own practices – possibly repeating the mistakes of the 'promoting good race relations' legislation in the 1960s. However, there are some encouraging signs, particularly the introduction of the new 'duty to promote community cohesion' in schools from September 2007, as a result of the Education and Inspections Act 2006, for which guidance has now been issued (DCSF, 2007).

The concept of 'social capital' is also discussed in Chapter 6, as it can complement both the theory and practice of community cohesion. Robert Putnam's notion of 'bridging capital' (Putnam, 2000), in particular, closely relates to 'cross-cultural' contact and some further ideas about how this might be built and the various forms, that it can take, especially as his more recent work (Putnam, 2007) suggests that social capital is diminished by increasing diversity, are developed in this chapter. Three areas are distinguished (see Table 6.1); associational, social and structural cross-cultural contact. Key policy areas are also discussed, notably education, housing and regeneration programmes.

There is still relatively little attention given to the social and psychological needs of communities, especially in respect of the host community, to help them to come to terms with change. There is also little by way of general education to enable people to relate to 'others', and, more importantly, to create and build commonalities between groups, rather than to reinforce and emphasise differences. Relatively little has also been done to explain the role and nature of inward migration (whether in economic terms, or on a compassionate basis in respect of asylum seekers escaping persecution) and to tackle some of the corrosive myths and stereotypes. The process of helping immigrants to settle and to adjust to their new circumstances is beginning to improve but is still very limited. Moreover, the ability of key agencies to provide a realistic level of local resources to reduce the competing demands between newcomers and longer term residents is still far from adequate. Further, these hugely complex issues require both strong and committed leadership and an investment in skills development at all levels, which has not yet been forthcoming (and have generally been left to voluntary organisations that often seem to survive by dedication and commitment alone).

Despite the difficulties, the practice is beginning to grow and is now being developed with greater confidence, as the successes become more and more evident. It is hoped that this book will contribute to that further development and growth – and, moreover, to the building of strong and positive relationships between communities, based on shared experiences and meaningful interaction.

2
The Journey to Community Cohesion

The Second World War marked a turning point in the nature of immigration and settlement. Many countries had absorbed successive waves of immigrants over the centuries, generally because of persecution in their homelands, or as a result of colonial exploitation and expansion. But the post-war period was characteristically different and was essentially about 'race'.

Prior to the War, most people in western democracies had had very limited experience of black people – then described as 'coloured' – and the black communities, such as they were, were very small and localised. By 1950, for example, there were only around 100,000 black people in the whole of Great Britain, mostly living in the London docklands area and other coastal cities. By 1968, the number of people from all ethnic minority backgrounds had risen tenfold, to 1 million (Daniel, 1968, p. 9). In Britain, and no doubt other western countries too, this sudden growth was in a world where white people still believed that they were innately superior to other races – and to foreigners generally. In a survey published in 1969 their 'pecking order' was quite clear with only 22 per cent of British people believing that they were on the same level as, or inferior to, people from Africa; 23 per cent took the same view in respect of people from Asia and 56 per cent and 69 per cent in respect of European and American people respectively (Rose *et al.*, 1969, p. 567).

In Britain, black people were settling alongside the almost exclusively white host population in considerable numbers, moving into their neighbourhoods, working in the same factories, using the same public transport, shops, schools and social facilities. Further, they were apparently intending to re-locate on a permanent basis and expecting to receive equal treatment as British subjects and citizens. Jobs were not only available to them, but their labour was needed to fuel the post-war re-building and expansion plans. For many British people, it mattered not that their fellow countrymen had, for years, exploited many of the countries from which the newcomers came, nor, that they had provided personnel to fight alongside them in the War, this was a change that challenged the very idea of the 'rightful place' of the British amongst the other peoples of the world. New policies, backed by new legislation and procedures to regulate these new relationships, were inevitable.

Across Europe, there was the same wind of change, with the former colonial powers like the Netherlands and Belgium, also drawing upon their former colonies to provide labour. Others focussed more on 'guest worker' schemes, which created the illusion that the newly established multiculturalism was reversible. Whilst each developed different models to come to terms with the changes, they have all struggled to emerge as cohesive societies and the difficulties continue to threaten the success of multiculturalism to this day.

Aliens and foreigners

The boundaries of nation states have become increasingly permeable as transport and communication links have improved and become more widely accessible. Foreigners were regarded as 'aliens', up to the early part of the twentieth century, with legislation framed accordingly. Foreigners were comparatively rare, especially outside the ports and major cities and their status and the level of tolerance towards them was often low, with little or no expectation of the granting of rights equal to those of existing citizens. With the exception perhaps of high-ranking nobles, foreigners were often treated with great suspicion and even contempt.

Foreigners had, however, been of sufficient number to form themselves into recognisable communities over many centuries, and in Britain, Jewish communities were the first to establish themselves as long ago as in the twelfth and thirteenth centuries, although they were occasionally the subject of anti-Jewish atrocities, including massacre and expulsion (Winder, 2004, pp. 34–9).

Many other groups found their way to Britain, including those known as 'gypsies', a term which might have been corrupted from 'Egyptians' (ibid., p. 42), who were the subject of many a harsh measure. For example, in Britain a law of 1713 provided that all persons 'pretending to be gypsies, or wandering in the habit or form of counterfeit Egyptians' would be whipped, given hard labour and sent to their place of last settlement, or place of birth' (Algerant, 2004).

Many came to Britain for religious reasons, especially protestants from Flanders and, most notably, the Hugenots, in the sixteenth century, escaping persecution in France. Whilst England was seen as offering religious toler-ance, the Hugenots nevertheless suffered terrible mob violence and the same fate befell some of the many groups of entrepreneurs and craftsmen who came from a range of European countries. These included Italians, who were not only the subject of vicious attacks, but also a new alien tax (Winder, 2004, p. 43). Diversity grew by degrees and included a small number of black people as a spin-off from the slave trade. According to Winder (ibid.) in his excellent book of the same name, all this simply reflected the British regard for all of the newcomers as 'Bloody Foreigners'. However, the racial dimension was of a different order:

> The contrast with previous generations of immigrants could hardly be more obvious. The European Protestants who fled Catholic whips had to suffer resentment, but they prospered mightily, and represent the sunny side of immigration. The Africans represent the opposite, the tragic side ... the greatest legacy of the slave trade was that Britain became infected with a racism that would dominate the twists and turns of migrant life in the future.
>
> Whatever lay at the root of British hostility to foreigners, through the slave trade it achieved a new and clearer definition. From now on, Britons would think of themselves as 'white', as if this alone was a suggestive and meaningful quality. (Winder, 2004, p. 111)

By the twentieth century, the migrant minority populations had become more substantial, and, in some cases, had developed into a critical mass, living within small enclaves of a number of cities, generally the busiest ports. For the most part these were assimilated into the host community and they struggled to maintain a distinct identity. The Jewish community was, perhaps, an exception and they became the most visible diaspora with a recognisable minority in a number of nations, partly by a process of self-segregation and informal communal control over their own communities (Rose *et al.*, 1969, p. 19) – and presumably because of the discrimination they faced. Between 1870 and 1914, about 120,000 Jewish people migrated to Britain, largely due to persecution in Russia (Castles and Miller, 1993, p. 59) and boosted the community to 300,000 by the end of that period (Solomos, 2003, p. 41). Jewish immigration into Britain was a hotly contested issue, the subject of protests and the subsequent cause of restrictions on entry, through the various Aliens Acts in the first quarter of the twentieth century.

Foreigners of any description, however, were inevitably regarded with suspicion, especially at times of international conflict, as much based on allegiance, as race. It was in this context that the Aliens Act of 1919 was passed to control which foreigners entered Britain:

> The Aliens Act was passed in a fit of post-war xenophobic hysteria as a sop to the 'Hang the Kaiser' lobby when all foreigners entering Britain were regarded as possible spies or, at best, degenerate undesirables. The philosophy behind the Act had been outlined by Lloyd George who had said, while electioneering in the 1919 election, that foreigners were going to be 'forced out of the country.' (Foot, 1969, p. 79)

However, the 1919 Act – the full title of which was the Aliens Restriction (Amendment) Act – had stemmed from the 1905 Aliens Order and had already been stiffened through the 1914 Aliens Restriction Act. It appeared to have been applied in a non-restrictive manner until 4,000 to 5,000 Jews entered Britain in 1914 and the War had added the security dimension to the new restrictions. This legislative period culminated in the Aliens Order in 1920, with continued restrictions on 'aliens', who could be refused entry, made subject to residential restrictions and deported if they became a burden on the State (Solomos, 2003, p. 42).

Following the Aliens Restriction (Amendment) Act 1919, Parliament passed the Special Restriction (Coloured Alien Seamen) Order 1925. Its purpose was to regulate the entry of colonial seamen entitled to seek discharge and domicile in Great Britain. Under the Order, if such seamen could not provide documentation proving they were British Subjects, they would have to obtain leave of an immigration officer before landing. The problem was that virtually no documentation was acceptable as proof to Immigration Officers. Anyone registered under this order became an alien – or had their nationality categorised as 'SEAMAN' – and was subject to the Aliens Order 1920, and the Aliens Restriction (Amendment) Act 1919. In other words, they could be deported (Joshua *et al.*, 1983).

The reason for the 1925 Special Restriction Order was that between April and August 1919, almost every seaport city with a black population – and in particular Cardiff, Liverpool, London and Newport – experienced violent racial upheaval with white crowds attacking black localities. People died in the riots in Liverpool and Cardiff (there were also race riots in April 1911 in Cardiff where a crowd of 2000 smashed and burned 21 out of 22 Chinese laundries in the city during a strike of the National Union of Seamen) (ibid.).

Within British society the Irish were also an identifiable and visible group and whilst being white, were generally regarded as racially and culturally inferior and were the subject of anti-Irish sentiment and, on occasion, to attack. This was despite the fact that they were citizens of the United Kingdom as a result of the Act of Union in 1800 and that they enjoyed freedom of movement and settlement even after the formation of the Irish Republic in 1922. Castles and Miller (1993, p. 59) estimate that the Irish made up around 3 per cent of the population of England and Wales and around 7 per cent of Scotland by 1851, and the number migrating to England, Scotland and Wales had amounted to around 630,000 by 1901 (Solomos, 2003, p. 38). The Irish nation was generally poorer with a far less developed economy and they were increasingly seen as a race apart during the nineteenth century, with anti-Irish and anti-Catholic sentiment remaining critical to the notions of 'otherness' that underpinned British national identity (Parekh, 2000, p. 21). They were not regarded as foreigners, however, for the purposes of the various Aliens Acts, which had been principally directed at Jewish immigrants.

Foreigners, or 'aliens' were, at best, tolerated and certainly not regarded as equal citizens. The indigenous population often sought to protect their superior position through higher rates of pay and restrictive employment practices. This particularly applied to seamen, who were obviously most likely to travel to and from British ports and was enshrined in legislation until the Second World War. The limited rights afforded to foreigners was only to be expected. Britain and a number of other white nations, exercised their domination of the world, in economic terms, and simply assumed the superiority of their race, language and culture. The fact that this domination had been achieved by the exploitation and colonialisation was of little relevance and simply reflected what they saw as the natural order of things. Racial superiority was assumed and, indeed, became supported by pseudo-scientific endeavour, for example, through the 'eugenics movement'. Eugenics, based on biological determinism and the selection of racial and other natural characteristics to reinforce and develop superior beings, was even supported by supposedly liberal and enlightened thinkers in the early part of the twentieth century. The use of 'science' and the development of popular mythology in support of racial and ethnic superiority are explored in Chapter 4.

The notion of equal rights between men and women had also not been established within nation states. In Britain, women were not granted universal suffrage until 1928, following partial enfranchisement in 1918. In many other ways women did not enjoy equal rights, particularly in respect of employment. In many other countries equal rights for women lagged even further behind. Voting and other rights and entitlements for both men and women had been closely tied to social and economic position – and especially property ownership – for centuries. The struggle for equal rights therefore, was not simply a matter of nationality and had always been linked to social class and economic position. Race added another layer upon which discrimination and protectionism could be based.

The focus of race relations, then, began with restrictive practices and protection of the superiority of the host nation and was based on the assumption that foreigners and aliens were subordinate and would remain so. Immigration controls were used to limit the numbers of these supposedly inferior beings entering the country and maintaining the advantage over them. However, it was also a matter of trust; nations were constantly at war with each other and all foreign nationals were therefore to be treated with suspicion, or even as a potential future enemy. In all this, the superiority of the white race was simply assumed, alongside the superiority of men over women and rich over poor. The idea of a natural 'pecking order' was still very evident in all social and economic relationships but this was about to be fundamentally tested and challenged.

The emergence of race relations policies

The rise of fascism in Europe in the 1930s was largely fuelled by anti-Semitic movements which attempted to scapegoat the Jewish community in a period of economic depression. In Germany it took on a new dimension – to try to establish the purity of the Aryan 'race', and its' supremacy over many others, including Eastern Europeans, gypsies, as well as Jews. Whilst the Nazis also regarded black and Asian people as, axiomatically, inferior in all respects, they were not the principal focus of their campaign, simply because they were not in their field of view and beyond the scope of their immediate 'pecking order'. The Jewish community on the other hand, had a significant presence in Germany and neighbouring European countries. They were easy to demonise and to present them as a threat. Their proximity mattered. The concept of racial hierarchy was not a simple issue of black and white ethnic groups, but entwined with historic differences and disputes over territory and national boundaries, as well as the various notions of religious and social superiority

The Second World War changed the political landscape in a number of different ways including the redefinition of 'race'. The days of empires and colonialism were coming to an end with the Independence of India, Pakistan and many other nations in the immediate post-war period. Their independence might have been expected to result in the severing of relations with the 'mother nation', but in fact, the people of the former colonies retained rights as 'subjects', which they were encouraged to exercise by taking advantage of the pressing labour requirements to fuel the post-war re-construction and economic expansion. The people of the former colonies and dependencies had acquired an understanding of the cultural and linguistic requirements of their former 'mother countries' and these affinities ensured a natural choice for the expansion of the labour market.

Meanwhile, in the aftermath of the War, the massive public expenditure associated with the defence industry and post-war construction, coupled with technological and industrial advancement created new conditions for the mass production of consumer goods and fashion items. The rapid expansion of the automotive and other manufacturing industries reshaped the workforce and with it, familial and residential patterns. The creation of the National Health Service in Britain and the development of other service industries to look after the new 'affluent workers', meant that immigration was required to provide the extra labour.

Immigration to Britain gathered in pace and the new communities were beginning to put down roots. By 1970, the BME population numbered approximately 1.4 million, a third of these being children born in Britain – and largely descended from the New Commonwealth countries of South Asia, the Caribbean and Africa. Significant inflows also resulted from the national crises in East Africa in 1968 and 1976 (Strategy Unit, 2003, p. 14). Nevertheless, there was a net emigration from Britain during the 1950s, 1960s and 1970s (and during the later period of the 1980s and early 1990s emigration and immigration were roughly in balance) (Glover *et al.*, 2001, p. 7). The discussion was therefore, not about numbers, it was about race and 'difference'.

The mass immigration of black and Asian people after the War made an immediate impact and attempts were made to restrict the influx almost as soon as it had started. This had to be balanced with the evident continuing need for labour and the need to keep faith with the people from the colonies who had been afforded special status as subjects and retained the right to enter and live in Britain. The same dilemma was evident in other European countries that also had a number of former colonies and dependencies. The first response of the British Government, again in parallel with developments in other European countries was, by degrees, to try to institute controls on the numbers of immigrants.

The 1948 British Nationality Act could control non-British subjects. Most immigrants from the colonies were, however, British subjects. In any event, Britain, like other European countries with a colonial history, were dependent on colonial labour to feed the post-war boom:

> Some scholars of migration have maintained that European policy makers deliberately sought to tap the reservoir of colonial labour to feed the post-war boom; this is a misunderstanding. It was rather the case that policy makers had little choice but to rely on (or, which was more often the case, to tolerate) colonial migrants. The United Kingdom and France present the clearest examples of this trend, but it can also be found in the Netherlands and Belgium. (Hansen, 2003, p. 26)

Both Britain and France had attempted to use administrative devices to try to skew its much-needed immigration towards white European people, rather than its former colonies and dependencies (ibid.). Solomos (2003, p. 53) supports this view and contrasts the UK Government's attitude to colonial immigration to that of people from Eastern Europe. He suggests that despite appearances, the period from 1948 to the 1962 Commonwealth Immigrants Act was not one of free entry and both Labour and Conservative governments used administrative measures to control black immigration.

Despite the ambivalence of governments, colonial migrants continued to move into Europe, partly because of the liberal attitudes of some politicians who could not bring themselves to impose a blatant racial dimension into controls and partly because of a mixture of guilt-ridden and paternalistic attitudes to their former colonial subjects. Enoch Powell, who became far better known for his racist views in the 1960s, was a Minister in the British Government who defended the form of citizenship afforded to people from the former colonies:

> Powell was against the British Nationality Act (1948) because it dispensed with subjecthood, because it recognised the independence of the Dominions and many of the newer Commonwealth ... countries were allowed to break away from the Crown ... (and) because it wrote into

British citizenship law the disintegration of the Empire. His opposition had nothing to do with the fact that it re-established the open door for all citizens of the Empire. (Foot, 1969, p. 18)

But the 'immigration problem' was on the agenda, almost from the time the Empire Windrush docked in May 1948 with over 400 Jamaicans. Black people were subject to abuse and assaults on a sporadic basis with race riots in Liverpool in 1948, Deptford, London, 1949 and Camden Town, London in 1954 (MacMaster, 2001, p. 178). By the time the larger and more sustained riots broke out in Nottingham and London's Notting Hill in 1958, legislation was all but inevitable. After the riots had taken place, a motion was passed at the Conservative Party conference, against the advice of the leadership and with a substantial majority, which called for immigration control (Foot, 1969, p. 34). The subject of immigration also attracted much comment in the British press with the Daily Sketch calling for an end to 'the tremendous influx of coloured people', and MPs from Labour and Conservative parties demanding controls in the House of Commons (MacMaster, 2001, p. 179).

In this hostile atmosphere, the possibility of supporting immigrants, helping them to integrate and to develop positive interactions with the host community was extremely difficult.

> MP's instead of seeking to tackle prejudice ... blamed the immigrants for those conditions of which they were the principal victims. Already in the 1950s government carefully avoided social and economic programmes that would have helped newly arrived West Indians to adjust to life in Britain and also reduced racial tensions, since it was feared that improved conditions would attract further immigration. (Ibid., p. 179)

The 1962 Commonwealth Immigrants Act sought to control immigration, but had a perverse effect. First, the threat of controls meant 'a violent upswing' in the flow of arrivals in 1961 and in the first half of 1962 (Rose *et al.*, 1969, p. 82). Second, whilst the Act took away the right to enter from all Commonwealth citizens, there was an increase in the number of arrivals because of the admission of dependents (ibid., pp. 77 and 87). In fifteen years the number of Commonwealth immigrants had increased from 336,000 in 1951, to 660,000 in the 1961 and 942,000 in 1966 (ibid., p. 97).

The general election in 1964 marked a turning point in race relations. This was partly out of the shock defeat of Labour's Patrick Gordon Walker by Conservative's Peter Griffiths, who had made some rather unguarded racist statements and was associated with the slogan 'if you want a nigger for a neighbour, vote Labour'. The electorate, it seemed preferred Griffiths's prejudice to the comparatively liberal views of Gordon Walker. This, at least, galvanised the Labour Government, with the Prime Minister, Harold Wilson committing his government to legislate to tackle discrimination and incitement to racial hatred – and, in passing, to condemning Peter Griffiths as a 'parliamentary leper'.

The new Labour Government soon introduced two legislative measures to deal with the 'race problem', despite continued heated debate along party lines (see for example, Pannell and Brockway, 1965). The Race Relations Act of 1965 established the Race Relations Board (RRB) to tackle discrimination and to take up individual cases and made it unlawful to discriminate on the grounds of race or colour in a number of areas, such as housing, places of entertainment and employment. It also created a new criminal offence of incitement to racial hatred. The 1965 Act was followed by the Race Relations Act 1968, which strengthened and extended the earlier measures. Although, the 1965 and 1968 Acts marked a significant step forward in race relations there was considerable and continuing doubt about their effectiveness (Solomos, 2003, p. 82) and the RRB itself recognised in its report in 1973, that the problem of discrimination was not just that of individual cases, but was also linked to systemic forms, which would require further legislation in later years.

Early integration measures

In the meantime, a slight change in tack had become evident from the setting up of the Commonwealth Immigrants Advisory Council (CIAC) in 1962. This produced a series of reports that recommended various means by which the welfare of immigrants might be improved, for example, in respect of education and housing. The National Advisory Council for Commonwealth Immigrants (NACCI) was also established two years later in 1964 and both were superseded by a new National Committee for Commonwealth Immigrants (NCCI), chaired by the Archbishop of Canterbury, in 1965. The NCCI supported a local voluntary network, including a number of 'inter-racial councils' in towns with significant immigrant communities, and provided information and support, as well as funding for professional staff working with the local committees. At last, it seemed some thought was being given to addressing the social needs of immigrants and promoting goodwill and integration.

The 1965 White Paper *Immigration from the Commonwealth* (The Prime Minister, 1965), which also presaged the 1965 Act, provided the impetus for the NCCI to deal with what was seen as the problem of integration, although this work was often overshadowed by the more controversial proposals in respect of immigration control. The Race Relations Act of 1968 introduced new measures to improve community relations through the establishment of the Community Relations Commission (CRC), with a network of local Community Relations Councils, replacing the NCCI. The new Commission widened the scope of the 1965 Act but its significance in terms of cohesion, was in its aim to promote good relations between racial groups and help develop more tolerance towards BME communities.

The 1968 Act had at least begun to recognise that Britain had become a multicultural community and that, as a consequence, the host community and the minority communities had to establish a rapport. This was largely seen as the 'integration of the immigrant' into the host community, rather than an acceptance of, and respect for, separate cultures. The policy of integration was still far from being universally accepted however, with Enoch Powell making his infamous 'Rivers of Blood' speech in the same year.

The CRC set up by the1968 Act was now in a position to pull together the many previous practical measures that were introduced in the 1960s and were consistent with the integration aims of the Act. Many of these had evolved by trial and error as professionals in the public services grappled with the day-to-day problems of immigration:

> a process of groping towards ad hoc solutions was as true of the local agencies of central government – offices of the national assistance board and employment exchanges – as of the departments of local government. (Rose *et al.*, 1969, p. 202)

These measures included special arrangements for the teaching of English to immigrants, which was the subject of a report by the Commonwealth Immigrants Advisory Council and various government circulars, until a nationally funded system was enshrined in section 11 of the Local government Act 1966.

Housing policy also evolved to tackle problems in both the private rented sector and in council housing with priority given in some cases to areas that had attracted immigrants (ibid., p. 258). Attempts were also made to disperse immigrants, largely in the context of schools, but the practice among Local Education Authorities varied, with some rejecting the policy outright and it mostly fell into disuse within a few years. Some attempts were also made to respond to the special health needs emerging from the immigrant communities, who often experienced the worst housing and social conditions, and faced discrimination in employment.

Rose *et al.* also describe some of the 'varieties of voluntary organisation which were set up to help solve "race" or "community" problems ... mainly focussed on local, borough or neighbourhood-based committees to promote "good relations" between immigrants and the native population' (ibid., p. 380). Some national bodies were also active, not least the church-based organisations, but they had little idea about the religious and other needs of the new communities, nor how to tackle the prejudices of the host community. Despite the good intentions of these local liaison committees and other initiatives, they failed to have a significant impact because of lack of commitment, leadership and resources. Their work certainly did not amount to a national programme and they were not supported by a clear vision, in which diversity would be valued and nurtured, suffering from a constant veering between acceptance and denial of multiculturalism.

Rose establishes that the Government conveniently saw integration issues as matters for local institutions and then quotes Mary Grigg (1967) to make his most powerful point that;

> the function of the liaison committee, which originally was to express the goodwill of the community, has now become a matter of grappling with the ill-will of the community ... [a] committee set up to cope with a limited local problem, can scarcely adjust itself overnight to understanding and tackling the local symptoms of a national disease

and, even more tellingly;

> they were built on a belief that there was nothing fundamentally wrong with the local community. (Ibid., p. 383)

Patterson (1969, p. 287) provides details of some of the 'non-governmental organisations concerned with immigrant and race relations'. These were poorly resourced and very patchy in geographic terms and did not even begin to provide a meaningful and comprehensive programme. For the most part they were focussed on 'immigrant welfare', but some local organisations did also aim to influence the general climate of opinion, by 'public education' (Westminster), 'promoting understanding and contact' (Oxford) and the 'reconciliation of neighbours experiencing racial friction' (Willesden and Brent). There were some more general, albeit limited, attempts by public servants to influence public opinion by trying 'to allay public fears about immigrants taking jobs and making demands on limited housing' (Goulbourne, 1998, p. 78).

These limited experiences provide important lessons for the development of the community cohesion agenda some forty years later (discussed in Chapter 6), which is also in danger of being under-resourced, seen as a worthy initiative for the voluntary sector and leaving institutional and structural reforms in the background.

Support was also targeted at the inner cities, where most immigrants lived, through the Urban Programme in the late 1960s and again a decade later. These measures rarely dealt with race relations directly, but were intended to tackle the poverty and deprivation in the areas of large migrant populations and improve conditions generally. Many of the areas have been targeted by a range of regeneration programmes on several occasions since that time.

But whilst Britain, France and the Netherlands were viewing their migration policies through the lens of their colonial past, countries such as Germany and Austria, developed 'guest worker' policies, which were based on the assumption that the guest workers would return to their country of origin when no longer required. This expectation was, in fact met in some cases, with large numbers of guest workers returning home in Germany, during the recession of the late 1960s (Hansen, 2003, p. 26). Many European countries followed the German approach with Denmark imposing controls in the same year (1973), and Norway, Belgium, Netherlands, Sweden, Austria and France in 1974 (MacMaster, 2001, p. 188). However, the strict immigration controls meant that migrants began to stay, for fear of not getting back in when the economy improved.

The immigration controls across Europe continued to have a racial element in that they were

> selective, allowing preferred 'white' migrants continuing access (and) most crucially, governments and political leaders of most major parties quietly concurred with a shared discourse that presented immigrants as the cause of deteriorating conditions in inner city slums, growing crime, educational failure, social and cultural dislocation and threatening racial tensions and violence. (Ibid., p. 189)

In European terms, however, Britain had made an early and more positive response to integration. The Netherlands, which had similar policies to Britain, adopted its integration measures only in 1981 and France and Germany maintained a piecemeal approach with specific actions often left to localities and voluntary bodies (Hansen, 2003, p. 32). In the United States, legislation had commenced earlier still, with the use of 'non-discrimination' measures in the 1940s and 'equal opportunities' measures in the 1950s. However, these relatively gentle persuasion methods failed to counter the obvious differences between blacks and whites, particularly in the South, and the more radical 'affirmative action' programmes began in 1961 and were reinforced in 1965 (Ratcliffe, 2004, p. 143). These were intended to redress past discrimination and the imbalance of the life chances in the black population by discriminating in their favour. Miscegenation laws, which prevented men and women of different races from living together even after marriage, were not finally expunged from Southern states until 1965, as result of a ruling by the Supreme Court, which had been in the making for nine years. In 1974 the Assisted Housing Programme began, with a strong interventionist approach to segregated areas, with subsidies provided to black families to enable them to move out of the inner city. This was extended into even more supportive measures, such as the 'Gautreaux' programme and over 50 mobility programmes across the country (CRE, 2002a, p. 14).

Meanwhile, immigrants were themselves inevitably putting down roots, marrying and having children who would only know that country. They were also investing in property and businesses, developing social networks and generally building new lives, despite both institutional and cultural barriers. For example, in Germany, where the number of foreign workers had doubled from 1.3 million in 1966 to 2.6 million in 1973, despite the discouragement of dependents, some did join their loved ones and families inevitably became established and children were born in their new homeland (Castles and Miller, 1993, p. 71).

France had also experienced a high level of immigration, with 2 million foreign workers and a further 690,000 dependents by 1970 (ibid., p. 70). This also had, inevitably, an impact on family settlement and integration:

> family customs were gradually falling into line with those of the majority French people from similar backgrounds ... the number of marriages between Algerians and French women tripled between 1965 and 1982 and partnerships between Frenchmen and Maghrebin women increased tenfold over the same period, although in the latter case such unions are forbidden by religion and constitute a form of betrayal. (Lewis and Schnapper, 1994, p. 69)

Many European countries, however, assumed that their guest workers and immigrants would return home and that citizenship would not be sought on a permanent basis. They continued to deny that they were at that point, inevitably and forever, multicultural nations. It was hardly surprising, therefore, that little real attempt was made to support immigrants, to dispel fears and misconceptions, promote tolerance and respect – let alone encourage cross-cultural contact.

In addition, the very concept of targeting minority communities to tackle the deprivation and discrimination they experienced proved difficult in some countries:

> In France programmes which address social inequalities do not specifically target ethno-racial populations. The French constitution clearly establishes the equality of individuals and necessarily implies equal treatment as the sole means of respecting the principle of equality. Affirmative action programmes that recognise equal rights but infer the existence of unequal needs and direct or indirect structural discrimination based on social, ethnic or sociological affiliation of individuals would in France threaten the balance of rights that govern democracy and form the very foundation of the Republic. (Gagnon and Pagé, 1999, p. 22)

In Britain the limitations of legislation, however, were beginning to be exposed. A Select Committee report on *The Organisation of Race Relations Administration* in 1975, suggested various ways in which the previous Acts could be improved and was followed by a White Paper in the same year (Home Office, 1975). The White Paper was something of a turning point in that it recognised that immigrants were 'here to stay' and the ensuing 1976 Race Relations Act therefore set out to strengthen anti-discrimination legislation. The 'rights agenda', would receive a boost as a result, but any attempt to change the attitudes that had underpinned a lot of the racist behaviour and discrimination, was downplayed.

The Act offered tougher action and, in particular, introduced the concepts of 'direct discrimination' where 'a person treats another person less favourably on racial grounds' and 'indirect discrimination' which is discriminatory in its effect on a racial group due to the difficulty that one group would have in complying with a particular requirement compared to another group. This had a beneficial effect as much of the discrimination had become less overt and the Act attempted to outlaw some of the more subtle means of discrimination which were the result of general rules and practices which might have seemed unrelated to any obvious purpose to discriminate.

In 1976 Race Relations Act also abolished both the Race Relations Boards and the Community Relations Councils, which had survived less than ten years. The Act amalgamated their role into the Commission for Racial Equality (CRE), which the Act had also created. The new Commission was given a mandate to tackle discrimination and to promote equality of opportunity and good relations between persons of different racial groups. Moreover, local authorities, by virtue of section 71 of the Act, were given a statutory duty to 'make appropriate arrangements' to fulfil the same ends in respect of the functions that they carry out.

The CRE subsequently built upon the earlier legislation's attempts to tackle discrimination and gave assistance to individuals pursuing complaints, who were for the first time allowed access to the courts and industrial tribunals. The CRE's powers extended to the carrying out of formal investigations of organisations in which it believed unlawful discrimination was taking place. These were substantial new powers for a new organisation set up against a background of continuing discrimination and unrest. It is hardly surprising then, that the CRE failed to pursue the CRC role from the 1968 Act in any meaningful way. This work effectively died with the amalgamation of the 1968 Act into the new 1976 Act – a span of just eight years.

The development of equalities programmes

The immediate impact of the 1976 Act was limited, with the machinery set up to implement the legislation also being somewhat ineffective, and did not produce the intended results. The expectations of the black community, in particular, were not met and the community remained disadvantaged in almost all respects (and recent reviews of employment opportunities and other key indicators confirm that BME communities remain in a significantly disadvantaged position, see later chapters). The unrest in the 1980s also indicated that the frustration in the BME community continued to grow.

Parekh's Report (2000, p. 264) takes a more generous view of the measures introduced, and touches upon the broader influence of the Act:

> we are convinced that the Race Relations Act 1976 has had a positive effect. Together with the Sex Discrimination Act of the previous year, which conceptually and politically paved the way for it, it has helped to curb the worst kinds of discrimination in employment and the provision of services. It has also made an invaluable impact on the general climate of opinion.

There is more general agreement that the 1976 Act did not deal with institutional racism and that many aspects of the implementation process needed to be strengthened. These were to feature in a later wave of legislation in the late 1990s.

Further, despite the 'cultural shift' heralded by the Act and the increasing recognition that ethnic monitoring and positive action programmes were legitimate means of ensuring fair play for BME people, the Race Relations Act was 'concerned essentially with the negative duties – the avoidance of discrimination as distinct from actively promoting equality of opportunity and recognising diversity' (ibid., p. 265). The BME communities were still to be seen as in need of remedial action and requiring intervention and support on their behalf. The focus was still also on the 'rights agenda' and the aim of 'promoting good race relations', carried over from the 1968 Act was largely ignored. Other than castigating the white community for acts of discrimination, there was little or no attempt to assist them to come to terms with multiculturalism and to provide education and positive multicultural experiences, nor to deal with the real challenges posed by the impact on public services that continued to struggle to cater for the needs of deprived local communities.

Service providers, however, did begin to focus on the fairness of provision. For example, a major and influential review of local authority housing was published on the Ministry of Housing and Local Government (MHLG) in the form of the Cullingworth Report in 1969. This Report, whilst taking a progressive view of race relations and recommending the introduction of ethnic monitoring with regard to housing allocations, at no point suggests any measures to assist cross-cultural contact, tolerance and understanding. Indeed, the Report even notes that the issue of whether ethnic monitoring should be carried out was the most difficult decision it had to make and concluded that, 'reluctantly but quite definitely was necessary'. This was, in Cullingworth's view, the means by which fairness would be demonstrated and ensured and, furthermore,

> we have assumed as an act of faith that records will be needed only for a short limited period. We may be proved wrong in this, but we look

forward to the day when policies have achieved their objective and colour is irrelevant in practice as it is in principle. (MHLG, 1969, pp. 161–2)

This 'faith' in systems and processes was shared by many public agencies at the time. It did not, however, immediately transform the fortunes of the BME communities, though ethnic monitoring has now become a widespread and accepted practice and has undoubtedly contributed to equal opportunities and, to some degree, to the changing attitudes and values. Gradually the practice of ethnic monitoring has been made ever more sophisticated. Most of the initial application was in Labour-controlled local authorities but has now been taken up by most other public agencies including government departments and by many large private sector employers. It was initially only applied to one or two key numerical measures in each service area, but has gradually been extended to a wide range of qualitative indicators. For example, in housing, whereas Cullingworth focussed on house lettings, most housing authorities will now monitor many other services, including the repairs service, access to community facilities and whether enforcement proceedings are equitably applied.

The main focus of attention in this period was, however, in relation to employment, where the different performance of black and white communities was most clearly apparent. Again, the spotlight was turned initially on public sector employers, like the police and local authorities, where it became clear that BME communities were visibly under-represented, both as a proportion of employees and, most especially, in senior positions. But relatively little was done in the workplace to gain acceptance of the new equal opportunities agenda and, as it was taken up initially by mainly left wing local authorities, it was often characterised in the popular press as 'loony left' extremism, with no general support. To the immense credit of these agencies, which not only stuck rigidly to their policies, but also, over time, gained widespread acceptance of their practices, the point has now been reached where ethnic monitoring is simply seen as part of the performance regime of any professional discipline.

Whilst the controversy revolved around the introduction of such systems and processes, however, little real consideration was given to how they might eventually become redundant or – in Cullingworth's terms – 'irrelevant in practice and principle'. Some measures were of course implemented to try to engender support for the development of equal opportunities work. For example 'race awareness' training was introduced, again largely in those local authorities at the forefront of the work. However, the approach was often confrontational and even intimidating. It was based on the assumption that the underlying cause of racism was to be found in the inherently racist attitudes of the white population. This view was often extended to encompass the notion that black and Asian people could not perpetrate racism, because they understood it only too well, having been on

LIBRARY, UNIVERSITY OF CHESTER

the receiving end of white racism. The challenge was therefore, very bluntly aimed at the white community, or even more directly, at fellow white colleagues in the same workplace.

A few public awareness campaigns were also attempted. The Greater London Council (GLC) was amongst the most determined:

> The centrepiece of the GLC's anti-racist strategy was the declaration of London as an 'anti-racist zone' and the announcement that 1984 was to be an anti-racist year in which the struggle against racism would be a continual and primary focus of the council's work. These commitments took the council into the realm of popular politics and relied on public awareness campaigning marshalled through billboards and press advertisements. (Gilroy, 1992, p. 181)

Equal opportunities programmes were introduced for staff in local government and financial support to ethnic minority groups and organisations were also developed, and by 1984, sixteen London boroughs had taken some action in this respect (ibid., p. 180).

Local authorities also borrowed the idea of 'contract compliance' from the United States to secure a contractual commitment to equal opportunities in the workforces of their contractors. Again, the Greater London Council (with the Inner London Education Authority) was amongst the first in the field, and this pioneering work was soon developed and promulgated by the Association of Metropolitan Authorities (AMA), which represented authorities in the major conurbations. They held a national conference in 1986 and produced a conference report and 'good practice' guide in the following year (AMA, 1987). Contract compliance activities, however, were constrained by the Conservative Government as a result of the Local Government Act 1988. This Act essentially stopped local authorities from taking account of what the Government defined as 'non-commercial' considerations in the award of contracts. Nevertheless, authorities were still able to check whether contractors had had regard to race relations legislation.

In 1980 and 1981 there were riots in Bristol, Liverpool, Brixton in London and elsewhere. The Brixton riots led to the appointment of Lord Scarman to head an Inquiry and his report was published in late 1981 (Scarman, 1981). Scarman's report will be best remembered for linking racial disadvantage and deprivation to the unrest and particularly to the problem of youth unemployment. Scarman also focussed on the poor relations between the police and the black community and proposed a significant expansion in police training in race and community matters and that consultative committees be established at a local level to improve communications between the police and local people.

Scarman moved the race agenda on significantly, in linking unrest to social conditions and by recognising the feeling of hopelessness and powerlessness in the black community. He also emphasised the need for improved communications at a local level. However, the report offered less in practical terms in respect of changing the attitudes and perceptions of the white population and the underlying causes of the racist attitudes and discriminatory behaviour. Nevertheless, the poor social conditions in urban areas recognised by Scarman were not addressed in any meaningful way and the overall economic position did not improve. Further riots took place in London and other cities with a significant black and minority population, such as Birmingham and Nottingham, in 1985. The reports that followed again referred to the problems of deprivation and inner city decay. However, attention was again focussed on policing and the poor relations between the police and the black community generally.

The Macpherson Report in 1999 followed the murder of a black teenager, Stephen Lawrence, in Eltham, south east London. Whilst the Report was wide ranging it will be remembered for establishing a commitment to tackling 'institutional racism'. Its political importance was considerable, demonstrating that the new Labour Government was at last getting to grips with its own governmental machinery. The Race Relations (Amendment) Act followed in 2000, giving public authorities a 'general duty' to prevent discrimination, promote equality of opportunity and to promote 'good race relations', as well as a 'specific duty' to draw up a race equality scheme in respect of their own functions. Whilst public authorities almost immediately began to draw up and publish their schemes to promote equality, few covered any specific aspects of 'promoting good relations'. The CRE's advice on this matter has also been very limited over the years and a substantial guide was not published until 2005 (CRE, 2005).

However, it was not just the CRE that failed to interpret its duty 'to promote good race relations' in a positive and pro-active way. Such measures were simply not on the agenda. Local authorities were generally developing their equal opportunities policies and focussed almost entirely on the 'rights agenda' and the tackling of discrimination and inequality, rather than attempting to change the attitudes and values of the white community. For example, the AMA produced a good practice guide on housing and race in 1985 (AMA, 1985) which specifically drew attention to the wording of the 1976 Act, including section 71. However, in making seven recommendations to its member authorities involving a number of changes to the processes and systems operating in local authority housing, including ethnic monitoring, allocations criteria, recruitment of ethnic minority staff and training, it failed to include any in respect of the 'promotion of good race relations' specified in section 71. Similarly, a Royal Town Planning Institute (RPTI) Guide *Planning for a Multi-Racial Britain*, actually produced jointly with the CRE (RTPI and CRE, 1983) made 36 proposals, none of which were to promote 'good race relations' other than the obscure aim of 'matching the process of participation and land use and development control policies to these diverse needs' (ibid., p. 82). Even a House of Commons Select Committee Report, *Racial Disadvantage*, failed to mention the social and psychological needs of communities, despite making 57 recommendations (House of Commons, 1981).

Addressing the underlying attitudes and values of the host community and helping them come to terms with the changes that the new diversity had brought was simply never on the agenda. In part, this reflected the overwhelming moral case for equal rights that simply had to be addressed, perhaps a lack of imagination in continuing to deal with the symptoms rather than underlying causes, but possibly an unwillingness to do so – was there an ambivalence in the minds of policy makers – do we really want to build a multicultural society, or just keep a lid on the more extreme behaviour?

The riots (officially classed by the Police as 'disturbances') which took place in 2001 in Bradford, Burnley and Oldham and involved the Asian community, again underlined the limitations of Britain's race relations strategy. But the unrest in these northern towns and cities had a somewhat different character to previous riots. First, on this occasion it was largely Pakistani and Bangladeshi Muslims that were involved (although the press invariably referred to them as 'young Asians', making no mention of their religious affiliation (Billig *et al.*, 2006)). They had been targeted by white racists in a similar way to the black community in previous riots and were generally second generation, born in Britain, who might have been expected to be more able than their parents to claim an equal stake in British society. They had also been the beneficiaries of over 40 years of anti-discrimination and equal opportunities legislation. Yet such factors had clearly had a limited impact and the riots were seen as the product of segregation over many years, the lack of any meaningful contact between white and Asian communities and the absence of any real stake in their local communities.

In relation to Bradford, the report commissioned before the riots took place, commented:

> the Bradford District has witnessed growing divisions among its population along race, ethnic, religious and social class lines – and now finds itself in the grip of fear. Few people talking openly and honestly about problems, either within their own communities or across different cultural communities. (Ouseley, 2001, p. 1)

The focus on equal rights had not been matched by any serious attempt to break down the barriers between communities and to develop a better understanding, which might have led to increased tolerance and trust. Of course, given the clear injustice associated with differential treatment based on race and the everyday reality of racism and discrimination experienced by BME communities, a programme of 'bridge building' between communities might have appeared a secondary consideration. The moral case for equal rights seemed overwhelming and simply assumed primacy in every debate. The arguments that had supported the original duty to 'promote good race relations' enshrined in the earlier legislation and which might have undermined racist sentiment and discriminatory behaviour, simply never regained prominence.

In some ways, the focus on the 'rights agenda' may have helped to perpetuate the very myths that the agenda was seeking to address, namely that disadvantaged individuals and communities need special treatment. Whilst the aspiration of this approach was simply to create a 'level playing field', the introduction of 'positive action' measures were particularly controversial even though they were designed to give people from minorities an equal chance, for example in respect of an employment opportunity. Such actions included training people in how to complete application forms and skill training courses to equip them with the necessary qualifications to apply for particular jobs. These measures were often seen by the white community, as 'positive discrimination' in favour of the BME community, even though positive discrimination is not permitted under British law, apart from in very limited circumstances. Nevertheless, they could be characterised as 'special treatment', especially by politically motivated groups who were opposed to any equality measures. Despite the controversy, positive action measures have undoubtedly succeeded in removing some of the inequalities inherent in British society.

The provision of special assistance to residential areas dominated by minorities has also been controversial. Even though BME communities are amongst the most deprived in Britain, white disadvantaged communities from neighbouring areas, have often seen these programmes in a very negative light – discrimination in favour of BME communities. Although there has been no evidence that resources have been directed to these communities on grounds other than 'needs', the perception remains. It is also possible that, over time, such areas become stigmatised creating a negative impression of the abilities and motivation of minority communities, which the programmes are designed to overcome. A somewhat more difficult problem has also been in the background, however, and that is the lack of openness and reluctance to justify the decisions made. This is again largely because of the belief that debates about resources and 'special measures' will be hijacked by racists, who are simply waiting their chance to create mischief. But without debate – and challenge – programmes cannot be established on the basis of real consensus or understanding and, because they are not understood, are perceived as 'politically correct' impositions (along with many other actions that are not acceptable to some), which are not based on genuine merit.

The failure to promote or create an open dialogue alongside equalities initiatives has led to the disengagement of some sections of the white community. The lack of justification for actions that promote the legitimate aims of minority communities to have equal opportunities, has also meant that the white community's attitudes and values have also not been challenged, joint understanding has not been sufficiently developed and the process of building acceptance of the new diversity brought by minority communities has been delayed. Rather, some white communities have seen diversity as a challenge to their culture, and that it is somehow being eroded and diminished, rather than being enriched.

Social cohesion and community cohesion

'Social cohesion' and 'community cohesion' have sometimes been used interchangeably. A distinction is discernible, however, in that 'social cohesion' has tended to be used more broadly and aligned particularly with general socioeconomic factors, whereas 'community cohesion' has emerged as a more specific term to describe the societal fractures which are based on identifiable communities defined by faith or ethnicity, rather than social class.

The term 'community cohesion' was effectively created in response to the riots in the northern towns of England in 2001. The term had been little used prior to that time and this was the first occasion it had been used to shape government policy. It appeared to have Canadian origins and actually grew out of the concept of 'social cohesion'. Lynch (2001) drew upon the definition used by the Social Cohesion Network, a part of the Canadian government, in 1996:

The ongoing process of developing a community of shared values, shared challenges and equal opportunity within Canada, based on a sense of trust, hope and reciprocity among all Canadians.

Lynch (ibid.) also referred to the work of Ferlander and Timms (1999) and Forrest and Kearns (2000) to underpin the development of the notion of community cohesion and in each case reflects upon the use of 'common norms and values' and 'shared interests' as principal components in the concept of community cohesion. Again, Lynch draws upon their use of the term 'social cohesion' and uses it synonymously with that of 'community cohesion'.

Forrest and Kearns's (2000) use of 'social cohesion', however, focusses on the social processes which underpin more general aspects of harmonious community relations – the degree of social capital, attachment to a place or area, inequalities based on wealth and access to services, social order and common values. They do not emphasise the divisions based on ethnicity and faith, although their 'domains of cohesion' can usefully be applied to establish whether societal fault lines do divide on this basis or any other 'common local interest'.

The term 'community cohesion' was nevertheless adopted for the British context, based principally on race and faith and used to underline the necessity to develop shared values across ethnic divisions, as a response to community conflict and unrest. This also represented a very different approach to reports into previous disturbances and unrest:

> It is easy to focus on systems, processes and institutions and to forget that community cohesion fundamentally depends on people and their values. Indeed, many of our present problems seem to owe a great deal to our failure to communicate and agree a set of common values that can govern behaviour. (Cantle, 2001)

The Community Cohesion Review Team, which had been set up to investigate the underlying causes of the riots, used the title 'community cohesion' to emphasise that changing attitudes and values were crucial to repairing the fractures between communities. This complemented other attempts to reinvent the concept of 'community', which Margaret Thatcher had seemingly earlier disavowed. David Blunkett, the then Home Secretary, was the driving force behind this 'reinvention'. In his book 'Politics and Progress' (Blunkett, 2001) Blunkett combines some communitarian strands and the work of social capital theorists to present his ideas of communities with strong social networks to bind people together across all potential divisions. His ideas gradually emerged through the subsequent establishment of a number of dedicated units in the Home Office to promote 'active communities' and 'civil renewal' to complement others dealing with 'faith', 'race equality' and 'community cohesion'. By 2004, David Blunkett's approach was more explicit, explaining that the challenge of community cohesion was not 'just to tackle inequalities' but to rebuild civic pride, promote citizenship and to enable and empower communities to do things for themselves (Blunkett, 2004). The 'Old Labour' notion of collectivism had been radically changed into a 'New Labour' concept of civic values and social responsibility.

Parekh (2002, p. 42) had also dealt more explicitly with models of cohesion when his Report was published in 2000. But whilst he is clearly relating these models to 'multi-ethnic Britain', he does not use the term 'community cohesion' to describe divisions along faith or race lines. Parekh sets out five models of 'cohesion, equality and difference'. These are constructed at a very general level of political culture and social norms, and whilst intended as 'theoretical discussion to clarify real life situations' they do not establish how communities would relate to each other, nor how such relationships are built, in a practical sense.

Social cohesion was also beginning to be used to emphasise the necessity of 'inclusion', and the determination to tackle 'exclusion': where individuals or groups were so disadvantaged that they could not effectively participate at any meaningful level of society. Tackling the problem of 'social exclusion' became a driver of social policy in the Blair Government from 1997. The Social Exclusion Unit (SEU) was created to develop and co-ordinate action across government. This followed the work by the EU in the early 1990s, which was itself derived from the work of Jacques Delors in France (Parekh, 2002, p. 76) moving across the Channel in the 1980s (Pilkington, 2003, p. 91).

Social exclusion has been defined as multiple disadvantage, which can be applied to individuals or communities that suffer 'unemployment, poor skills, low incomes, unfair discrimination, poor housing, high crime, bad health and family breakdown' (SEU, 2004, p. 4). The principal focus of action, however, has been 'on whether or not people are in or outside the labour force' (Pilkington, 2003, p. 95). It has not, then, been associated with any particular ethnic group or culture, and was criticised as a result by Parekh (2000, p. 82) who generally regards the social exclusion policies as 'colour blind'.

In conceptual terms, 'social exclusion' remained firmly linked to social class and poverty:

> Social inclusion is often treated in rather crude economic or employment terms, with inclusion being defined in terms of possession of minimum wealth or a job. Its opposite, social exclusion is defined either by the absence of these characteristics or as the process by which specified targets are denied these attributes. (Ferlander and Timms, 1999, p. 7)

The SEU responded, in somewhat uncertain terms to the earlier criticism, accepting that some groups 'remain cut off from service reform' and instance the Pakistani and Bangladeshi communities (Tyler, 2004). Nevertheless, the main focus of their work remains that of addressing the fractures in society along class or economic lines – 'social cohesion' – with little by way of specific programmes specifically targeted at ethnic minorities, which are just one part of 'multiple disadvantage' (see, for example, Social Exclusion Unit, 2004).

Class and race have never been easy to disentangle, either conceptually or in practice. Racial minorities have often been presented as an 'underclass', and seen in Marxist terms as simply the most exploited of the working class. But race and class are clearly separable variables, even though black and ethnic minorities are, in general, amongst the most economically and socially disadvantaged. There is also a huge variation in the social and economic positions, both within and between, BME communities. Substantial sections of those communities are, on any objective analysis, positioned within middle and upper classes. Others have remained in working class jobs and are indistinguishable in social class terms from their white neighbours. However, this does not mean that they do not suffer occasional racist abuse and discrimination. Yet in some areas, most notably in the most deprived areas of our inner cities, black and ethnic minorities are clearly set apart from their white working class counterparts, socially, economically – and in many cases – physically.

Visible differences may have a great deal, or very little, significance and can also help to set minorities apart and can add another layer to those based upon social and economic divisions, or they can stand alone. In many multicultural areas, with a high degree of interaction between people of different faiths and ethnicities, for example, visible differences may be irrelevant with people more attuned to other characteristics, perhaps in terms of social class or occupation. On the other hand, they may well be the most obvious and distinguishing feature of a community and help to underpin separation, though often compounded by further differences in religious practices, language and lifestyle. The nature of 'difference' is discussed further in Chapter 3, but it is important to note here that the extent to which particular communities are identifiable will have an impact on the possibility of societal fractures, especially as in Britain and other Western nations, the prevailing culture is that of the majority white community and difference is generally judged against that backdrop. Visible minorities have popularly become denoted as 'non-white' (Karim, 1996, p. 2) and some local authorities in Britain, like the London Borough of Hackney, have even adopted the term 'visible minorities' in preference to 'BME' population. (The term BME has itself recently been challenged, with some organisations now preferring BAME – Black And Minority Ethnic – to emphasise that not all minorities are 'black'; whilst others have simply used ME – minority ethnic, which has the same effect and perhaps reflects the increasing diversity of the population as a result of a new wave of immigration.)

Visible differences may therefore be a means by which communities are identified and by which society is stratified. These may also be a factor in the 'fear of difference' which is also discussed in Chapter 3 and this fear of others, is a fundamental part of community cohesion. It recognises, as many commentators have suggested, that these fears are socially and politically determined, or are constructed by 'in-groups' to define themselves and their relationships to others, or 'out-groups'. The social and psychological issues therefore have to be addressed as part of any attempt to establish mutual trust and respect and are the basis for good relations between different groups. Community cohesion will therefore also embrace other identifiable communities, such as travellers and has been extended to divisions based on age (Wilmore, 2005), and wherever 'difference' and the 'fear of difference' is apparent and irrespective of whether it is entwined or entirely separable from economic position.

'Social cohesion' has been described as a 'murky concept' (Pahl, 1995, p. 354) and has certainly been used in a number of different contexts. It is often linked to 'social capital' to help describe the 'glue' that holds societies together. In this sense it is used as an expression of a positive community spirit, where the social networks effectively support a particular community or place. Some argue that, in this form, social cohesion has been in decline for some time, particularly as a result of social and economic changes, for example, the emergence of the individual 'affluent worker' in the new manufacturing industries, detailed by a number of sociologists, principally, Goldthorpe and Lockwood in the 1960s, who also plotted the demise of working class solidarity and collectivism. They set out the decline of the traditional type of working class community, or the 'urban village', founded upon the residential stability and social homogeneity, which was undermined by the growth of privatised home-centred lifestyles. Others doubt whether this form of social cohesion was really any more effective 50, or even 200, years ago (Pahl, 1995, p. 350).

The concept of *social capital* is now much more widely used in the development of social policy and is increasingly being used to describe the extent and nature of community relationships, based on the belief that where social capital is strong the cohesion of the community will be reinforced. The British Government's review of social capital (Aldridge and Halpern, 2002) found an overall decline in social capital in countries such as Australia and the United States, a more stable or even rising picture in the Netherlands, Sweden, Japan and Germany and a more ambiguous picture in Britain.

This study illustrated the difficult debate about what actually constitutes social capital and extended the notion to include indicators such as 'trust' (which showed a decline over time in Britain) and to others, such as 'volunteering' (which remained stable). Bolstering social capital, in any form, is nevertheless now seen as fundamental to the success of community policies.

Robert Putnam's seminal work on social capital, *Bowling Alone* (Putnam, 2000), which presented a substantial body of evidence to demonstrate how social networks had been in decline for some time and that the strength of community ties and norms has reduced as a result, undoubtedly helped to establish this new direction. His work can be related directly to community cohesion, as he also demonstrated that social capital levels are inversely related to the extent of diversity in a wide range of cities and towns in the United States. However, Putnam (2000, p. 22) developed the notion of 'bridging capital' as a means of defining the contact between unlike groups of different ethnic origin, and where the lack of contact between ethnic groups was seen to fundamentally undermine cohesion.

Despite the lack of any clear and generally accepted definitions for each of these terms, there is now an emerging consensus which will hopefully support a basic division between 'social cohesion' and 'community cohesion' along the following lines:

- **Social Cohesion** reflects divisions based on social class and economic position and is complemented by social capital theories relating to the 'bonding' between people and the presence of mutual trust. It is seen to be undermined by the social exclusion experienced by individuals or groups, again generally defined by their social class and economic position.

- **Community Cohesion** reflects divisions based upon identifiable communities, generally on the basis of faith or ethnic distinctions, which may reflect socio-economic differences. It is also complemented by the social capital theory of 'bridging' between communities. It is undermined by the disadvantage, discrimination and disaffection experienced by the identifiable community as a whole and by lack of trust and understanding resulting from segregation and social separateness.

The relationship between social capital and community cohesion is discussed further in Chapter 6.

The various reports produced in response to the 2001 riots all agreed that the fragmentation of communities along faith and ethnic lines and that the lack of contact between those communities which were also divided by different levels of disadvantage and discrimination, was a major and underlying cause of the unrest.

In Bradford, Herman Ouseley's, Report (2001, p. 6), which was commissioned prior to the riots, came to the same conclusion:

The key concern in the District is that relationships between different cultural communities should be improving, but instead they are deteriorating. There are signs that communities are fragmenting along racial, cultural and faith lines. Segregation in schools is one indicator of this trend. Rather than seeing the emergence of a confident multi-cultural District, where people are respectful and have understanding and tolerance for differences, people's attitudes appear to be hardening and intolerance towards differences is growing. The situation is hindering people's understanding of each other and preventing positive contact between people from different cultural communities.

In Oldham, Ritchie (2001) made similar comments (pp. 7 and 9):

The divisions are now such that we have to ask the question whether people in different communities actually want to have much to do with one another.

and

There must be substantial interchange between people of different ethnic backgrounds which go beyond the purely commercial, and there must be a premium on more communication and interaction at all levels.

In Burnley, it was a similar story, with the Task Force indicating that they were told that Asians and whites lived separate and parallel lives, compounded by segregation in schools and in the workplace (Clarke, 2001, p. 6).

The Cantle Report took a national view based not only a review of the towns that had riots, but also on observations in a range of other towns and cities in England. Nevertheless, in order to illustrate the concept of 'parallel lives' it used a graphic example from Burnley:

> The extent to which ... physical divisions were compounded by so many other aspects of our daily lives was very evident. Separate educational arrangements, community and voluntary bodies, employment, places of worship, language, social and cultural networks, means that many communities operate on the basis of a series of parallel lives. These lives do not seem to touch at any point, let alone overlap and promote meaningful interchanges.

A Muslim of Pakistani origin summed this up:

> *When I leave this meeting with you I will go home and not see another white face until I come back here next week.*

Similarly, a young white man from a council estate said:

> *I never met anyone on this estate who wasn't like us from around here.*

There is little wonder that the ignorance about each others' communities can easily grow into fear; especially where this is exploited by extremist groups determined to undermine community harmony and foster divisions. (Cantle, 2001, p. 9)

The government then, responded immediately and positively to the Cantle and other reports (Denham, 2001, p. 2) and firmly created the link between 'community cohesion' and 'race' and embedded it into Government policy:

> This report is a key step in the process of building stronger, more cohesive communities, reflecting the Government's commitment to civil renewal. But it is just the beginning. Our central recommendation is the need to make community cohesion a central aim of Government, and to ensure that the design and delivery of all Government policy reflects this. We recognise areas affected by disorder or community tensions, there is little interchange between members of different racial, cultural and religious communities and that positive measures will have to be taken to promote dialogue and understanding. We also take on board the need to generate a widespread and open debate about identity, shared values, and common citizenship as part of the process of building cohesive communities.

and

> There are no easy answers or quick fixes to the deep fracturing of communities on racial, generational and religious lines now evident in parts

of Bradford, Burnley and Oldham. The causes are multi-layered and complex, and tackling them will require sustained effort over several years, across Government working in partnership with local agencies and people, if our most fractured communities are to become cohesive ones, uniting people around a common sense of belonging regardless of race, culture or faith. The development of effective policy responses must be truly inclusive, involving all sections of all local communities.

Denham, therefore, reinforces the point that community cohesion is about the fault lines in communities, not only in respect of ethnicity or race, but also on religious grounds (as for example in Northern Ireland) or for any group visible by cultural or other identifiable characteristic. Subsequent work has also focussed on other groups, for example, on travelling communities and on inter-generational conflict (see, for example, Home Office/Vantagepoint, 2003).

However, relatively little work has been undertaken in respect of the host white community, even though they have often felt threatened by their increasingly multicultural society and have been prepared to express racist views and practice discrimination to protect what they see as their identity and to maintain their advantageous position, particularly in the housing and employment markets. Even after forty or fifty years of multiculturalism, many white communities still do not accept the idea – let alone the reality – of multiculturalism and are unwilling to see it as an enrichment, of their lives. In Britain, this is often manifest in the support for the British National Party (BNP), or other extreme right wing groups although this support has been relatively modest compared to other European countries where support for the extreme right has often been in the range of 15–20 per cent (and higher in some cases) in national and regional elections. Nevertheless, remedial programmes have often been targeted at BME communities, as a response to their disaffection and disadvantage, and there has been a lack of will and confidence to challenge the attitudes and values of the white community and the underlying causes of prejudice.

Not all commentators have responded favourably to the emerging notion of community cohesion. McGhee (2003, p. 400), for example sees the idea of building reciprocal relationships and a shared vision as 'unobtainable ideals', but concedes somewhat grudgingly, that with enough funding and community support, the 'turn-around from bonding to bridging might work selectively' and 'be all for the better'.

Burnett was much more cynical and saw community cohesion as ignoring material deprivation of BME communities and the problems of policing. Further, the reports following the riots in 2001 were no more than a 'thinly veiled attempt to control those non-white communities designated as a risk to Britishness' (Burnett, 2004, p. 8). Moreover, community cohesion strategies are 'naive and insulting' to Asian communities (ibid., p. 13).

Burnett's interesting views seem to have ignored, however, three fundamental points. First, that the development of community cohesion was not simply based on changing attitudes and values. The Reports following the disturbances were all concerned about the lack of equal opportunities for some sections of the population and the poverty and disadvantage so very evident in the areas. For example, Cantle (2001, p. 10) referred to the 'lack of hope and the frustration borne out of the poverty and deprivation' and drew attention to the unequal opportunities in respect of housing, employment and education. Similarly, Ritchie (2001, p. 12) contrasted other cities with Oldham and the lack of economic opportunities stemming from the decline of traditional industries. Denham, in responding for the government, also saw this as a key issue (2001, p. 15).

In fact, it is difficult to conceive of a cohesive society in which the gap between rich and poor is not only clear and apparent but is also identifiable with particular classes or groups. The perpetuation of that divide over time, especially on an inter-generational basis would suggest that those sections of society are subject of structural factors that frustrate legitimate aspirations and expectations. The disengagement of these disadvantaged groups would mean that they did not believe they had an equal stake in society and that an equal stake would be almost impossible to achieve, whatever effort they made. It would also be difficult to persuade them to believe in a vision of an inclusive society and that they shared a sense of belonging. This would apply to groups divided by class, race or faith and to both white and BME communities.

Second, the reports did not simply focus on the BME communities and the changes that they might have to make to become somehow 'more British', and placed a particular emphasis on the need for the white host community to change and to become more comfortable with diversity.

Third, the essence of community cohesion is not to develop interaction between communities and to try to change peoples' attitudes and values for its own sake, even though this may be laudable in itself. Rather, it is to try to break down some of the prejudice and intolerance of others that allows discriminatory behaviour to continue and fester. It is an attempt at longer-term change to improve the life chances of those constantly faced with prejudice and discrimination and is not simply focussed on controlling behaviour in the short term – an approach that has clearly had limited impact over the last 40 years of such legislation. Again, such attitudinal change is inevitably targeted more at the majority or host population, who have had most difficulty in coming to terms with diversity, than at minorities.

A number of organisations and individuals have been tirelessly campaigning against racism and discrimination and rebutting all and any attacks on black and minority ethnic people over several decades. Given the history of race relations in the UK, a robust approach has certainly been necessary on many occasions and indeed racial discrimination is still unfortunately prevalent today. And, with regard to equal opportunities, there is, to coin the phrase used by the CRE as the title for its last review of the state of race relations, 'a lot done – a lot to do' (CRE, 2007). But, the consequence of this continuous and defensive position is that there is often a knee-jerk and antagonistic reaction to any new policies, or even discussion, in respect of race relations and immigration, lest it should again be misused by the extreme right and racists of all descriptions as a means of stirring up resentment and hostility towards minorities.

It was almost inevitable that the concept of community cohesion would be similarly viewed with suspicion when it appeared in 2001. For some commentators, it was seen as an attempt at blaming BME groups for the riots and poor race relations generally, when the real problems were simply those of poverty and disadvantage and institutionalised racism. The Institute of Race Relations has maintained a view which has been typical of a simplistic stance.

> Now the fight against racism could be put on a back burner ... it exonerated government policies and institutions of the racial discrimination that prevented integration and implicitly blamed minority ethnic communities for the lack of cohesion. (Bourne, 2007, p. 5)

This response was despite the fact that virtually all reports into the riots and their causes actually specifically drew attention to structural inequalities. None 'blamed ethnic minority communities', no quotations from the reports were produced as evidence, it was somehow 'implicit'. Similarly, Burnett and Whyte (2004) seized the opportunity to attack what they saw as the new policy thrust of 'New Labour's New Racism'

> the term 'community cohesion' masks a double-edged sword. The rhetoric proposes an agenda for revitalising community and improving social and economic opportunities for all. The sharp edge of the sword explicitly seeks to rid the country of difference.

Again, no quotations were produced from the original reports, nor from the more contemporary community cohesion guidance. They chose to ignore the explicit statement on community cohesion, widely adopted by the main governmental and non-governmental bodies (see Figure 2.1) which set out the valuing of difference and diversity as a key aim.

The term 'parallel lives' coined by the Independent Review Team after the riots in 2001 (Cantle, 2001) was also viewed suspiciously, even though the Report made it very clear that white communities had no contact with BME groups, as well as vice versa and carefully illustrated this point (and the very concept of 'parallel lives' was developed explicitly to indicate that 'many' communities were involved). But still 'critics sensed in the debate the possibility of deprived communities being blamed' and it was even 'implicitly assumed' that this could be 'condoning criminality' (Harrison *et al.*, 2005, p. 85).

The 'assumptions' and 'sensing' went still further as the highly attuned defensive mechanisms kicked in and any discussion about segregation and self-segregation was also seen as a threat. Up to this point 'self-segregation' had simply been seen as the product of justifiable protectionism and had been used by academics with alacrity. But now 'the cohesion discourse' and the subsequent speech by Trevor Phillips, 'Sleepwalking in to Segregation' (Phillips, 2005) was seen as an attempt at blaming ethnic minorities for 'not wanting to integrate'. Simpson took this argument to a rather tortuous extreme and sought to describe any suggestion of increasing self-segregation as a 'myth' (Simpson, 2003). However, any attempt to restrict the discussion to such limited terms is unlikely to succeed (and is returned to in Chapter 3). And there is clear evidence that a degree of 'self-segregation', as generally attributed to minorities is real and remains an expressed preference (and has even been acknowledged in the studies of critics like Simpson and Phillips (Simpson *et al.*, 2007; Phillips, D., 2005)). Similarly, the reduction of the white population, which is of a very substantial nature in some cities and can be attributed to 'white flight' to some extent at least, is also acknowledged by those same critics (ibid.). White flight could just as well be described as a form of self-segregation, or perhaps more aptly, 'self-separation'. The polarisation of communities, along ethnic lines, has also increased because of differential natural factors and may well have been exacerbated by further in-migration of minorities and out-migration of the white majority, though it is likely that firm evidence will only be provided by the 2011 Census. There is however, some proxy evidence, particularly from school composition and other local data which indicates an increasing level of segregation as a result of all of the above factors (Johnson *et al.*, 2006; iCoCo, 2007).

However, the concern about whether segregation, and self-segregation, is increasing rather misses the central point of the cohesion debate, that is, that separate communities do exist and that they often develop in fear and ignorance of each other, with little or no contact between them. Also, the debate about spatial distribution fails to recognise the separation in social and many other spheres, which contribute to 'parallel lives'. The question of why segregation exists and whether or not it is increasing may be debatable, but it is vital to recognise that whatever the cause, a number of societal consequences will result.

Again, we must distinguish between clustering and supportive networks, with permeable boundaries, and very distinct separate and segregated communities. Some level of self-segregation is probably inevitable, but also desirable, as clustering of distinct groups often provides support systems (as Cantle, 2007, has described and Cheshire, 2007, has noted). But, there is a very considerable distinction between ethnic clustering which is permeable, overlapping with other networks and integrated through employment, schooling or in other ways, and exclusive 'no-go' areas in which different groups remain in their own comfort zones and lead parallel lives. The community cohesion 'discourse' of segregation etc., is, in any event as much a criticism of the host community, who themselves seek to remain separate and to reinforce such separation through 'white flight'. As suggested earlier, the concept of community cohesion, together with any apparent critique of the multicultural model, is sometimes wrongly interpreted as an attack on minorities, to which an automatic and rather unthinking, defence is needed. This emphasises, once again, the need for a much more open debate about these issues, unbounded by some of the previous fears and defensive positions – updating our multicultural model is not the same as abandoning it. Indeed, if we fail to update it, the model may well become untenable, particularly in an era of 'super diversity'.

Whilst some of the 'old soldiers' of the race debate continue to fight on familiar battle grounds, the nature of the debate has moved on to different territory – and one which no longer revolves around a simple black and white paradigm. Over the last few years, the impact of EU migrants, in particular, has begun to be felt, raising some very familiar and some very new issues of identity and diversity. Whilst accurate figures are difficult to come by and national projections and local estimates are frequently disputed (iCoCo, 2007) around three-quarters of a million national insurance numbers have been allocated to foreign nationals from 2002/03, most of which have been given to EU nationals. Not all of these foreign national workers will remain in Britain on a long-term basis, but the scale and pace of recent migration has generated a considerable interest in how to avoid some of the past mistakes of separate development and to encourage integration. The Audit Commission produced a report to help local authorities and their partners manage change by developing local services and appropriate strategies. Emphasis was placed upon giving support to migrants to help them settle-in and to improve communication and understanding. This was followed by more comprehensive advice to local authorities (iCoCo, 2007c) which also emphasised support to the 'host' community to enable them to come to terms with change. Other advice and guidance has been developed for particular communities, for example in respect of the Roma community, one of the most demonised in the press and media (Oakley, 2005). There has been little criticism of this new approach to integration, based upon practical measures and little suggestion of homogenisation, or assimilation, despite the much greater emphasis upon the requirement for migrants to learn English, to avoid ghettoisation and promote cross-cultural interaction.

The criticisms of the concept of community cohesion do not appear to extend to its practice, which they largely ignore. They therefore fail to consider whether it is more successful, or likely to be, than some of the previous approaches, which have clearly failed to develop real equality, or a society 'at ease with itself'.

Formalising community cohesion

The various reports into the 2001 riots did not formalise the definition of 'community cohesion' and, rather, described a range of activities that were designed to close the gap between communities, to engender a common sense of purpose and to encourage positive interaction between different groups so that tolerance, understanding and respect would develop. It was left to the various agencies of local and central government to respond:

> The challenge facing us all, since the publication of the Cantle and other reports, has been to translate our understanding of the issues raised into practical action to improve the situation on the ground. This action needs to tackle the causes that lead to conflict and to guard against circumstances that could lead to the fracturing of communities. (Local Government Association *et al.*, 2002, p. 5)

The Local Government Association, together with the Home Office, Office of the Deputy Prime Minister, the CRE and the Inter-Faith Network then went on, in their 'Guidance on Community Cohesion' to, somewhat cautiously, set out a 'broad working definition' of community cohesion, exactly one year after the publication of the original reports – see Figure 2.1.

The Guidance covered a wide range of measures to create a common and inclusive vision, in which diversity was genuinely valued and celebrated and more practical measures on regeneration, housing, education, sports and cultural services, community safety and policing, employment and working in partnership with faith communities and other organisations and groups was encouraged.

This definition has subsequently been adopted and used by local authorities and the various arms of Government. Many voluntary and community organisations have also adopted the definition. It has since been incorporated into a large number of local community cohesion strategies and in a number of cases is part of the formal agreements between local and central government for funding priorities. Many local authorities now have designated

---

The formal definition of community cohesion adopted in Guidance issued by the British Government and others is that a cohesive community is one where:

- there is a common vision and a sense of belonging for all communities;
- the diversity of people's different backgrounds and circumstances are appreciated and positively valued;
- those from different backgrounds have similar life opportunities; and
- strong and positive relationships are being developed between people from different backgrounds in the workplace, in schools and within neighbourhoods.

Figure 2.1   Definition of community cohesion

Source: Local Government Association, Office of the Deputy Prime Minister, Home Office, Commission of Racial Equality, *Guidance on Community Cohesion, 2002*.

community cohesion officers and lead elected members and a performance framework in place to measure progress.

However, at the time the concept was first promulgated at least one commentator preferred to have the 'traditional' approach to racial unrest in the form of a special programme of resources directed at the disaffected communities (Bodi, 2002). Others have regarded the definition as 'minimalist' and suggest a more demanding vision, drawing upon an Anglican tradition to 'put another's interest before your own, where you care for one another' (Bonney, 2003, p. 2). A similar approach is taken by another faith-based organisation who again emphasises 'that all humans are part of one family' and arguing that cohesion must go beyond 'mere tolerance' and also beyond the concept of 'a community of communities' to 'a deeply held and lived sense of human oneness' (Leith, 2002, p. 3). They also argue, in furtherance of the communitarian concept of 'diversity within unity', that 'diversity without unity is division; unity without diversity is uniformity' and that both extremes should be avoided (ibid.).

Most recently, the Commission on Integration and Cohesion (CIC, 2007) has reinforced support for the concept of community cohesion and has suggested an even wider definition, to include trust in local institutions, the rights and responsibilities of individuals and recognising the contribution of new arrivals. If this extended definition is accepted by Government, it takes cohesion into a wider realm of social capital and citizenship. The practice of community cohesion has been developed from the reports into the disturbances, which contained a large number of recommendations. The Cantle Report (2001) alone contained 67 recommendations, which were largely of a practical nature, but also recommended that work be undertaken to establish clearer principles of citizenship following a national debate and that programmes be established to promote cross-cultural contact and mutual respect and tolerance. The Home Office responded by establishing the Community Cohesion Unit in 2002, to co-ordinate the government's work on community cohesion and to develop and implement new approaches. The unit was complemented by an independent Community Cohesion Panel, which established about a dozen 'practitioner groups' to develop guidance and best practice in all of the major areas of government and local government activity.

The panel continued until June 2004, when it published its final report, *The End of Parallel Lives?* (Cantle, 2004) summarising the progress to date and suggesting what further work was required to develop the policy and practice of community cohesion. The panel raised a number of crucial questions about the way in which community cohesion was being implemented, and in particular, whether it was being sufficiently 'mainstreamed' with clear institutional and structural change to support it. The Report also suggested ways in which citizenship might be developed on a more pervasive and inclusive basis and how the government should ensure that 'settlement' is properly managed, rather than relying on a policy of 'managed migration'.

Further, it was proposed that local authorities should be given the lead role in both these areas and 'not only co-ordinate the provision of resources but also address the social and psychological needs of communities'. A wide range of other recommendations were also made and these were fed into the government's emerging strategy, *Strength in Diversity* (Home Office, 2004) which was published a month or two later in the form of a consultation document and firmed up into a final strategy in 2005 under the title of *Improving Opportunity, Strengthening Society* (Home Office, 2005). This brought together the race equality and community cohesion approaches into one strategy built around four themes:

- tackling inequalities and opening opportunities for all,
- promoting inclusive notions of citizenship, identity and belonging,
- eradicating racism and extremism,
- building community cohesion.

The recent Government Select Committee Report on Terrorism and Community Relations (House of Commons, 2005, p. 60) has also urged that 'the Government's proposals for community cohesion should be implemented with vigour'.

The CRE's response to the government's consultation document was also influential and represented a change of direction under the leadership of the Chair, Trevor Phillips. This acknowledged the CRE's dual role of enforcing the Race Relations Act and changing social attitudes, and the need to tackle the segregation and the confusion about identity (CRE, 2004). For the first time since the CRE was established in 1976 it was ready to address a broader-based agenda and to focus upon the underlying causes of prejudice, as well as the discrimination and inequalities that result. The CRE published guidance on 'promoting good race relations' in 2005 (CRE, 2005) which also helped to reinforce the cohesion agenda. However, the government decided to subsume the CRE into the new Equality and Human Rights Commission and the CRE was one of a number of equality bodies transferred to the EHRC in 2007. The effect of this on the community cohesion agenda remains to be seen, but presently appears positive.

The government was also able to build upon what it had learnt from the 'Pathfinder' scheme, launched in April 2003, backed by £6million in 14 local areas (with a further 14 shadow areas) to experiment with ways of 'breaking down the barriers between and within communities'. These new programmes were intended to be 'at the cutting edge of social policy, testing new methods of engagement' (Home Office and Vantagepoint, 2003). However, many of the schemes had the look of previous approaches to tackling equal opportunities, suitably tweaked to obtain additional funding, rather than being genuinely new and challenging, reflecting the then limited expertise in the emerging community cohesion agenda.

A further development in June 2003, was the publication of *'Building a Picture of Community Cohesion'* (Home Office *et al.*, 2003), which set out to guide local authority and their partners as to the measurement of cohesion at a local level. The aim was to establish a baseline in each area, so that trends could be established. The guidance proposed a mixture of 'hard' indicators, such as the number of racial incidents recorded by the police, and 'soft' indicators, such as 'the percentage of people who feel that their local area is a place where people from different backgrounds can get on well together' and 'the percentage of respondents who feel that they belong to their (area)'. As such, it helped to emphasise that 'community cohesion' was as much about attitudes and values as it was about those from different backgrounds having similar life opportunities.

Similarly the *Guidance on Community Cohesion* published in 2002 (Local Government Association *et al.*) helped to promote the notion that the development of an inclusive vision for local areas, in which 'unity in diversity is the theme' (p. 13) and where strong political and community leadership is required to establish community cohesion is based on the need to change attitudes and values. The *Guidance*, of course also recognised the need to tackle disadvantage and discrimination at the same time. The *Guidance* has become one of the most well-used source documents on community cohesion and was expanded, updated and re-published in 2004 (Local Government Association *et al.*, 2004). More strategic guidance, aimed at the leadership of local authorities, was produced by the same agencies in 2005 (LGA and IDeA, 2005) with complementary messages.

The Race Relations (Amendment) Act 2000, which came into force in April 2001, had also given an added, if unintended, impetus to the community cohesion agenda. This required local authorities and other public sector agencies to have regard, in everything they do, to not only promote race equality and tackle discrimination, but also to promote good relations between people from different racial groups. Similarly, new European laws on equality, such as the Racial Equality Directive and the Employment Equality Directive in 2003, were intended to, not only prohibit discrimination, but also to promote more positive measures, including measures to counteract the trend of ethnic segregation in important areas such as education and employment (European Monitoring Centre for Racism and Xenophobia, 2002).

Significantly, the Audit Commission, which inspects local authorities and assesses their performance, both in terms of service delivery and leadership of the community, included the concept of community cohesion in its inspection regime in 2005 (and also reviews performance in terms of diversity and equality). The new duty upon schools 'to promote community cohesion' also came into force in 2007 and Guidance has now been issued by the government (DCSF, 2007).

Gradually, then, the conceptualisation and practice of community cohesion has been formalised and the definition (see Figure 2.1) adopted in early

2002 (LGA *et al.*, 2002) has been widely used and reinforced in official publications and by non-statutory bodies over the last five or six years. The
emerging practice (see Chapter 6) has also been based on this definition but
recently given a significant boost by the publication of the CIC report *Our
Shared Future* (CIC, 2007) and by the publication of further examples of
emerging practice (CIC, 2007a; 2007b).

Whilst the concept of 'community cohesion' is presently a British one, it
is possible that synergy is also emerging at an international level and elements of similar practice are to be found in the work on inter-ethnic conflicts in other countries. These attempt to build mutual confidence and trust
between rival communities. In India, for example, pioneering work is
described by Varshney (2002), including that of Bhiwandi, a town just outside Mumbai. Bhiwandi has been segregated into Muslim and Hindu areas
and was infamous for the riots and conflicts between the two communities
in the 1970s and 1980s. In 1988, however, a new police chief decided to
tackle the conflicts in a different way and:

> (he) argued that instead of fighting fires when they broke out, it was bet-
> ter for the police to bring Hindus and Muslims together to create mutual
> understanding. The aim was to set up durable structures of peace. If the
> Hindus and Muslims could meet each other often enough and discuss
> common problems, a reservoir of communication and perhaps trust
> would be created. (Varshney, 2002, p. 293)

Despite riots in Mumbai and elsewhere after that time, the peace in Bhiwandi
endured. Varshney is also able to provide similar examples of successful
interventions in Northern Ireland, South Africa, the former Yugoslavia and
the United States.

Further examples of tackling even the most deep-seated divisions between
communities by fundamentally changing attitudes can be found elsewhere.
In west Jerusalem a project that commenced in the Nisui school has reached
into the wider communities. It uses the folklore and traditions of Jewish and
Arab families to bind together the two groups. It does not attempt to resolve
the conflict, but does attempt to break down the barriers between the communities who are sometimes fearful and often ignorant of the 'other'. The
project aims to challenge the stereotypes portrayed on both Israeli and
Arab television and appears to have had some success in developing positive
inter-action (Taylor, 2004).

The British Council has adopted 'intercultural dialogue' as one of its four
priority themes and is developing programmes in a wide range of countries.
The European Union is sponsoring the European Year of Intercultural
Dialogue in 2008 and has already supported a wide range of activities and
programmes to showcase during the year.

It is also possible that some similarities between the community cohesion agenda and the work developing under the banner of 'peace, forgiveness and reconciliation' in South Africa, Rwanda and elsewhere, can be found. The Western world watched, almost with incredulity, as Nelson Mandela held out the hand of forgiveness to the white minority that had oppressed the majority black and coloured population when apartheid collapsed. Yet, it is not clear whether the West has been prepared to learn any lessons from these bold new processes.

Meanwhile, in the former riot torn towns and elsewhere in Britain, schemes to break down the barriers between the communities, by developing cross-cultural contact and understanding, have now been underway for several years. These range from encouraging more mixed intakes in schools and challenging the stereo-typical occupational patterns, to developing cross community youth programmes and even the more 'banal encounters' of joint cookery classes. In each case, it is often the first occasion in which people from one community have had any meaningful contact with the other.

However, as the accepted definition of 'community cohesion' suggests, community cohesion involves tackling structural problems as well as the social and psychological needs of communities and is, therefore, a wider process than simply developing cross-cultural contact. The emerging practice, including promoting equalities and tackling discrimination, is discussed in Chapter 6.

3
Changing Conceptions of Multiculturalism

'Multiculturalism' has been used to describe a wide range of circumstances and is understood and interpreted in a number of different ways. As a result, it no longer has any real meaning, other than at a very generalised level and in political terms. This chapter attempts to explain some of the various ways in which the term has been used and also suggests some new interpretations of 'difference' within modern multicultural democracies.

Many societies would certainly be described as 'multicultural' if a very simple definition, based on the presence of a number of different ethnicities, faiths and cultures, were to be adopted. However, this would say very little about the relative size of the different groups, their similarity, in terms of beliefs, values and behaviours, both within and between the minorities and in terms of their relation to the majority group. It would also tell us little about their socio-economic position, in terms of education, employment, housing and other areas, again, in relation to each other and in relation to the host community. The crude numbers would also tell us nothing at all about the most significant determinant of successful multiculturalism – whether the distinctiveness of each cultural group is tolerated, accepted and celebrated, within a societal framework which also manages to create a common bond. Judgements about the success of multiculturalism have also generally been very focussed on the minority communities, rather than on the host, or dominant, community, yet the extent to which the host community can adapt to the challenge of accommodating diversity in their midst is often particularly crucial. Sandercock (2004, p. 16) sums up this position:

> Empirically, many societies and many cities can be described today as multicultural. But very few countries have embraced an *ideology* of multiculturalism. (Sandercock's emphasis)

Characteristics of multiculturalism

In numerical terms, most of the developed countries would be classed as 'multi-cultural'. However, the number of people from ethnic minority

68

backgrounds in each country is not always well documented and different forms of classification and measurement are used in each case and, in some countries, the relevant statistics are in short supply. Multicultural societies are classified in different ways and there has been confusion between people who are 'foreign born' and those classed as 'foreigners' (Stalker, 2001, p. 14). However, both have often been used as a crude proxy for 'ethnicity'. Foreigners may lose their foreign status when they become naturalised, taking up citizenship, although they would remain 'foreign born'. Some 'foreigners' may also be of the same ethnicity as the host population and not be perceived as different in any respect, other than their formal citizenship status. Much of the focus of race relations policy has then continued to be on 'migrants', and then often failing to distinguish economic migrants from those escaping persecution, who may be seeking asylum and who subsequently become refugees.

Each country has different rules about the transition from 'foreigner' or 'migrant' to citizenship, and both the way in which they are recorded and what citizenship actually represents will vary. Each category may be an expression of the multicultural nature of the country in some way or another, but will be open to different interpretations and may not compare directly with the demographic characteristics of other countries. However, most of the Western democracies do now have significant ethnic minority populations, accommodating around 60 per cent of the world's 175 million migrant population: 56 million live in Europe and 41 million in North America. In the ten years from 1990 to 2000, there has been a 28 per cent increase in migrants to the most developed countries (UN, 2002 and UN, 2002a).

As suggested above, the migrant population does not reveal the full extent of diversity and can be calculated in different ways. For example, in the United States, the 'migrant stock' was estimated at 35 million by the UN in 2001 – or 12.2 per cent (ibid.) – whereas the 'foreign-born' population was calculated at 26.3 million in 1998, equivalent to 9.8 per cent (Stalker, 2001). However, the Hispanic and black population was put at nearly 30 per cent in 2000 by Iceland (2002), based on the work of his colleagues from the US Census Bureau, as follows:

> The nation has become markedly more diverse over the last few decades. The proportion of the population that is non-Hispanic White declined from 83.5 per cent in 1970 to 75.8 per cent in 1990, and to about 69.1 per cent in 2000. By 2050, this figure is projected to decline to about 52.5 per cent. The trends are even more visible in some of the nation's largest cities: 6 of the 10 largest cities were 'majority minority' in 1990. (Iceland, 2002)

Stalker (2001) basing his estimates on a mixture of sources, suggests that the number of foreign citizens in selected countries in 1998 ranges from

1.2 per cent in Japan, to 1.8 per cent in Spain, 3.8 per cent in the United Kingdom, 5.6 per cent in Sweden, 6.3 per cent in France and to 8.9 per cent in Germany. In Canada it is 17.4 per cent and higher still in Australia at 23.4 per cent. However, given that immigration to at least some those countries has been evident for at least 50 years, the BME population will inevitably be higher, as they will either be citizens, or classed as 'foreigners' rather than 'foreign-born'. For example, in the UK the 2001 census calculated the BME population at just under 8 per cent (ONS, 2003), see Table 3.1.

The term 'multicultural' also embraces faith divisions, which may or may not coincide with an accepted ethnic division. In Northern Ireland, for example, there is a relatively small ethnic minority population which is over-shadowed by the dominant division within the same ethnic group, based on Protestant and Catholic affiliations. In the Ukraine the religious division between the Catholics in the west and the Russian Orthodox group in the east is reinforced by linguistic differences – Ukrainian and Russian speaking people respectively. In other cases, for example the rivalries between Sikhs and Muslims are clearly shaped by both ethnicity and faith (although in Britain, Sikhs are categorised as an ethnic group and Muslims are not).

The number of minorities and whether they are constituted by reference to ethnicity, faith or other factors will also shape our notion of 'multiculturalism'. Until relatively recently a number of developed nations have had no more than a handful of principal minorities in any significant number, whereas recent immigration has provided a much richer pattern of diversity. In the United Kingdom, the Census 2001 (ONS, 2003) illustrated a limited range of ethnic groups, totalling 4.4 million (see Table 3.1) with the *other* category at 230,165 (0.4 per cent of the total) concealing a very wide variety of groups (over 30 were listed in the summary of how write-in answers were allocated). Terms like 'Asian' or 'black', in themselves, also cover a range of ethnicities and other differences. In numerical terms, the traditional countries of emigration are very dominant, but this picture is now changing with a very different pattern of immigration emerging particularly as a result of

Table 3.1   Minority ethnic population of the United Kingdom, 2001

Ethnic origin	Nos.	%
White	54,153,898	92.1
Mixed Race	677,117	1.1
Asian/Asian British	2,331,423	4.0
Black/Black British	1,148,738	2.0
Chinese	247,403	0.4
Other	230,615	0.4
Total minority ethnic population	4,635,296	7.9

Source: *Office of National Statistics* (ONS) (2003), *Census 2001* (London: ONS).

inter-ethnic and other conflicts in recent years. There are now over 300 languages spoken in London schools and over 100 in many of Britain's other principal cities. 'Multi' – culturalism is, therefore, becoming to mean something very different in terms of the spectrum of difference it embraces.

Census information alone provides relatively limited information about the dynamics of community relations. In the United Kingdom the proportion of BME population has grown significantly and stood at 7.9 per cent in 2001. In England it was slightly higher at 9 per cent, having risen from 6 per cent in 1991 (ONS, 2003). (The 'growth' in the BME population since the last census was, however, partly as a result of the addition of the 'mixed race' category, which was not available in 1991.) The BME population for the United Kingdom now stands at over 4.6 million people (see Table 3.1) many of whom are second or third generation. Indeed, 87 per cent of England's population were English born, with 3 per cent coming from other parts of the United Kingdom (ibid.). There are no accurate estimates for the number and composition of the population since 2001, but with the wave of EU in-migration, together with out-migration of British citizens and natural growth, the BME population will have grown by at least 1 million (iCoCo, 2007).

However, the number of people from ethnic minority backgrounds only partly describes 'multiculturalism' and this will also depend upon their size, composition and distribution. Minority communities are often highly concentrated in separate geographical areas, with rigid employment patterns, segregated education and separate social spheres, making the possibility of interaction with the majority community (and with other minority communities) much reduced. In other words, where communities are living 'parallel lives' within the same nation state, it would be difficult to assert that multiculturalism really features in any meaningful way in the daily life of either the majority or minority populations.

This form of separation is apparent in most European countries where, to a greater or lesser extent, there is also an extremely uneven population distribution of BME and migrant groups and which are generally heavily concentrated in the larger cities and ports. In the United States, segregation is generally regarded as more prevalent, Cashin (2004, p. 42) sets out a number of measures under which 'less than 4 per cent of Americans live in stable diverse communities' and as many as 19 per cent on other scales. In Scandinavia, the concentration of minority ethnic communities can also be found, and Harsman (2006) identified a clear pattern of ethnic segregation in communities in Stockholm, which has intensified over time.

In Britain, London accommodates around 50 per cent of the entire BME population and has the highest concentration of ethnic minorities, with boroughs such as Newham, reaching 60 per cent. Cities such as Birmingham and Leicester are also moving towards a BME majority population (ONS, 2003). Further, within those cities, the BME community are largely to be found in the inner core areas, generally in the older terraced housing. Other European cities often have similarly distinct BME communities similarly concentrated, either in areas of relatively new social housing in Amsterdam, or on estates on the periphery of cities like Strasbourg. Nevertheless, the pattern of separation is similar. By the same token, the white population is, unsurprisingly, not evenly spread. In Britain, the highest proportions of those describing themselves as 'white British' are to be found in the North East, Wales and the South West and with around 150 local authority districts having a white population of 98 per cent or more (ONS, 2003). In many of these areas, the white population is so dominant that it could be described as 'mono-cultural'.

Virtually all parts of England have witnessed a growth in the proportion of BME population, suggesting that dispersal and integration is taking place. So, for example, many of the 150 districts referred to above have typically seen the BME population double in percentage terms between 1991 and 2001, even though it remains at under 2 per cent. This generally amounts to a few hundred people and less than a thousand in most cases. However, the growth in areas which already had a greater concentration of BME population has been significant in percentage terms and very evident in numerical terms. The percentage of 'non-white' residents in the London Borough of Brent, for example, has risen from 101,212 (41.6 per cent) to 144,186 (54.7 per cent) over the same decade and in another London Borough, Newham, from 86,802 (40.9 per cent) to 147,761 (60.6 per cent) (ONS, 2003). Those districts that already had a BME population of above average levels in 1991 have typically experienced growth of many thousands, usually amounting to tens of thousands.

Over the last ten years a familiar pattern has emerged. Black and minority ethnic people have become more dispersed into very predominantly white areas, but in very small numbers, remaining a very small proportion of the population and, at the same time, BME people have become even more concentrated in the areas which already had a substantial community. Not surprisingly then, the longstanding patterns of distribution have simply been reinforced. In 1961, London contained 47.2 per cent of the BME population and the West Midlands conurbation 14.3 per cent (Rose *et al.*, 1969, p. 101) which is almost identical to the comparable figures of 47.6 per cent and 13.6 per cent (Strategy Unit, 2003, p. 5) some forty years later (the comparison may not be exact as the boundaries of these conurbations may also have changed over that time, but will be largely co-incidental).

Within towns and cities, it is often the same pattern with highly segregated, or mono-cultural areas, which have often reinforced the original settlement patterns. Neighbouring communities may have no contact, again living 'parallel lives' and often in fear and ignorance of each other. This separation appears to have become compounded in recent years by the reduction of the white population in some mixed areas, often accompanied by a rise in neighbouring and less mixed areas. This may be attributable, in part at least, to 'white flight', which together with the structural and social barriers which inhibit BME movement to white areas will add to increasing segregation or concentration of distinct communities (this is discussed later in this chapter). The patterns of settlement, have not only shaped interactions at a number of levels, contributing to stereotypes and prejudices but have, to some extent, also determined our conception of 'multiculturalism'.

Separateness and segregation

The socio-economic structure of societies will have a significant impact on the way in which multicultural communities are structured and how minority and majority groups relate to each other, in physical and other terms. The host community, in general, hold better positions, are more affluent and are proportionately less concentrated in the lower socioeconomic groups. More choices will therefore be available to them in both the economic and social sphere and it is to be expected that one manifestation of this will be that they gravitate to the more affluent and higher priced housing areas. This will also be true of members of the ethnic minority community who have had the same opportunities to become upwardly mobile and have not been inhibited by the insecurity of moving into predominantly white areas. However, social stratification and differentiation do not simply follow class patterns and can often be aligned with race, faith and other factors.

The divisions created by faith are particularly significant in many parts of Europe and are often entwined with ethnic and class divisions. In Northern Ireland, for example, where faith divisions were underpinned by economic factors, with many years of discrimination against the Catholic community, segregation is extreme in some areas. This is no longer simply a reflection of the economic positions of the different communities and is maintained as a means of combating the perceived threat to the political or religious integrity of that community and to resist its disintegration. To that extent segregation has succeeded, but by hardening internal cohesion, each segregated community has lost the freedom of greater differentiation within it and the freedom to openly make relationships outside it.

Many aspects of daily life in Northern Ireland are also segregated, for example, Catholic participation in sport is almost wholly through the Gaelic Athletic Association; shopping patterns are also often separate; Catholic and Protestants also use separate auctioneers, solicitors and estate agents and around 95 per cent of children are served by separate school systems. None of these differences are principally attributable to social class and simply ensure that the integrity and identity of each community continues. However, they are also representative of the competition between two communities for more advantageous and privileged access to social and economic positions. The denial of opportunities and rights to one community is simply a means of creating, or protecting, a superior position for the other.

In many European countries, faith divisions have accounted for many of the long-standing divisions, which are still apparent in discriminatory practices and behaviour today. Within Europe, two religious divisions, in particular, have shaped the course of European history: the battles for supremacy between Catholics and Protestants and the persecution of the Jewish community. Similarly, the division between Europe and its immediate neighbours has often been characterised by the hostile relationship between Christians and Muslims. As those neighbours have increasingly become a part of Europe, by immigration to the predominantly Christian countries, so Islamophobia has become an increasing concern. Again, such divisions have been used as a means of maintaining an advantage for one group, as much as for cultural or identity protection.

Differences between the host community and immigrant communities may well be compounded by differences between minority communities. In Britain, the relationship between some minority communities has been difficult with occasional conflict, for example, between Black Africans and Black African-Caribbeans and between Sikhs and Muslims. The riots in the Lozells area of Birmingham in 2005 were caused by tensions between black and Asian communities. More recently, clashes between new migrants and more settled migrants have been recorded and a number of opinion polls and other research has shown that the existing BME community is almost as likely as the white community to oppose further inward migration. The levels of inter-ethnic enmity often reflect long-standing divisions and historic differences based on former relationships in heritage nations, but continuing in their new home nation. Again, this may have reflected a form of protectionism in which each community originally seeks to develop and maintain its position, but having constructed the myths and conceptions about each other, the prejudice has taken over from the origin of the conflict and difference.

This is somewhat removed from the traditional Marxist view of class which defined divisions along economic lines. Marx believed that class revolved around the relationship to the means of production and that the basic distinction was between those that owned capital and those that sold their labour, with a further distinction for the landlord class. These objective divisions, Marx suggested, could not be reconciled with whatever they thought about their positions – their 'class consciousness', and was characterised as 'false consciousness' – their subjective values denied their objective position. The concept of 'class' has been debated by many sociologists over the years, with some supporting and refining the Marxist position and with others suggesting different stratification theories. However, the concept of class has generally remained closely related to economic position, especially in terms of disposable income and accumulated wealth. This is, in turn, closely tied to occupation and educational attainment upon which more highly paid jobs often depend. Class has therefore become an inadequate means of understanding social stratification, whether in relation to ethnic and faith divisions or more generally. John Rex (1961, p. 136) has pointed out that:

> The most striking fact about studies of 'social class' in contemporary sociology has been the confusion of two analytically distinct conceptions, on the one hand the concept of class as used by Marx and on the other the concept used by Lloyd Warner and others to refer to hierarchical groupings in small communities. ... it must be pointed out at once, however, that the two concepts are only analytically distinct ... what we have to do now is to look at the models implied by each of these concepts in turn and seek to understand the way in which class and status systems intersect in actual social situations.

A few years later Rex, with John Moore (1967), went on to do precisely that in a separate study of 'race community and conflict'. They established the existence of 'three different groups differentially placed' in the initial settlement of the city. These were the upper middle class, 'characterized by their possession of property and capable of living without communal and neighbourly support'; the lower middle class 'aspiring to the way of life of the upper middle class, but enjoying only relatively inferior social facilities including housing', and the working class 'which finds security in communal, collective and neighbourly institutions fashioned in the course of struggle against economic adversity'. A further stage of development, through the emergence of the suburbia, occurs when the lower middle classes, forsake the centre of the city and yet another when the working class exercise their political power to demand a new public sector (council housing) suburbia. This is not simply a conception of 'housing classes', and as Rex and Moore explain, there should be 'no unitary concept of the host society, but see it as compounded of groups in a state of conflict with one another about property and power, as well as of groups with differing styles of life arranged in a status hierarchy' (Rex and Moore, 1967, pp. 8–14).

The relationship between class and race is dynamic, in which 'several processes seem to operate':

> class conflicts which are inherent in the situation because of shortage of facilities may cross-cut ethnic conflicts ... secondly, the children of a particular ethnic group may, through their school contacts move into a different social world ... thirdly, since the available means of association (for instance, churches, and political parties) are not historically geared to the existing conflict situation ... (and) ... may serve to blur the lines of conflict. (Ibid., p. 17)

Rex and Moore's work in the sixties brought a strong sense of reality to the academic discussion about class. They demonstrated that, whatever concept of class is used, it must be seen as being dynamic and constantly shaped by conflict and social interaction within and between different groups. Moreover, they present 'culture' as an independent variable, which does not depend upon the possession of power and property and where value systems wield considerable influence. However, the nature of multiculturalism in a given society can only be understood in relation to the way in which it has been shaped by class and the general pattern of income distribution and wealth.

Multicultural societies have, then, been marked by segregated areas and separateness in a number of social and other spheres. These may relate to divisions based upon social class, but ethnic and faith divisions are separable and even independent. Different patterns of settlement and interaction are to be found not only within the same country, but also within the same town or city. In Britain it had been assumed that segregated areas were gradually being broken down, but the report into the riots in 2001 (Cantle, 2001) found increasing evidence of 'parallel lives', in which physical separation of different communities was compounded by a complete separation in education, employment and in other spheres. In many parts of the United States, the problem of 'ghettoisation' has long been recognised and de-segregation policies have been attempted. They have had limited success and segregation remains so pervasive that there seems to be an acceptance of the notion of the 'mostly balkanized neighbourhoods of race and class' (Cashin, 2004, p. 29).

A more fundamental issue is whether a 'separate but equal' policy is ever likely to be tenable, given that the experiences of distinct communities are not the same, they are resourced and governed under different regimes and by different people holding very different positions of power and influence in society and with little understanding, or commitment, to equal standards. Cashin (ibid., p. 298) takes the view that, in practice, 'through separation and segregation we are institutionalising and perpetuating inequality'.

In most European countries the black and ethnic minorities are also concentrated in particular sections of towns and cities, with a similar separation of many aspects of neighbourhoods, especially in respect of housing and schools (Bloomfield and Bianchini, 2004, p. 29). Only in the large and 'international cities' referred to earlier, does the neighbourhood separation seem to be less evident, but even here, divisions in many other aspects of daily life and the lack of equal opportunities, can actually reinforce divisions and reduce opportunities for meaningful contact and exchanges.

The term 'segregation' now also has a limited value. The literal meaning implies an enforced, or involuntary, separation of people on the basis of group identity – usually ethnicity or faith. The 'enforcement' may be regulated by the state or imposed in practical terms by the creation of such financial and institutional barriers that choice to move to other areas cannot be freely exercised. In this sense segregation would be unlawful in Britain as it constitutes direct discrimination under Race Relations legislation and would also be effectively unlawful in those countries that are signatories to the UN International Convention on the Elimination of all Forms of Racial Discrimination (CRE, 2002a).

'Segregation' is now rarely used in the sense of enforced separation and has become more generally used to describe an area, which is so dominated by one group, that it is effectively mono-cultural, or dominated by minority ethnic groups and set apart from the majority community. In this sense, the physical separation is still sufficient to create a process of separate development, with most aspects of daily life confined to that area or constrained by other institutional and structural barriers, such as educational and employment patterns which cater mainly or solely for that group. Some areas, described as 'segregated' are in reality more fluid with people interacting at different levels, living in one area, working in another, perhaps worshipping in yet another area, attending a college or university in a different region and so on. Moreover, communications cut across communities and increasingly bring people together in a wide range of different ways. Television is, of course, widely accessible and the internet is becoming almost universal in the developed world and at least allows 'virtual' contact with others. The press and media are now no longer catering for national audiences and may have international or even global perspectives. Business, academic bodies and tourism have also increasingly developed on a global basis. People from different cultures can often be 'observed' through these mechanisms and may well feature in both positive and negative ways, with new international role models in areas such as politics, the arts, science and sport. All of this suggests some form of inter-action with people from other cultures, even if it is indirect. However, modern communications can work in the opposite direction to integration, by providing the opportunity to maintain external frames of reference that reinforce cultural heritage, rather than the 'bridging' of cultural divides (Lloyd, 2003, p. 94).

The term 'self-segregation' has been increasingly used to describe the emerging patterns of separate development, though there is no accepted definition of how the many different strands of daily life actually constitute a segregated or self-segregated area. Further, the 'voluntary' nature of self-segregation does not fully recognise that the 'choices' people make are in reality constrained by the institutional framework, by structural and economic factors, as well as by the prejudice of landlords, employers and local people and by the discriminatory activity of housing market institutions, such as estate agents (Phillips, D., 2005, p. 31). Further, self-segregation is often the result of negative choices by people who only feel safe in an area dominated by their community, or who have little chance of accessing facilities and services that cater for their needs outside such areas, as well as those that make a positive commitment to only live in an area made up of people who are 'like them'.

Ouseley, in his study of Bradford (2001, p. 16), commented:

> different ethnic groups are increasingly segregating themselves from each other and retreating into 'comfort zones' made up of people like them-selves. They only connect with each other on those occasions when they cannot avoid each other, such as in shops, on the streets, at work, when travelling and, perversely, in Asian-owned restaurants by choice. Education in schools that are racially self-segregated is the most vivid reflection of this state of affairs.

and

> self-segregation is driven by the fear of others, the need for safety from harassment and violent crime and the belief that it is the only way to promote, retain and protect faith and cultural identity and affiliation. (Ibid., p. 10)

Few studies have actually sought the views and preferences of the local community themselves. However, Simpson *et al.* (2007, p. 8), whilst emphasising that many young Asian people wanted to live in mixed areas in two Northern towns in England, their research 'clearly shows that White and Asian young adults identify and favour areas partly in terms of factors they associate with racial composition', but, again, whether this is on the basis of a free or constrained choice is less clear.

Terms such as 'segregation' and 'segregated areas' are therefore of limited value in describing the separation of different groups within multicultural societies. It is suggested an analysis of the 'layers of separation', which create distance between minorities and between the minority and majority groups, should be developed (see Table 3.2). These 'layers' are, of course, often inter-related. For example, residential separation may well help to structure other areas of separation, such as in respect of schooling, but does not, in itself, imply a complete lack of interaction between groups. Breaking down 'segregation' into layers of separation will also allow more specific policies to be developed which can address each area and to understand how far each is genuinely built upon choice. Some responses may be based on closing structural divisions, whilst others require intervention in the social sphere.

The 'layers of separation' offer a more complex basis of 'segregation'. For example, how far are language and communications shared between all groups, and are debates and discussion able to cut across cultural and religious boundaries? Are there, at least, some national press and media outlets in common, or do they divide along cultural lines with little room for common understanding? Similarly, do faith boundaries reinforce other areas of

Table 3.2 The layers of separation

Layer	Area of potential separation
Language	minority and majority languages written and broadcast media formal and informal communication systems
Faith and beliefs	forms and places of worship religious instruction frame of reference (and diaspora) festivals and holidays
Education	schools and related networks supplementary and nursery schools further education and training (all in respect of both intake and curriculum)
Leisure	informal events and activities cultural, artistic and musical preferences sporting interests and club/league organisation
Employment	occupational structure business development patterns advisory and support networks
Housing	housing areas and neighbourhoods financial and professional support
Lifestyle	trading and shopping patterns of travel and communications
Social structure	support to elders gender equality and roles family and kinship patterns friendship, volunteering and support networks

separation, both in terms of incidental and social contact between different groups and in terms of more fundamental beliefs and values? Do separate housing areas create different social spheres and generate separate school populations? Are higher and further educational opportunities different with consequently different employment structures? And are social and leisure patterns similarly separate and distinct?

The concept of 'parallel lives' (Cantle, 2001) was based on separation in all or most of the above layers, in which geographic separation of minority and majority populations is compounded by a lack of any meaningful contact in any sphere, such as employment, faith, education or leisure and cultural activities. Many people have no knowledge of other cultures and often have to rely upon myths and stereotypes to define that relationship. The separation on all, or most, of the spheres of daily life therefore has profound implications for the way in which each community views each other and is inevitably a denial of any multicultural reality. This does not only apply to the relationship between the majority and minorities, but also to the relationship between minorities. Further, the existing patterns of separation will, to some considerable extent, determine the way in which each group sees itself. The present position of each group therefore influences aspirations and can become self-fulfilling.

However, the separation of different groups in respect of some of the layers will not necessarily militate against a cohesive society. Indeed, from the perspective of trying to preserve some sense of cultural identity, some degree of concentration of cultural commonalities in particular areas is probably essential. The existence of 'critical mass' of one community in a given area will, for example, create a sufficient level of demand for particular products in local shops, provide viable congregations for temples, mosques and churches, ensure the maintenance of second languages and bring a reasonable level of attendance to cultural events and activities. A 'critical mass', or clustering, does not mean that neighbourhoods are exclusively the preserve of one group or another, as is often evident in many towns and cities. A local community can support many different cultures and lifestyles, in which a rich and diverse environment flourishes. However, if it begins to move towards the preserve of one community, even if that community is still in a minority, it may reach a 'tipping point' at which it develops into a downward spiral to rapidly become a mono-cultural area. This tendency is not in any way limited to the black and minority ethnic areas and mono-cultural communities, using the same range of 'layers of separation', are also to be found in white areas. Indeed, areas dominated by the white community have often been the least open to change and the barriers to creating more mixed areas have, as yet, proved to be too difficult to overcome.

Further, segregated environments are, not only created by people moving in, but also by people moving out. The concept of 'white flight' has now become quite well established in Britain, although there are disagreements about how extensive it is and few attempts have been made to measure it. Dorling and Rees (2003, p. 21) suggests that this 'flight' constitutes 'white, ethnically and probably partially racially motivated self-selecting migration' which has led to a 'very large (41 per cent) increase in the spatial polarisation of people labelling themselves as 'white' (and that) the segregation between white and all others is growing'.

According to a study commissioned by the Office of the Deputy Prime Minister (University of Newcastle *et al.*, 2002, p. 49):

> the higher the proportion of out-migration from the places with the greater presence of non-white people conforms to the much reported push factor as white flight

The reduction in the white population between 1991 and 2001 in a number of British cities is very substantial and whilst it cannot simply be attributable to white flight, it does raise serious questions about whether the country is 'sleepwalking into segregation', a phrase used by Trevor Phillips, Chair of CRE in a speech in 2005 (Phillips, 2005). Critics of Phillips accused him of 'blaming minorities' for segregation, though this was not the tenor of his speech and the movement of the white population suggests that where the concept of 'segregation' is based upon the *concentration* of different groups, Phillips' contention has some validity. Over the period 1991 to 2001, Census data reveals that the white population reduced by around 43,000 in Manchester, 90,000 in Birmingham and 340,000 in London. Over the same period, the BME population increased by around 15,000, 58,000 and 600,000 respectively. Other cities and areas experienced similar change. Based on 'natural factors' – birth and death rates – the white population would have been expected to remain the same and whilst the BME population would have grown, due to a younger age range and higher fertility rate, it was also augmented by in-migration in some areas. A considerable amount of change is therefore accounted for by population movement. Again, it is difficult to say that the change in the white population is due to 'white flight' or whether it is due to other factors, such as higher levels of social mobility. And the Census data also indicates that a small outward movement from the BME population will have taken place at the same time, increasing the diversity of predominantly white areas.

However, whilst there is some acceptance that the result is a more ethnically concentrated population, and therefore there is more 'segregation' in the general way that it has become understood, Simpson (2003) has argued that segregation is not actually increasing and justifies this by utilising a definition based entirely upon whether minority in-movement has taken place and discounts the change in the composition resulting from natural factors. Further, he focusses almost entirely upon the movement of minority populations and also appears to discount the out-movement of white households which inevitably changes the ratio – and concentration – of minority to majority populations. (He also seems reluctant to describe any part of this as 'white flight' despite many studies which attribute at least some of the movement to this phenomenon, though his recent work (with others) and based on the expressed views of both white and BME residents, accepts that this is a reality (Simpson *et al.*, 2007)). Simpson's attempt at a re-definition of segregation, based upon why, rather than whether, it exists, flies in the face of all measures of segregation which are defined by some form of concentration of populations or their ratio to each other, based upon a static measurement, calculated by an index.

Some evidence also supports the view that there are a growing number of minority ethnic 'enclaves' (Poulsen, 2005). The study looked at 16 UK major cities and found that Pakistani and Bangladeshi communities were increasingly separated and isolated and this will continue to increase over time. Simpson (2003) also set out an analysis of the ethnic minority population of the city of Bradford, which demonstrated that the number of enumeration districts with a 'South Asian' population of over 75 per cent had increased from 29 in 1991 to 77 in 2001 and those with 25 per cent to 75 per cent 'mixed South Asian and others' increasing from 152 to 163. (Nevertheless, he reached the somewhat surprising conclusion that Bradford had become 'more mixed', seemingly on the basis that the result from the indices he employed on an overall basis was almost unchanged.)

Other reports have concluded that segregation is not increasing. *The State of the Cities* Report, for example concluded that for the period 1991 to 2001, 'the pattern of distribution of ethnic minority (sic) across particular cities barely changed across the decade' (ODPM, 2006). Differing results are not altogether surprising given that a number of indices are used to measure segregation and they are applied at different levels, from whole cities, to neighbourhoods, wards and enumeration districts. An acrimonious disagreement, dubbed the 'Index Wars' (Carling, 2006) has emerged over this very issue with, on the one hand Simpson (2003) attacking what he sees as the 'myth of segregation' (and self-segregation) whereas, on the other hand, Carling (2006) seeks to demonstrate that such claims 'cannot survive critical scrutiny' and chastises Simpson for a 'political struggle for the correct position rather than (or in addition to) a technical struggle with recalcitrant numerical data'.

The debate about whether segregation is increasing, or whether the UK is 'sleepwalking into segregation', as suggested by Phillips, has been hindered by the lack of data and the way trends can only be analysed on the basis of Census data, up to 2001. The population of the UK has changed profoundly since 2001 and more contemporary studies, such as those focussed on school populations (see below) and very recent attempts at localised mapping (iCoCo, 2007) and the Office of National Statistics (ONS) projections in 2007 are needed.

Keeping track of population dynamics, is in any event, extremely difficult as the Census is only conducted on a ten-year cycle and even then, the most disadvantaged groups are generally under-recorded. The Community Cohesion Panel (Cantle, 2004) also commented on the limited evidence on 'concentration and segregation' trends and recommended that the Office of National Statistics be given the task of mapping and monitoring these trends in order to inform future policy. There are now signs that this task is being addressed with the Office of National Statistics now recommending new approaches (ONS, 2006) but is still the subject of debate, particularly with local government agencies, anxious for better local statistics on the nature and composition of their local populations.

However, some compelling evidence has begun to emerge from the study of school populations both in terms of changing composition and in comparison to the neighbourhood or area which they serve. A study of 'parallel lives and ethnic segregation in the playground and the neighbourhood' (Burgess *et al.*, 2004, p. 1) found that:

> on average school segregation is greater than the segregation of the same group in the surrounding neighbourhood.

The possibility of such segregation in schools, in which the local neighbour-hood is no longer automatically reflected in the school population has clearly accelerated since the advent of 'parental choice', in which parents are no longer expected, nor required, to choose their local neighbourhood school. Race and racism, may well have become a factor in such choices, as the (Burgess *et al.*) study suggests. However, there are now many anecdotal reports of parents moving home in order to live in particular neighbour-hoods to increase their chances of gaining a place in a 'good' school (whilst parental choice in theory takes no account of the parents address, when a school is over-subscribed, which nearly all good schools are, the school will generally give priority to local families). As a consequence, house prices have risen in the 'catchment areas' of these good schools, pricing poorer families out of the market. The impact on school and neighbourhood segregation has, as Burgess *et al.* noted, been subject to very limited scrutiny with little contemporary evidence available.

Using recently released data, Johnson, Burgess *et al.* (2006) have now been able to explore the extent of ethnic segregation in schools and whether it simply mirrors that found in local neighbourhoods. Unlike their previous studies the new data enabled them to base their conclusions on an analysis of every school in England, focus on much smaller and more relevant areas and to utilise a graphical concentration profile. Their initial analyses:

> show national patterns of both residential and school segregation, with the clear suggestion that the latter is greater than the former, especially among those of South Asian ethnicity.

Segregated patterns of university provision have also been documented recently:

> During 2004/5, 18% of all accepted applicants to undergraduate HE courses were ethnic minority students. Students of Indian origin made up the largest number of non-white undergraduates (4.4%). There are 53 higher education institutions with less than 5% ethnic minority students. About 20 have more than 40%. Half of the Russell Group universities have fewer than 30 black students of Caribbean origin each, and there are more black Caribbean students at London Metropolitan University than at the whole of the Russell Group put together. (CRE, 2007)

Social segregation also seems to have been increasing in recent years. The CRE has been monitoring trends in friendship patterns across ethnic groups. On this basis segregation is increasing, from an already significant level (Phillips, 2005).

The institutional drivers of segregation have received relatively little atten-tion. The CRE (2002a, p. 12) carried out an investigation into some estate agents in Oldham in 1990 and found that discriminatory practices were a causal factor in racial segregation in the town, with white customers being advised to buy in white areas and where Asian prospective buyers were advised to buy in Asian areas. Similarly, the Chartered Institute of Housing (Ratcliffe, 2001, p. 82) study found a number of structural and psychological barriers in a report on Bradford's housing and, in particular, the practice of 'blockbusting' by estate agents, in which they contact neighbours once a nearby house has been sold to an ethnic minority family, suggesting that their own property's value may decline.

Rattansi (2002, p. 99) also refers to the racism of building societies and the 'panic-inducing tactics' of estate agents that promote 'white flight'. However, much of the evidence is anecdotal, with relatively few studies in this area and most reports relying upon the perceptions of local residents. Similarly, there have been a limited number of studies of the social rented sector, but with some evidence of discriminatory practices found in the past (CRE, 2002a). In the United States, the evidence is stronger, particularly the 'very prevalent' use of 'racial steering' by the real estate industry and the practices which support it, by developers, insurance companies and financial institutions (Cashin, 2004, p. 10).

Segregation and separation – whether at the spatial, social or any other 'layer' – does matter and is a significant barrier to community cohesion. It entrenches differences and creates a real or perceived constraint to learning about, and understanding of, other cultures. Moreover, it allows prejudicial attitudes to, at best, go unchallenged by any form of real experience and, at worst, for ignorance to grow into demonisation of the 'other'. The evidence in support of this contention is already clear and growing stronger as a result of both academic research and the development of community cohesion practice. This is further discussed in later chapters.

The degree of 'difference'

The spatial and structural nature of multicultural societies and the way in which they are separated at different levels is only one part of their varied nature. The term 'culture' has been used very loosely to embrace a wide range of differences, some of which may reflect fundamental values, and may be even more difficult to reconcile. Most modern democracies are used to accommodating different cultures. But what exactly do we mean by culture and how different are minority cultures from either the predominant culture, or from one another? There is no easy definition and it is difficult to determine what particular characteristics would be sufficiently meaningful to create an identifiable 'culture'. Could 'culture' be based on a distinctive form of dress, or a separate musical tradition? Does the use of a minority language, with a particular historical literary style, create a culture? Is it created out of a separate historical and developmental process? Or is it the product of distinct belief and value systems? All of these things would create cultural differentiation, though together – and perhaps with other differences – they may fall into what Rex (1961, p. 47) describes as the classic sociological definition of 'culture':

> Laws and customs, the content of education and currents of opinion may all be readily included in Tylor's classic definition of culture as 'that complex whole which includes knowledge, art, belief, morals, law, custom, and any other capabilities acquired by man as a member of society'.

Raymond Williams, in his seminal work *Culture*, was no more helpful in the sense that he defined the most common general meaning of culture as 'the whole way of life' of a distinct people or social group (Williams, 1981, p. 11).

The content of separate and distinct cultures and the boundaries between them are, then, difficult to define with certainty and are inevitably subjective, defined by the individuals and groups themselves – and by the perceptions of others.

Ethnic differences are often linked to cultural differentiation, simply by the visible differences which permit identifiable boundaries to be drawn. However, an ethnic differentiation may not necessarily define a different culture. Many middle class and second-generation black and ethnic minority people, including those of mixed race, living in a predominantly white, but multicultural country, may perceive that their 'difference' relates only to their heritage and that in all other respects their culture is effectively the same as the prevailing culture. That does not mean that they do not value their heritage, but perhaps see it as of historic importance, rather than defining the present. Again, this emphasises that the definition of 'culture' is subjective, changing over time, as different aspects assume greater or lesser importance in the light of national and international events and developments. Whether a culture is said to exist depends upon the sense of belonging to a particular group, and whether that group is distinctive enough to be recognised by others. It is not coterminous with faith or ethnicity (which is also in a state of flux) and will depend upon a range of indicators that are thought to define 'culture'.

Like many terms in the discussion of race and diversity, the concept of 'culture' has a number of different meanings and the sociological definition, based around the idea of prevailing norms, is not the same as that used in common parlance, which is generally linked to the areas of art, literature and music – the notion of 'improving the mind'. 'Culture' has also been linked to heritage and in this more popular sense, cultural differences are not only tolerated but thought desirable and sometimes even regarded as quaint or endearing. So, when does a 'cultural' difference become understood as something more significant and fundamental and to represent a threat to others? Are we really challenged by visible or stylistic differences, or is it only when they appear to underpin an alternative value system? Or, when do those stylistic differences symbolise deep-seated fears and prejudices, which we have learnt over the years?

The preservation of 'difference' is not always seen to be desirable by either majority or minority groups and minorities would themselves actively seek to eradicate them in some areas – particularly those that create disadvantage in economic terms – for example, by seeking equal access to all jobs and ending discrimination in the employment market. Most minorities complain, quite justifiably, about the way in which discriminatory practices confine them to stereotypical occupations, often at a lower socio-economic level. Similarly the active promotion of the host community's language, or languages, is generally accepted as a means of ensuring that everyone can participate on an equal basis, particularly in a political and economic sense but it does not mean that other languages should not be protected and used to maintain cultural differentiation.

The 'right to be included' is very different from the language of assimilation, which has tended to emphasise compulsion and requirement, even though the direction of travel and the role of the state may be the same. For example, the development of the *European Inclusion Index* (Leonard and Griffith, 2003) promotes a competitive approach to integration, at some levels, between members of the European Union, in which 'laggards' will be subjected to 'overwhelming' peer pressure. They recognise, however, that this cannot be done in isolation and whilst immigrant communities will have to 'respect the identity of their host society' they will also be expected to develop a 'sense of integration' in at least some key areas:

> strengthening the codification and implementation of the rights that contribute to a sense of belonging to a single community such as those of association, access to education, political participation and freedom of movement. (Ibid., 2003, in Foreword by Vitorino, p. 5)

Leonard and Griffith go on to distinguish what they describe as 'thin and thick definitions of citizenship and inclusion', in which the 'thick' indicators are regarded as essential elements of a multicultural community and demonstrate that it is open to newcomers and 'allows' integration. They set out four 'dimensions of integration', against which member states will be measured and they also distinguish between short- and longer-term objectives for integration. These are

'economic', in which the short-term objectives are gaining a job and financial independence and the longer term are career advancement and income parity;

'social', in which the short-term objective is access to institutions and establishing social networks and the longer term is diversity within those networks and engaging to change those institutions;

'cultural', in which the short-term aim is to adapt various aspects of lifestyle and the longer term is re-defining cultural identity and;

'political', in which the short term is participating in elections and the longer term is the participation in political parties and movements.

This again, attempts to move the debate on to a more mature stage about precisely which differences should be narrowed and which should be maintained.

The relationship between minorities also needs to be seen in this context and is fundamental to tolerance and acceptance of the 'other'. In some areas this is already becoming the more fundamental issue, as the number of people from different minorities exceeds the host population and begins to define 'multi'culturalism in a completely different way.

However, it is both the number and degree of such differences, which will be the most important consideration in determining the extent of adaptation that both the majority and minority populations have to make and how easy it will be for mutual toleration, respect and acceptance to be established. The 'domains of difference' can be framed around a number of key areas, such as visible and linguistic differences, economic position, shared experience and history, faith and beliefs, and a number of lifestyle issues (see Table 3.3).

Groups that are significantly different from other minorities, or from the majority group, in just one or two domains will inevitably find it easier than those with compound differences to establish common bonds, if only because of the limitations of communications and the separation of lifestyles. We also need to recognise that there is often as much 'difference' within each identifiable group as between them. The present focus on the Muslim community in many countries, for example, generally assumes a high level of internal coherence and commonality, whilst in practice there is a huge variety in ethno-national characteristics, cultural heritage, theological traditions, kinship patterns and organisation – and political views.

The term 'culture' is used to encompass all of these differences, though some are more deeply ingrained than others; some relate to fundamental values and others to pragmatic and practical lifestyle choices, whilst still more are about political and economic systems and processes, rather than culture or heritage.

The extent and nature of 'difference', however, has not been considered as significant in many studies of multiculturalism. Parekh, for example (2002) suggests that the adaptation of Britain over the years has been constant and that Britain has long since been 'multicultural' because it adapted in response to the large regional variations and particularly the cultures of

Table 3.3   The domains of difference

Domain	Variability
Visible differences	Colour of skin and other physical attributes. Style of dress and appearance.
Linguistic differences	Commonality of majority/minority language, and second/majority language. Regional and social class dialects and common expressions/ways of speaking. Linguistic tradition.
Different experience and history	History of cooperation/conflict, with other minorities and majority, including impact of colonial past. Similarity of stage of industrial and technological development.
Difference in faith and beliefs	Religious beliefs and patterns of worship. Mythology and values. Internal or External frame of reference, diaspora networks.
Differences in political and civic engagement	Democratic and political traditions, e.g. freedom of expression and association, toleration of competing ideologies, representative structures, etc. Separation of public and private realms and secular/non-secular polity. Regulatory and rational-bureaucratic framework. Equality within and between groups, e.g. gender, class and caste.
Economic differences	Accumulated wealth and assets. Income and employment. Formal education and skills. Entrepreneurialism, business and networks.
Lifestyle/social differences	Food, culinary arrangements and diet. Artistic and musical traditions. Family, kinship and settlement patterns.
Symbols and ceremonies; social behaviours	Rites of passage. Celebratory and other events. Social behaviours, customs and courtesies.

Scotland, Wales and Ireland. This is, of course, true, but the degree of difference posed by the different indigenous cultures within the British Isles is significantly less apparent than by more recent migrants (and some long-standing diaspora groups) from other parts of the world. Indeed, this might be little more than the representation of sub-cultural differences, rather than separate or 'multicultural' differences, as the variation stems from the same overarching tradition (though the countries of Wales and Scotland and England would, no doubt, see themselves as representing more than 'sub-cultural' interests) but the line between 'sub-cultural' and 'cultural' differences is not distinct.

A higher 'degree of difference' is not a recent phenomenon and has been evident between different groups for some time For example, one of the longest standing British immigrant groups, the Orthodox Jewish community, continues to have a considerable degree of difference and has maintained separation from the host community and other minorities for some time. A similar higher level of differentiation is presented by newer immigrant communities, such as those from some African and Asian countries, whose level of difference is significant in almost every domain. However, a higher level of difference does not, in itself, threaten successful multiculturalism, but does imply different forms of engagement and agreement between the host and migrant communities. A higher degree of difference may also inhibit interaction between communities, as there will inevitably be less common ground and less opportunity for relationships to develop, at least in any direct sense. This continued separation may well result in higher levels of ignorance, fear and intolerance, whereas shared values will only arise from shared experiences, understanding and knowledge. 'Culture' is also dynamic and constantly changing, in both the host and migrant communities and as a result of the interaction between them. Greater differences cannot therefore be regarded as a barrier to mutual trust and acceptance in all circumstances and for any length of time.

From the perspective of multiculturalism, however, the key issue at this point is that 'multiculturalism' can encompass widely differing cultures, or very limited differences – and more often a mixture of wide and narrow differentiation at the same time. It is therefore possible to establish a considerable spectrum of multiculturalism. Whilst the 'degree of difference' can be distinguished, at least in the form of a theoretical model, it is perhaps, more difficult to determine the even more crucial issue of the willingness and the ability of the host nation – which will include established minorities – to cope with cultural variability. This will depend, in part, upon the extent to which the host nation has a history of, and a developed propensity to, tolerate and accept 'difference'. Britain is often seen as a tolerant and accommodating society with its own version of multiculturalism renowned for its principles of fair play. This tradition is sometimes contrasted with other European countries, which have been less willing to allow cultural diversity. However, the tolerance associated with such traditions are extremely difficult to measure and compare, except by way of anecdote and example. The French ban on headscarves, worn by Muslim children in schools, has been contrasted with the British acceptance of them, but such examples can be misleading as, in this case, where the French secularist tradition is clearly a consideration (though the timing and circumstances of the ban raise questions about the motivation behind the ban).

The concept of 'tolerance' may also depend on generalised views, which may mask the proportion of extreme views arguing either in favour, or against, change. For example, is a society where 90 per cent of the population are supportive of minority cultures and 10 per cent of the population vehemently intolerant of them, better than a society with say, 60 per cent supportive and 40 per cent being ambivalent? In Britain, the CRE (2002, p. 7) commissioned an opinion poll and discovered a high level of popular support for the idea that 'it is important to respect the rights of minority groups'. Seventy-eight per cent agreed, with 9 per cent disagreeing and 13 per cent uncommitted. Similarly, 57 per cent felt that 'We should do more to learn about the systems and cultures of ethnic groups', with 27 per cent disagreeing and 16 per cent uncommitted. The substantial majority expressing what appears to be positive views can only be welcomed, but does not deny the existence of a significant minority who could seriously threaten community harmony if their attitudes were manifested in behaviour.

Attitudes obviously also vary in relation to a number of factors, such as social class and location. In fact, given the uneven distribution of minorities across countries like Britain and their over-representation in poorer areas, it would be surprising if this was not the case. That is not to suggest that more tolerant areas are always to be found in multicultural towns and cities, although there is some evidence that this is the case. For example, recent support for the far right BNP in Britain has come from white areas with very small BME communities and they have made headway in various small towns and rural areas. A large proportion of the support for Jean Marie Le Pen's National Front has also been traditionally found in the rural areas of France.

Societies have developed a range of models to cope with 'difference'. This range is often presented as a spectrum from 'assimilation' to 'co-existence'. Assimilationist models would argue that the characteristics of minorities are simply absorbed into the dominant culture of the majority. This would entail the loss of minority languages, traditional dress and other outwardly identifiable characteristics, as well as the adoption of political economic and social norms that are determined by the majority. In more extreme forms, it may entail the suppression of separate faiths and distinct lifestyles. In less extreme forms, with limited or no provision to support them, differences may nevertheless soon be expected to wither away. However, the assimilationist model may not be even-handed, in the sense that the uniformity it implies may not extend to the provision of equal rights and equal opportunities to minority communities, particularly in respect of employment and other public services. Racism and discrimination may well linger on and prejudices continue in both the private realm as well as the public realm.

Assimilation may well be no more than a one-way street, in which cultural identity is traded for second-class citizenship.

At the other end of the spectrum from assimilation, the co-existence model assumes that different communities would co-exist with little or no contact or common ground between them. Legal and administrative processes would only provide a minimal of overall framework within which communities will function and inter-relate, and even this will be applied in a 'sensitive', way, allowing the separate community customs and mores to largely govern their own behaviour.

Co-existence can, therefore, mean that the nation has very little by way of common bonds and that the groups operate largely according to their own rules.

The Communitarian Network does not support either extreme:

> Two approaches are to be avoided: promoting assimilation and unbounded multiculturalism. Assimilation which requires minorities to abandon all of their distinct institutions, cultures, values habits and connections to other societies ... is sociologically difficult to achieve .... It is morally unjustified because of our respect for normative differences, such as to which gods we pray.
>
> Unbounded multiculturalism – which entails giving up the concept of shared values, loyalties and identity in order to privilege ethnic and religious differences, presuming that nations can be replaced by a large number of diverse minorities is also unnecessary. It is likely to provoke undemocratic backlashes .... It is normatively unjustified because it fails to recognise the values and institutions undergirded by the society at large, such as those that protect women's and gay rights. (2002, p. 2)

The Network goes on to expound its own approach of 'diversity within unity', in which each group is free to maintain its own distinct sub-culture, whilst maintaining a respect for the basic values and institutions and shared framework of society. A strong measure of loyalty to the heritage nation of different communities would also be accepted 'as long as this does not trump loyalty to the society in which (they) live if these loyalties come into conflict' (ibid.).

However, whilst this seems to move us along a path towards some sort of consensus, the Communitarian Network are unable to give more than the barest details of what this actually means in practice and fall back on the usual examples of differences that need to be resolved – forced marriages, female circumcision, religious holidays and a common language. Even on these basic issues, Wolfe (2002, p. 31) suggests that there is no real clarity and cites the work of Parekh, who has done more than most to promote acceptance of multiculturalism in his report on *The Future of Multi-Ethnic Britain* (2000). Wolfe believes that Parekh, whilst being a supporter of

'Diversity Within Unity', actually takes a very liberal view bordering on the co-existence model:

> Ever conflict averse, Parekh believes that the 'dialogically constituted multicultural society both retains the truth of liberalism and goes beyond it. It is committed to both liberalism and multiculturalism, privileges neither, and moderates the logic of one by the other'.

Wolfe does, at least, prefer Parekh's attempts to define those issues which are likely to conflict, to that of the 'group of normative political theorists who, in defence of what they call multiculturalism, would redefine citizenship to the point where it would not be worth much of anything' (ibid., p. 26). Pilkington (2003, p. 268) takes a similar view to Wolfe and believes that Parekh has 'still left us with how the competing claims of difference and equality can be recognised'.

The very term multiculturalism has become problematic and provokes different responses from different communities (Alibhai-Brown, 2000). It has also been found to have little resonance with the white community, who sometimes believe that it, and similar terms such as 'diversity', principally refer to the BME community and do not include them (IDeA, 2002, p. 5). Malik (2002, 2002a), more fundamentally, has questioned the whole basis of multiculturalism in that it has entrenched divisions, placing too much emphasis on instrumentalised differences and too little on universal values. He also supports Nathan Glazer's (1997) view that inequality has been institutionalised as a result. Malik (2002) therefore calls for difference to be treated 'with a bit more intolerance and a little less respect'.

Perhaps for this reason the practice of multiculturalism has also recently been questioned, most notably by the then Chairman of the Commission for Racial Equality, who demanded 'the scrapping of multiculturalism' (Phillips, 2004a). For Phillips, the conception of 'a community of communities' implied too much separateness, or 'co-existence', and he proposed 'that immigrant communities should become more integrated into a society that celebrates and tolerates differences between people but has a core of "Britishness" that binds us together' (Phillips, 2004b). The CRE subsequently preferred to use the term 'an integrated society' in preference to 'multiculturalism' (CRE, 2004). The new approach by Phillips and the headlines that they generated, came as a surprise to many people involved in race relations; his new definition of multiculturalism appeared to be very similar to previous articulations made several decades earlier, Phillips had simply exposed the gap between the multiculturalism rhetoric and reality and the practical failure to define the relationship between communities in any meaningful sense. Despite many years of various forms of multiculturalism, in many countries, segregation and separateness had not been defeated and had even increased in some respects, with a consequent continued lack of trust and reciprocity.

In terms of describing the relationship between different groups, the somewhat more historic term of 'cultural pluralism', has also proved to be no more satisfactory than 'multiculturalism'. Again, the vision was hard to question, especially in one of the earliest expositions, attributed to Roy Jenkins (1966) the then Home Secretary, at a time when racism and intolerance were very prevalent:

> Integration is perhaps rather a loose word. I do not regard it as meaning the loss, by immigrants, of their own national characteristics and culture. I do not think that we need in this country a 'melting-pot', which will turn everybody out into a common mould, as one of a series of carbon copies of someone's misplaced vision of the stereotyped Englishman.
>
> I define integration, therefore, not as a flattening process, but as equal opportunity accompanied by cultural diversity in an atmosphere of mutual tolerance. This is the goal. We may fall a little short of its full attainment, as have other communities both in the past and in the present. But if we are to maintain any sort of world reputation for civilized living and social cohesion, we must get far nearer to its achievement than is the case today. (Jenkins, 1966)

This established the liberal tradition from which multiculturalism flowed and created the expectation that a single political culture would emerge, in which immigrants would enjoy the same rights, within the limits of the fundamental societal values, whilst their distinct 'culture' would be protected in social spheres. This model is to be found in 'liberal' states with high levels of immigration, such as Canada, Australia and the United States. It has, again, been contrasted to the 'assimilationist model' in which the distinctive cultures of migrants are soon lost. However, it may also be contrasted with the 'integration model' that for some, amounts to much the same thing, and 'whereby adaptation assumes a more gradual form' (Gagnon and Pagé, 1999, p. 17).

The pluralistic model can also be used to denote 'both unity and diversity in the public sphere' as well as diversity in the private sphere (Ratcliffe, 2004, p. 6). Malik (2002a) attacks pluralism with the same vigour that he challenged multiculturalism. He suggests that:

> A truly plural society would be one in which citizens have full freedom to pursue their different values or practices in private, while in the public sphere all citizens would be treated as political equals whatever the differences in their private lives. Today, however, pluralism has come to mean the very opposite. The right to practice a particular religion, speak a particular language, follow a particular cultural practice is seen as a public good rather than a private freedom. Different interest groups demand to have their 'differences' institutionalised in the public sphere.

Distinguishing the public and private spheres is not however any easy task either at a theoretical or practical level. Many of the 'domains of difference' (see Table 3.3) cross this divide and, in practical terms, Ratcliffe (2004, p. 6) illustrates the difficulty through the example of Islam, which 'transcends the public-private divide, being intrinsic to the way a Muslim lives her/his life'. Nevertheless, it is this conception of multiculturalism in which separation at all levels, based on a community of communities model, is likely to prove most problematic as it inevitably pushes it towards the end of the co-existence axis.

The separation of public and private realms, however, is also put in doubt by Gagnon and Pagé (1999, p. 17) and Castles (1997, p. 119), who favour a more complex model than is often suggested by the spectrum from 'assimilation to co-existence' (and for which more liberal interpretations of multiculturalism and cultural pluralism stand somewhere in between). They suggest minorities are, in reality, integrated according to a 'differential exclusion' model in which full participation in a society, in some areas, for example, through employment and as a taxpayer, does not automatically confer citizenship rights in others, such as the right to vote, nor acceptance in social arenas. Countries like Germany, where such policies have been quite explicit, may fit this model but, in fact, differential exclusion (or inclusion) is the norm in most multicultural societies, whether or not it is an intended policy objective.

It is suggested therefore that a successful multicultural society will never be based simply on a series of distinct cultural norms with a few over-arching core values to tie them together, important though this is. To develop a meaningful debate, in which the competing claims of equality and difference can be addressed, a generalised discussion about 'multiculturalism' is no longer adequate. It will be necessary to examine the 'domains of difference' in each case and seek to narrow those that perpetuate fundamental barriers, whilst maintaining genuine cultural distinctions. This will require more integration at some levels, whilst rigorously protecting others. In particular, higher levels of integration will be required within the political and economic spheres, to ensure that people can engage with each other on an equal footing, to build mutual trust and respect and to create more equal opportunities. This will inevitably have some impact on other spheres, however, for example, through a rigorous development of a common language (or languages) to ensure constant communication between communities, whilst maintaining linguistic differences within communities to underpin cultural differences.

The most common response to these dilemmas has been to develop the notion of 'citizenship'. The UK, along with many other countries, have introduced tests for new citizens which generally question the knowledge of historical events, common expressions and national traditions. These have been supported by citizenship ceremonies to publicly celebrate the new citizenship of the individual concerned and 'citizen days' and other events have been introduced. The teaching of citizenship in schools is to be re-invigorated following the Ajegbo Report (Ajegbo, 2007). The Commission on Integration and Cohesion (CIC, 2007) advocated the introduction of a citizenship week and *The Governance of Britain* Green Paper from the new Ministry of Justice (SoSJLC, 2007) advocates a number of new measures, including the production of a 'British Statement of Values', as a means of using citizenship to improve national identity.

These differences are also closely linked to the question of identity (which, together with values and citizenship are further discussed in Chapter 5) and 'culture' is often used as the main determinant, but without really defining the separate elements. Much of this debate assumes that people think of themselves as having a definable 'culture', and if they do, that it is a signifi-cant enough part of their life to contribute to their identity. In particular, 'culture' is often equated with a faith or ethnicity, but many people have no faith, or it plays a limited role in their lives, and whilst all people have an ethnicity (or a mixed, dual, or multiple ethnicity) it may not be significant to them. They may therefore not wish to see themselves identified with any particular community in these terms and define themselves by reference to their occupation, political views or social circumstance. Individual or group affiliation may therefore be more important, than what is generally under-stood as a cultural or community interest. This is particularly the case for the white majority populations who often see others as having an ethnic iden-tity, rather than possessing one themselves and for people whose religious associations are often in the private realm, or those with relatively little observance, in a formal sense at least.

The role of the state

The role of the state is clearly crucial in the way multiculturalism is both envi-sioned and regulated. In modern multicultural societies, however, it has gener-ally been developed as a means of regulating the behaviour of individuals, rather than attempting to control, or change, the private beliefs and views that give rise to that behaviour. Most legislation has been directed at the prevention of discriminatory acts, though the public expression of extreme views are also liable to regulation, given that they could incite unacceptable and illegal behaviour. The 'incitement of racial hatred' is, for example, now generally regarded as a crime – and as a necessary curtailment of the right to freedom of expression. The state has also developed a more pro-active role in many coun-tries, by attempting to promote good relations between faith and ethnic groups and by more subtly influencing attitudes. Further, the state has also developed a role in the distribution of resources between groups, based on a notion of 'fairness' which reflects a variety of political, economic and social needs.

None of this is new, in the sixteenth century, Queen Elizabeth I is reputed to have distinguished between the public and private realms. She had no desire to commence her reign with a punitive regime against Catholics and declared that 'I would not open windows into men's souls'. In other words, their private beliefs were of no concern of the state and what mattered was their public actions and behaviour. Such a tolerant attitude may have had more to do with her tenuous hold on power than genuine liberal views, but the distinction is significant and one that modern democracies now take for granted. The separation of church and state generally represented a turning point in the freedom of religious minorities to hold private beliefs and to practice and to preach, but religion has remained a key issue in societal divisions and, all too often, in the persecution, of minorities.

The modern democratic state may, however, appear to support particular religious beliefs by retaining a link between operation of the state, and the traditionally dominant faith or denomination, through an 'established' church. Britain provides a good example of this arrangement, as the ruling monarch, distinct from the government of the day, is also head of the Church of England. The link can be significant in a number of ways, for example through the preference given to Christian bishops in appointments to the House of Lords. However, the importance of the formalities may be over-stated, given that the importance of the Christian faith and its obvious place in the public sphere in the United States, where there is no established church, contrasts with the British tradition. In practice, the formal link in Britain has also been counter balanced by trying to ensure more informal arrangements, with the Queen visiting temples and mosques and demonstrating an inclusive approach. This has also been significantly supported by the statement from Prince Charles, in which he describes himself as the 'defender of faith', rather than of *the* faith. In fact, what distinguishes a modern democracy from an authoritarian and oppressive regime is the freedom to hold personal beliefs, to support the faith of choice and the freedom to express views in support of that faith.

Nevertheless, the state can wield considerable influence over beliefs and values, and that influence can be exercised in a number of tangible ways. Parekh (2000, p. 42) suggests five theoretical models of multiculturalism, (these are not based on actual examples of approaches taken by nation states). They encompass the spectrum from 'assimilation' to 'separatist' and the role of the state is seen as a key determinant in each case. The state may be culturally neutral, promote a single culture and expect adherence, or allow each community to regulate its own affairs. Within the five models, Parekh (ibid., p. 46) also illustrates what he sees as the problematic links between the 'mono-cultural public realm with a multicultural private realm'. To illustrate this he uses the example of public holidays, which are based on the majority religion (and began as *holy* days) with no statutory provision being made for the minority religions. An individual from a minority religion, may not be able to fully celebrate and respect his or her faith, except by choosing to take annual leave, but even this is usually at the discretion of the employer. Parekh therefore raises the question as to whether all faiths, should have equal status, rather than just the freedom to practice. It is difficult to argue against such a view, especially where ancient and anachronistic laws, such as those de-barring Catholics from the monarchy, are still on the statute book. The practicalities of such an approach are, however, a little more problematic, given that, many faiths now make up multicultural societies and public holidays for the key points in all calendars would be difficult to accommodate. In many European countries the Christian dates are now losing their religious significance for most of the population and are often celebrated on a secular basis. This is part of a wider trend, in which not only is religion increasingly falling out of the public realm but religious observance is also in decline. As mentioned earlier, this is not the case in the United States however where faith is in the public domain and an increasing number of people believe that the churches should be involved in politics (Micklethwait and Wooldrige, 2004, p. 150).

The state may, then, permit religious freedom, whilst at the same time exhibiting an historic preference for the cultural norms that underpin the majority religion. But support for other religions has been provided in significant ways by both protecting the freedom to practice and by outlawing discrimination based on religion, in some spheres. This form of intervention is now to be found in all modern multicultural societies and not only aims to prevent discrimination but will also provide for redress. Most European states have long since had such provisions, though with varying degrees of coverage and impact. Two recent European Union Council Directives have attempted to establish a more consistent and higher standard, particularly, to coincide with enlargement of the Union in 2004. The Racial Equality Directive and the Employment Equality Directive were transposed by member states into national law in 2003 and subsequently applied to new member states. They also establish a framework for monitoring progress in member states and provide for organisations to be established to promote equal treatment. A characteristic of a modern multicultural country might therefore be said to be one where the state had intervened to protect minorities against discriminatory behaviour, on account of their race or faith. There may be considerable debate about the extent and nature of such legislation, how far it is actively promoted, how effective it is and whether it is enforced and monitored. Nevertheless, the aim of such legislation is to try to ensure that there is equitable and fair treatment of all citizens and groups.

In some cases, however, the principle of 'unequal treatment' has been enshrined in law. This recognises that treating everyone the same is not necessarily the most equitable arrangement and that uniformity would take no account of legitimate cultural differences. For example, Britain has made a series of legislative and other accommodations in line with the guiding principle of cultural pluralism and racial equality: the Motorcycle Crash Helmets Act 1976 and the Construction (Head Protection) regulation of 1989 enables

Sikhs to wear turbans instead of safety helmets. Within the Criminal Justice Act of 1988 the law on carrying knives in public places exempts Sikhs carrying them for religious reasons. Matters surrounding burial, such as designating areas of public cemeteries for specific religious communities and permission for burial in a cloth shroud instead of a coffin, as well as the speedy issue of death certificates within 24 hours in order to allow people to comply with Islamic law, have also been taken forward in support of diversity.

More controversially, some countries now have, or are considering, making 'inciting religious hatred' unlawful, to parallel the provisions in respect of race. In establishing such freedoms or providing protection against discrimination and intimidation, the actions of the state may well be helping to shape public attitudes by creating a moral climate and values, which individuals then internalise. Generally, the fact that the government of the day is throwing its weight behind such measures will help to legitimate the idea of respecting difference.

However, a distinction may be made between those measures which are intended to prevent discrimination and those that promote the interests of a particular group and the individuals that belong to it, even if this is only to try to create a more level playing field. These have proved to be more controversial. The cumulative impact of a series of actions designed to legitimate what is seen as special treatment or the conveying of an advantage to one group, may also provoke a negative reaction among some other sections of the population in the longer term. The 'affirmative action' programmes in the United States are perhaps the most obvious example, despite having been used to correct an imbalance in the historic representation of black groups in particular spheres, such as employment. However, there are many examples of 'positive action' programmes, in Britain and elsewhere, which give some form of special help or privilege to members of those groups in order to create a more equal chance of success in any subsequent allocation of resources or offer of employment. The advancement of, and acceptability of, legislation in this area would appear to revolve around the principle of 'fairness', a concept that will change over time and vary according to the particular circumstances and context.

Whilst, it is certainly the case that black and minority ethnic people are generally disadvantaged in developed multicultural nations and that equal opportunities are far from established, this should not be taken to imply that there is a consensus about what constitutes 'fairness' and how the state should bring it about. Wolfe (2002, p. 30) is concerned about 'those multiculturalists that assume justice is whatever works to the advantage of the weaker' and that the championing of minority rights and culture is an automatic reaction on their part. This, in Wolfe's view, also assumes that the state will be neutral on many key areas of difference and that by not resolving any conflicts the state would implicitly or explicitly tolerate the variety of practices involved. He believes that this approach undermines any real sense of nationhood or citizenship. Those that argue for a neutral state, he suggests, presume that any emphasis on 'patriotism, assimilation and unity is unjust and that a celebration of diversity is the opposite' (ibid., p. 27). Wolfe asserts that the state has to be 'fair', rather than neutral and recognise that:

> in pursuit of fairness, the impact of liberal procedures will fall differently on different groups: insisting that religion be relegated to the private sphere, for example, discriminates against those who prefer to live in a society in which religion is present in the public sphere. But all laws favour some and disfavour others ... merely showing that a law burdens some more than others cannot itself be taken as an indication that oppression exists. (Ibid., p. 34)

The pursuit of fairness generally implies, however, that the state's role is one of deciding between competing views and claims – a sort of referee. In this mode the state could assume an objective position in which the views of all minorities and the majority could be assessed in an open and dispassionate way. In fact, the starting point for most norms and legislation is lost in the mist of historical precedents (and accidents). The notion of fairness is thus circumscribed by all that has gone before – and much of that will depend upon the mono-cultural majority position that dominated the nation state for so long. To minorities, this may be another way of saying that the public institutions are 'institutionally racist' with, again, the most often cited example being the way in which our public holidays and working week are constructed around the Christian calendar. To Wolfe and others, the state has a legitimate right to maintain some cultural advantage for the majority and it has to decide upon a minimum common culture in order to maintain some identity and common purpose.

The centralising and monolithic tendencies of state must also be recognised. However much diversity is tolerated, it will always be in tension with 'the disciplining and normalising regime of governance (which) runs through the whole panoply of social policy in the UK' (Lewis, 2005, p. 543).

The question of whether minorities must adapt to the prevailing culture and vice versa, and whether the state intervenes on their behalf, or simply reinforces the position of the majority, is therefore again crucial. A distinction must, however, be made between the adaptation required of individuals and of the groups to which they belong. It is Barry's view (2001) that 'groups have no rights, only individuals do'. However, whilst it is true that it is only individuals who can exercise rights, they are only able to do so because of the recognition given to the faith or culture of which they are members. This does not imply that all groups and cultures are treated equally, merely that certain areas of 'difference' are given protection by law, or that discrimination is prevented on the basis of those differences.

The state's most important role is, however, to ensure fairness and social justice and to represent the interests of all citizens and sections of the community. In a multicultural society, this will require constant and open debate, facilitating acceptance of the principles – and reality of – multiculturalism and, in particular, to ensure at least a reasonable measure of agreement over acceptable and unacceptable areas of difference. This has been difficult in the past, given that the history of race relations has been dominated by prejudice and discrimination. Consequently open debate has been limited in case the arguments are used to fuel racism and succeed only in condemning the distinctiveness of minorities and pressurising them to give up their heritage – with the implication that their failure to do so will result in their own exclusion.

The British government has, at least, recognised the necessity of joining the discussion and in bringing together and developing, for the first time, race equality and community cohesion strategies, believes that it is their 'role to lead an honest and robust debate, in which people freely express their views' (*Strength In Diversity*, Home Office, 2004, p. 1). The Government suggests that it will also not shy away from the even more controversial questions in respect of migration and recognises that the discussion about migration has often been abused by racists:

> How can we ensure that we have an open debate around how to manage migration and prevent abuse of asylum which doesn't fuel prejudice against black and minority ethnic communities. (Ibid., p. 18)

There may be no perfect response to such a question, nor to the wider issue of which differences should be narrowed and which should be respected and promoted – but any vacuum is soon filled by racists and extremists seeking to exploit difference, rather than make diversity work.

4
Prejudice, Discrimination and the 'Fear of Difference'

Prejudice is an antipathy towards another person based upon pre-existing belief or opinion, resulting from some form of social categorisation or membership of a particular group. It relies upon a stereotypical characterisation, or generalisation, of others, which is not grounded in evidence or experience. In this sense, prejudicial views are not based upon rational judgements and are inherently unjust. In some cases, the views held about the members of another group are so exaggerated and misconceived that they become almost laughable. However, it is easy to dismiss them as the product of ignorant and closed minds as they can often be part of a social system which creates a hierarchical order, justifying discrimination in order to preserve the position of the superior group.

Various scientific theories have been deployed, in the past, to justify the unjustifiable. Some psychological theories also rely upon ideas about 'authoritarian' personalities and other disorders to explain prejudice and discrimination. However, discrimination is sometimes a rational, if unacceptable, means of protecting the interests of one group at the expense of another. In any event, as Runciman (1995, p. 215) suggests, we need to question whether any beliefs can be usefully described as 'irrational': 'we do not need to invoke rationality in order to report or explain them.' The 'fear of difference' is part of a wider culture in which barriers are put up around groups and the separateness gives rise to the myths and stereotypes, upon which prejudice depends.

National and international order

Each nation has its own hierarchy of nations, in which, not surprisingly, it puts itself at the top, with other nations ranked below. The 'pecking order' will often reflect little more than ancient stereotypes about other nations – and their nationals. Ethnicity may be a factor, though it is often the neighbouring nations, which share ethnic characteristics and with whom there have been long-standing territorial and other disputes, that feature somewhere towards the bottom of the list and with whom rivalries persist.

Some rivalries will endure over many years, but they often change, along with each nation's view of their supposed superiority, to reflect a new perceived threat, a peace concordat or new trade economic relationships. For example, in the early part of the twentieth century as Britain lurched towards war, the Germans became the British public enemy number one, supplanting the Jews (Winder, 2004, p. 202). Similarly, whereas once the Irish were despised by the British (or, in particular, the English) and regarded as being of lower intelligence, they are now increasingly treated with respect as European equals, with their 'intelligence' viewed positively as a somewhat creative trait. In the same way, most European nations looked upon the nations of the Far East as being poor and primitive and only capable of producing cheap and shoddy goods. Now, they are the powerhouse of technological invention and many trade names treated as a hallmark of quality.

The perception of other nation states, however, reflects more than simple rivalries and competition. Perceptions reflect a particular view of historical development. The military and economic domination by the white nations is relatively recent, over just the last five hundred years or so, since the start of the European global expansion. The most advanced ancient civilisations were generally black or Asian, a history that has been conveniently forgotten, or reinterpreted. Some of the black and Asian nations were, in fact, amongst the most powerful and advanced civilisations of their time. The Moors, Incas, Chinese and Egyptians, for example, all represented civilisation and power in their time as did the, perhaps less well known, six significant African civilisations dating from 800 BC (Yeboah, 1998, p. 107). However, the white nations' mental picture of power and success is not presently represented by black history and is reflected in colonial power and industrial and technological development. In the late nineteenth and early twentieth centuries, this world view became supported by racialised notions of national identity which were pertinent outside the colonial context and were used to underline the national identities of nation states in Europe (Solomos and Back, 1996, p. 47).

In fact, the idea of a world classified into separate 'races' is relatively recent (Banton, 1977, p. 27) and was used in the nineteenth-century Europe largely as a way of justifying the exploitation of black labour. Despite Darwin and various other studies, as early as 1840, that concluded that human beings all belonged to the same race (ibid., p. 31) the process of racialising the world gained ground:

> Europeans first developed the race concept as an interpretation of their own history. Having racialised the West, their successors proceeded to racialise the rest of the World. (Banton, 1977, p. 54)

The science of racism which also developed and became prevalent at this time was used to confirm notions of superiority of one group of 'races' over another. Whilst now discredited (see 'The Science of Racism' below) it was both used to support colonialism and justify economic exploitation (Yeboah, 1988, p. 51) and to give credence and scientific authority to popular mythology (ibid., p. 54).

The hierarchy of nations, then, reflects the prevailing values of the nation state (or groups of states) constructing the hierarchy. For the developed nations of the North, this will often simply reflect their social and economic history together with more present-day perceptions of the value of techno-logical development and economic growth and possibly, perceived threats from economic competition, conflict and, more latterly, from terrorism. From the perspective of the poorer nations, however, such as those in the South, the hierarchy will often be reversed, in which the values of the nations of North, largely uncontested as a global 'brand' since the fall of the Communist Block, are often despised for what is seen as their misuse of power and wealth, their greed and exploitation and their materialism. These perceptions are dynamic and change as international relations improve or deteriorate and as economic and cultural positions develop, though, no doubt, some long-standing and ingrained attitudes and prejudices linger on for many years, crossing generations and becoming lost in the mists of time.

'Race' and nationality are closely entwined and from the perspective of the nations in the North, it is the poorer nations of the world, which generally have black populations and are presented through the daily images of conflict and poverty on the television screens or in the print media. This reinforces their perception of superiority, even if those same white nations have had a history of colonialism and exploitation in those very states. Thus, North America will, in general, assume its superiority over the South American nations, aided by the flow of migrant labour which constantly serves to demonstrate to them the desirability of its own economic model and the 'failure' of the southern nations. Europe shares a similar view of the South, again aided by the flow of migrants from southern Europe, North Africa and sub-Saharan Africa. Both North America and Europe, however, now look towards the Asian nations and their people with a little more ambivalence, as some Asian countries rapidly develop into the new techno-logical hothouses, whilst others continue to be dogged by hardship and poverty. But in overall terms, the white nations can continue with their perception of superiority in both 'race' and nationality, as long as 'superiority' is judged against their own development model and standards.

The present day measures of power and success have been usefully codified by the United Nations Development Programme (UNDP) in the form of a 'Human Development Index' (HDI), which it calculates each year. This is published as a Human Development Report (UNDP, 2004) and pro-vides a clue to at least some of the perceptions which nations have of one another. The HDI combines basic areas of human development, including life expectancy, adult literacy, levels of education and GDP per capita, and the results are not surprising. Norway is at the top of the list closely followed by Sweden. Australia, Canada, Britain, the United States and France are all in the top 20, along with Japan as the only Asian country. By contrast, all of those categorised as 'low human development', the bottom 35 nations, are black or Asian. When considered separately, the Report's assessment of GNP per capita tends to give even more weight to the domination of the white nations (ibid., p. 184). Further, the Report's index of development trends (ibid., p. 143) demonstrates how it is only within the last 30 years or so that a few Asian nations, such as Singapore and the Republic of Korea, have begun to penetrate the white nations' top league. Some studies have also demonstrated a link between socio-economic position and stereotypes, not simply between nations, but between ethnic groups and even between men and women (Brown, 1995, p. 85).

This is not, therefore, a simple black versus white issue. The divisions within the black and Asian states also reflect a hierarchy in which each nation tends to place itself at the top and others – especially neighbouring states with which rivalries have long existed – some way below. Colombians look down on Venezuelans, the Somalians believe they are superior to the Yemenis and the people of Hong Kong were confident that they were better than the Chinese – which made the prospect of 'take over' by them even more alarming. And, in the same way, between white nations, the Swedes look down on the Danes, the French have traditionally thought themselves superior to the Spanish and New Zealanders will want any other nation to win the latest sporting event, as long as it is not the Australians. For the most part, these 'inferior' nations believe that exactly the reverse is true. Hierarchies do not simply follow or relate to economic power positions, directly or inversely, but do reflect them to a significant extent. They also represent the extent to which other nations are perceived as a threat or rival to economic success and well-being generally. These perceptions then form part of the socialisation processes and is often of a very subtle nature and is part of the popular culture, for example, in humour, art and sport.

The hierarchies within nation states are no less obvious and the discrimination and disadvantage suffered by minority ethnic or faith groups across the globe is well documented. In modern multicultural societies, which lay claim to meritocratic values, fairness and equal opportunity (and even where racial discrimination is unlawful), this is no less acute. Unequal opportunities and unequal life outcomes are commonly found in the areas of housing, education, employment and the criminal justice system. These inequalities have been well documented in other publications and it is not intended to rehearse them here. The extent and nature of these inequalities are, however, profound and long-standing. Minorities have struggled against direct and indirect forms of racism and discrimination, with perhaps, economic disadvantage being the most significant. For example, Wrench *et al.* (2003, p. 5) regard the much higher rates of unemployment of minorities in many

European countries as 'typical' and where they may well be double, treble or even quadruple, the rates of the host community. And at the same time, hate crimes and xenophobic violence persist, with nearly 13,000 such crimes in Germany in 2002, 3500 prosecutions in Sweden and 7300 in the United Kingdom (UNDP, 2004, p. 74).

A part of the prejudicial views that each nation has of others is due to socialisation processes we all experience. These are often very subtle and may depend upon the way in which nations are portrayed in the media, through films and television, or as a result of their economic position and technological development. Similarly, immigrants from particular regions and countries will be viewed through the same lens and will often face suspicion and discrimination purely as a result of these preconceived ideas of their ability and worth.

As the white nations of the North, have become more multicultural – and even to the point where it is now possible to contemplate the time when the US population has a black majority – attitudes may be expected to change. However, the pattern of inequalities between nation states has been perpetuated within those nations and the white communities remain the most powerful and wealthy section of the population and will continue to dominate international value systems for some time to come.

The science of racism

Science has helped to support a racialised view of the world by attempting to provide a rational justification for supposed differences which were aligned with national boundaries and ethnicity, and would now be regarded as inconsequential or spurious. Science has thus been used to support a series of misconceptions and myths, and to perpetuate the idea of a natural order and a 'rational' justification for the domination of one group by another – and even to justify the most appalling of atrocities. Divisions and conflicts are now so dominated by mythology and prejudice that they become more than sufficient reason to continue, with the original dispute or basis of the conflict, completely lost or forgotten.

The science of race is relatively recent and the 'attempt to classify the human species into a range of biological subgroups, did not emerge clearly until the eighteenth century with the work of Linneaus, Buffon and Blumenach' (MacMaster, 2001, p. 12). MacMaster describes the work of these 'founding race theorists', who developed complex classification systems, and points out that their conclusions were often the result of little more than comparative physical anthropology and the observation of different groups. Such theories sat unhappily with the seminal and, at the time, revolutionary work of Darwin who sought to demonstrate the evolutionary development and interconnectedness of all humankind, in his *On the Origins of the Species* in 1859. He demonstrated that all men were related, though his views of evolution and the 'survival of the fittest' gave succour to those who still clung to the idea that some 'races' were 'more equal than others'. The separateness and inferiority of black and Asian races was also taken for granted in white scientific and political thought and considerable 'scientific' endeavour was devoted to proving the inferiority/superiority of 'races' that divided the developed nations of the day, even to the extent of delineating those groups that no longer receive any serious classification, such as the Anglo-Saxon, Celtic or Nordic 'races'. Dozier also points to the spurious classification systems developed at the time:

> Nineteenth century ethnologists in Europe and America even classified whites into different races. One popular scheme identified three white races: blond, blue eyed Teutonics (deemed the superior race); brown-haired Alpines; and slender, dark-haired Mediterraneans ... . The immigration laws of many countries, including those of the United States, reflected pronounced racial preferences, even among 'whites'. In early nineteenth-century America, for example, Irish immigrants were often classified as blacks. (Dozier, 2002, p. 143)

Such distinctions continued to be pursued for many years and perhaps, most notoriously, in the 1930s by the Nazis, in their search for the perfect and illusory Aryan race to try to prove their own superiority, whilst attempting to dispense with what they portrayed as inferior 'races'. The apartheid system in South Africa was also founded on the development of a spurious classification system, using visual differences, supported by tests, such as whether the thickness of human hair would hold the weight of a pencil, to try to add a pretence of objectivity where visual differences were limited. Classification systems have always broken down when applied in respect of 'mixed race'. Generally, people of 'mixed race' have been classified as 'non-white' whatever their visual appearance and characteristics, which can be very variable, or simply added into a 'coloured' or 'black' category.

The treatment of people of 'mixed race' condemns millions of people to a position of having no identifiable heritage and a lack of identity and standing, as though they are of no race at all. The 'mixed race' category becomes a general 'dump' category for those that do not fit in with any particular heritage and, indeed, those of 'mixed race' have historically been regarded in a derogatory way, with such terms as 'half-breeds', or 'half-castes', to point to their lack of racial purity. The term 'mixed race' is itself regarded as derogatory by some and the alternatives of dual or multiple heritage have been preferred. This lack of recognition in the 'identity stakes', the confusion in the minds of the individuals themselves about where they belong – and especially the reaction of others to them, rarely attracts the attention it deserves. Yet, people of mixed race are anxious for public recognition of both their existence and the difficulties they face. An article in *The Guardian* in

September 2006 (Smith, 2006) attracted a huge response and pointed out that mixed race people had not even been counted in the Census prior to 2001 and that 'if you are not Black or Asian, you're not an ethnic minority with any particular needs'.

The confusion, again, stems from the idea of race being biologically determined – race is somehow 'in the blood'. Years of intermixing has proved that this is not the case and has made not a scrap of difference to the life chances of the individuals concerned, but still some seek, in many areas of the political and cultural environment, to emphasise the differences borne of the most minute of distinctions, rather than the overwhelming similarities.

The advancement of science has been partly responsible for changing conceptions of 'race'. But so too has globalisation and the increasing pace of migration and resettlement of people. At the height of the British Empire, the British began to see themselves as a 'race' (Winder, 2004, p. 171) and the Germans certainly aimed to define themselves as a master race in the 1930s. Many of the racial categories referred to earlier revolved around geographic and national boundaries and as these have broken down, so the racialised concepts have withered away. 'Race' based on national boundaries and national identity, has moved to one based, first, on international reference frameworks and, second, towards internal ethnic divisions which underpin power struggles within nation states. The international categories we now employ tend to be much wider, such as European (which is often used synonymously with 'white'), Asian, black, or even gypsy or Romany. Within nation states, these are often used to represent the political divisions and to distinguish past and present conflicts and competition for resources.

The present conceptions and classifications of 'race' are, then, no less politically and culturally determined, than in the past, but simply represent our present perceptions of 'difference'. For example, within Britain, the 'white' category is subdivided into 'Irish' and 'British' ethnicity and the *Guide for the Collection and Classification of Ethnicity Data*, goes on to suggest the allocation of 'write-in' answers in respect of 'Northern Irish', 'Cypriot', 'Gypsy/Romany', 'Baltic States' and others, to the same 'white' category (ONS, 2003, p. 52). The Census also added a question on religion as it was felt that 'one of the more defining characteristics for some ethnic minorities is their religion' (ibid., p. 14). Indeed, much of British anti-discrimination law treats groups like Jews and Sikhs as ethnic groups, simply because of past history – and the contradictory nature of these conceptions has been the subject of much criticism by British Muslims, who have a much more limited protection and are not treated as an ethnic group or separate 'race'.

The idea of separate 'races' is now almost entirely discredited, but it is still difficult to entirely dispense with the term as a descriptor of different groups, especially as it is built into popular mythology and enshrined in various forms of legislation. With the advancement of genetic sciences, particularly the mapping of the human genome, any argument on this point may well completely subside, as it is now possible to assert with even greater certainty that the concept of 'race' has no scientific or genetic basis and that many of the differences in physical appearance result from the tiniest of genetic divergences, perhaps only a single gene that determines skin colour (Dozier, 2002, p. 142).

> modern science has shown that human races are an illusion, genetically speaking, and racism is just a particularly venomous form of us–them stereotyping. Most of the genetic variations amongst humans – 90 per cent or more, according to some estimates – occurs within racial groups, not between them. This means that there are likely to be far greater genetic differences between two randomly selected 'Caucasians' than between a randomly selected 'Caucasian' and an African-American. (Ibid., p. 144)

It is therefore already possible for the idea of 'race' to be dismissed as simply a 'social and political construct' (Gilroy, 1992, p. 38). However, as a form of differentiation, it is now being replaced by 'ethnicity' (Pilkington, 2003, p. 18) and it is not yet clear whether this will also become recognised as being socially and politically constructed. The 'primordialists' still see ethnic characteristics as 'fixed, fundamental and part of the circumstances of birth' and can be contrasted with the 'instrumentalists' who see identity as 'contingent on circumstance and fluid' (ibid.). But the differences between ethnic groups are often, at best, superficial and often entirely socially defined.

For example, in Rwanda, the murderous conflict has been based on the differentiation of two ethnic groups, the Tutsis and the Hutus. Yet, membership of these two groups has been variable over the years and it was only through colonialism that the divisions were 'firmed up, instrumentalized and substantiated', with the Tutsis promoted to the 'master race', by the Belgian administration. For lack of a cultural distinction between the two groups, a Tutsi was defined as 'someone with more than ten cows' (Meyer, 2001, p. 35).

The differences between ethnic groups have always been open to manipulation, even if not completely manufactured. In Sudan, the genocide of the black African population by so-called Arab Militiamen or Janjawid, appears to have been engineered, or at the least, not prevented, by the Sudanese Government. The roots of many conflicts are difficult to ascertain and to know whether they are culturally determined or spawned by political elites. Meyer suggests (ibid., p. 56) that such difficulty arises with regard to conflicts between the Serbs and Bosnians in the former Yugoslavia, the Hindus and Muslims in Mumbai, and the Tamils and Sinhalese in Sri Lanka. In each case, however, culture and conflict reinforce each other, providing justification and popular support.

'Ethnicity' is increasingly used to replace racial classification and whilst this may have the benefit of emphasising our commonality as one human race, it has become a new means by which political and cultural constructs of race can be portrayed. The new importance attached to 'ethnicity' is constantly emphasised in the *Guide* (ONS, 2003) with the 'common ancestry', 'physical appearance' and 'skin colour' forming a key part of the classification system. This, again, implies some form of biological trait or distinction, which is of a more semi-permanent state of being. Malik (2001) challenges any such use of ethnicity, which he says 'in many ways, is race after an attempt to take the biology out (and) in postwar years ethnicity has indeed come to replace race as a politically acceptable means of describing social differences'. The significant differences are, then, simply the ones that we individually and collectively decide are significant. We cling to the idea of permanence through the use of such terms as 'race', 'ethnicity' or 'heritage' which are used to emphasise physical differences as well as much more nebulous concepts, such as a shared history and other cultural and social dimensions.

Religious differences are even more clearly those that we construct for ourselves and yet are also increasingly used to define divisions and are often more salient (Pilkington, 2003, p. 21). This has become particularly true in respect of the Muslim community in white nation states, since September 11. 'Muslim' is not an ethnic identity, but their religion has begun to be defined in that way in many countries, by both the host nation and by Muslims themselves. Right wing extremists have also attacked Muslims as a proxy for attacking black and Asian people in those countries where it is unlawful to discriminate on the basis of race. Consequently, Muslim organisations have sought the same protection from discrimination and incitement of hatred as is presently available to ethnic minorities. The racialisation of faith is, like the conception of ethnicity, a political and social construct.

However, such a view is certainly not universally agreed upon, partly because of the whole history of the science of racism which lingers on and continues to exert influence on our thinking.

The Eugenic movement would not have accepted a political or cultural definition of 'race' and had a very different starting point. Eugenicists attempted to develop a science in support of *racial determinism*, in which 'race' was biologically determined and no amount of social, cultural or environmental exposure could undo the basic order and hierarchy. MacMaster (2001, p. 41) suggests two directions in which it has been used:

Eugenic ideas were widely debated in Europe from 1860 onwards, although the term, which means 'good in birth' or 'noble in heredity', was not invented by Francis Galton until 1883. The movement has been frequently analysed in relation to *negative* eugenics, which emphasized the most controversial forms of suppression of the racially feeble, and the *positive* eugenics, which promoted steps to encourage or enhance the birth rate of the biologically superior individuals or groups. Negative eugenics has received more attention from historians since its methods have laid the basis for the worst excesses of National Socialism.

and

Negative eugenics proposed the drastic termination of the 'breeding' capacity of individuals or groups that were perceived to carry hereditary traits that would damage the future biological fitness of the race-nation .... . This led to the logic, often pushed to the extreme, that programmes of social reform, health care, education and general welfare were radically dysgenic since not only could they not improve the genetic quality of the sick and degenerate, but they also ensured their 'unnatural' survival.

Not surprisingly, the genetic movement also applied their theories to the problem of 'class'. The lower orders were seen as lowly bred and that their potential expansion – working class families tended to be much larger than those of their 'superiors' – would result in the eventual outnumbering of the middle class. And industrialisation had created a mass working class, concentrated in the major cities, linked to the expanding labour requirements and developing their own radical political identity through the trade union and other movements. To the Eugenicists, the working class were considered primitives, biologically determined with inherited characteristics, a different and savage race, rather than a product of their social circumstances (ibid., pp. 35–44).

Whilst the Eugenicist movement was largely discredited in the latter part of the twentieth century, scientific thought and evidence continued to be presented in an attempt to suggest that differences between groups were due to genetic differences. For example, anatomical studies were used to try to create another form of scientific 'proof' of the existence of different races during the nineteenth century (Banton, 1977, p. 31), in which many comparisons were made between body shapes and, particularly by craniology, comparing skull size and shape, these were said to give rise to different 'temperament and mentality' (ibid., p. 38). However, much more effort, and over a longer period, was devoted to the racialising of the concept of 'intelligence', where various studies purported to show that racial differences were biologically determined and that they gave rise to real differences in performance and capability.

Charles Darwin's cousin, Sir Francis Galton, also spawned a particular strand of the Eugenicist model, based on what Daniels and Houghton (1972) described as 'the loosest kind of scientific theory'. This followed a subjective examination of the family background of 400 high achievers, or 'geniuses' to assert that the 'genius' trait is hereditary. Galton's book, *Hereditary Genius*, published in 1883, made overtly racist assertions, but still established him as the 'founding father of intelligence testing' (Hudson, 1972, p. 12). Psychology subsequently became a battle ground, however, between those that relied on the biological and physical sciences and those that related to the social sciences. The school of 'psychometry' was based on the former and gave rise to a series of tests, such as K-factor assessments, Ink-blot interpretations, V-factor test results and intelligence tests, which achieved new heights in the early years of the Second World War and were applied to forces personnel to assess aptitude and capability (Daniels and Houghton, 1972, p. 69). This form of psychology simply added to the idea that the capability of individuals – and groups of people – were fixed and based on hereditary factors, which created a natural order in society. The 'nature versus nurture' debate has continued to the present day and psychometric testing, particularly in relation to recruitment and employment selection processes, has become more sophisticated and common place, though still regarded with suspicion by some black and ethnic minorities.

Arthur Jensen successfully reignited the debate with an article in the *Harvard Educational Review* in 1969, by focussing upon apparently persistent IQ differences between blacks and whites in the United States. Jensen argued that compensatory educational programmes had failed to close the differences and that these differences therefore had a genetic origin. Hans Eysenck created a similar furore in Britain, with his *Race, Intelligence and Education* in 1971, although he did not rule out the impact of environmental factors. The 'science' employed by the likes of Jensen and Eysenck, has, however, been challenged and found to contain flaws and biases (MacMaster, 2001, p. 219) as has the work of Sir Cyril Burt who attempted to prove an hereditary basis of intelligence with a study of twins, later found to be a 'scientific fraud' (Yeboah, 1988, p. 240). Such 'science' is no longer taken seriously if, for no other reason, than the evident success of black people in every field of human endeavour – perhaps representing some sign of social progress since the debate raged in the late 1960s and early 1970s. In all this, it is sometimes forgotten that an intelligence test measures no more than what is included in the test itself and it remains a simplistic scale by which complex processes are measured:

> This process is clearly evident in the attempt to reduce the notion of measuring intelligence to the result of an IQ test. Here the whole of cognition, language, thought and conceptualization is reduced to a single figure which expresses an individual's standing relative to his peers. (Richards, Richardson and Spears, 1972, p. 180)

However, the debate about the genetic origin of differences in intelligence was subsequently used to question the worth of social programmes to tackle poverty and inequality and even to revive 'biological' explanations of social phenomena, such as the propensity of black minorities to criminality (Rex, 1972, p. 176) or to particular types of 'grave offences' (Pannell and Brockway, 1965, p. 29). Perhaps, ironically, Enoch Powell, one of the most notorious opponents of migration in the same period, argued his case on cultural differences and 'territoriality' – the undermining of the host culture – rather than any sense of the innate inferiority of immigrants (ibid., p. 177). Nevertheless, the idea of the innate inferiority of some groups has persisted and is perhaps most evident today in the ideas about criminality, for example, with regard to the 'stop and search' debate about policing methods in Britain and has become part of the mythology surrounding notions of inferiority of black and minority ethnic groups.

The search for scientific 'proof' in either direction will always be illusory. 'Intelligence' is just one of many differences between individuals and there is still no agreement about exactly what it is, let alone how to measure it. There are many examples of so-called geniuses who excel in one area, yet seem to lack the basic common sense which would enable them to prosper at a human or social level. Similarly, some people who appear to have a high intellectual ability do not have the 'streetwise' ability to avoid difficult situations nor do they necessarily possess the entrepreneurial skills of 'dyslexic failures', like Sir Richard Branson. The very idea of intelligence is socially and culturally defined and the tests merely represent those views. It is, of course, possible that our intellectual and personality differences are shaped by our genetic background as individuals, but given the cultural and environmental differences that exist between ethnic groups they can never be isolated in any scientific way. What we do know, however, is that many long-standing immigrant groups have become integrated, and even assimilated, over time into the culture of the host community, effectively eradicating those cultural and environmental differences and, with them, any serious debate about innate inferiority. Groups that were once disparaged and demonised are no longer the focus of any attention. The focus of our current concerns are almost always about new migrants, about which relatively little is known and myths abound, or where the 'degree of difference' between the migrant and host community has remained significant, including cultural and social differences, so that their 'environments' remain distinct.

John Rex's views about the way such arguments change and develop is still pertinent today:

> The crux of the sociological argument about racist biological theories therefore is this. On the political level, societies may pass through periods in which there is no great need for any kind of theory which emphasise the differences and incompatibilities between different ethnic or religious or 'racial' groups. In such periods, popular maxims and anecdotes will affirm the essential similarities between men, and informed opinion will deplore the political behaviour of the small minority of disturbed persons at home who are 'prejudiced' and of governments abroad which work on a basis of racial supremacy. As strains in such a society develop however, there is a groundswell of opinion in which popular maxims and anecdotes guiltily [sic] and uneasily, spotlight racial differences. (Rex, 1972, p. 176)

The perception of 'environment' must also go beyond cultural dimensions and can be linked to serious structural differences and particularly to poverty and deprivation. Poor health, poor diet and poor housing is clearly responsible for many aspects of personal development, particularly during childhood. Similarly, upward social mobility, educational success and good health have all been linked to economic position and social stability. The impact of the physical and social environment on the development of an individual is very significant and is even more marked when taken over a greater period of time and when the transgenerational impact is considered (Richards, Richardson and Spears, 1972). It is therefore important to constantly fit the discussions about supposed inferiority/superiority debates into a dynamic model, in which, over a period of time, the performance of individuals and groups, our perception of that performance and our perceptions of what is politically and socially important in that performance model, will change and develop.

'Race' has therefore been used to classify people, in a variety of hierarchical patterns, and has been constructed on the basis of, religion, nationality, social class, ethnicity – as well as physical characteristics, particularly skin colour – to present a deterministic model of social relations. Various attempts have been made to provide a scientific validity for such differentiation and to present such differences as the 'natural order', which will, in turn, justify slavery and forced labour, segregation, discrimination, the denial of basic human rights and equal opportunities – all in an attempt to maintain and institutionalise the domination and superiority of one group over another.

Social psychological models

Early psychological explanations of group behaviour focussed upon personality differences; that the behaviour of one individual is determined by the motivation of another. In terms of prejudice and racism, concepts such as the 'authoritarian personality' have been advanced, the most influential advocates being by Adorno *et al.* (1950). In their view, the authoritarian personality was the product of harsh parenting and is particularly susceptible to the development of extreme views and irrational beliefs. The authoritarian personality type apparently develops rigid views and is intolerant of any deviant or nonconformist behaviour. They are supposedly deeply conservative, intolerant of difference, not only in respect of ethnicity, but are also likely to be sexist and homophobic. However, despite some much later studies which have found a link between authoritarianism and prejudice against women and mentally ill people, as well as ethnocentrism, the evidence has been equivocal (Brown, 1995, p. 24).

In any event, the existence of a particular personality type is unlikely to offer any real explanation of the racism by groups or large sections of a given population, though it may offer something in respect of the background and development of leaders of extreme or fanatical groups who are implacably opposed to any tolerance of difference and not open to reasoned or reasonable arguments. No one would seriously argue that the millions of people across Europe who regularly vote for extreme right wing parties all have an authoritarian personality – whether or not due to harsh parenting or some other deep seated psychological problem. A social context is essential and social psychologists have shifted towards the examination of the social processes involved in the interaction between groups.

The possibility of a large group of people sharing a personality type may be unlikely, though the idea of an 'authoritarian community' in which people have a very similar and limited experience of others, does need to be considered. Such a community may have become very insular and been subject to limited change over a period of time, with little movement in or out, even on a temporary basis, and with little opportunity for active engagement with others. In addition, if the general level of both formal and informal education is also low, members of that community would neither have the means to develop higher level educational skills and understandings of others, nor the ability to 'imagine the other' through literature, through the performing arts or other media, which Scarry (1998) suggests could be important. It seems reasonable to suppose that a substantial number of people in such areas, could have developed a fixed and limited conception of others and their 'fear of difference' and prejudicial tendencies are mutually reinforcing.

This may also have an impact on the way in which we categorise people, especially as groups are created by a process in which each individual attempts to make order of a complex world, by reducing the infinite variety of people and objects into some sort of category (Allport, 1954). These categories may depend upon a wide range of variables, but we may begin to make judgements about those categories of people, which may pose a potential threat, those that are benign and those that are likely to be supportive and helpful. Positive or negative attitudes (prejudices) are formed in respect of whole groups of people, simply because of the sheer difficulty of making judgements about each person on an individual basis, bearing in mind the need for a quick decision in certain circumstances, especially when we first encounter a stranger and there is a need to respond in some way or another. This categorisation can develop into more rigid patterns of group 'favouritism' and the concept of 'in-group' and 'out-group' explains how close-knit membership, or even simple emotional attachment to one group, the in-group, can lead to unfavourable views of another group, the out-group. According to Dozier (2002, p. 40) this is what a number of anthropologists like Claude Levi-Strauss and biologists like Edward O. Wilson and others have developed into the 'binary instinct' which utilises the natural, or innate, intuitive process to create order within our minds, about who we feel safe with. It is a primordial us–them distinction, a fairly crude classification, based on stereotyping to decide who is not 'like us'.

Such distinctions are not simply based on ethnicity, and each area of difference is reinforced by social processes:

> societies everywhere break people into in-group versus out-group, child versus adult, kin versus non-kin, married versus single, and activities into sacred and profane, good and evil. They fortify the boundaries of each division with taboo and ritual. To change from one division to the other requires initiation ceremonies, weddings, blessings, ordinations and other rites of passages. (Ibid., p. 41)

Social identity theory, then, is based on the assumption that we have a natural tendency to place ourselves in one group and to socially categorise people in relation to that group, often on the basis of an immediate judgement. We then apparently favour members of our own group, at the expense of members of other groups. According to Tajfel (1970) such favouritism will develop irrespective of whether one group is in competition with another group for resources, or on any other basis. However, more recent work has shown that this is a very complex issue with perceptions about in-groups and out-groups being dependent upon pre-existing information and stereotypes (Poppe and Linssen, 1999) and perceptions of status (Nesdale and Flesser, 2001). This 'natural instinct' may therefore be heavily conditioned by social factors, or even if the result of some immediate visible clues and signals, may soon be subject to developmental processes.

Various studies have also considered the impact of cross-cultural or inter-group contact and the way in which attitudes to 'others' is shaped by that contact and by lack of contact. The lack of any previous experience of an 'out-group', for example, may mean that the development of contact between the 'out-group' and the 'in-group' is more difficult to establish because of anxiety and prejudices which have not been explored and broken down. Information about the 'out-group' can help to reduce those fears and improve the likelihood of more positive relations developing through contact. Even when the initial contact reinforces the pre-existing prejudices, this may be broken down over time as trust and empathy develops through repeated contact (Pettigrew, 1998, pp. 65–85). A substantial body of research now shows that contact between groups can reduce prejudice (Brown, 1995, p. 268) and that in some cases, the frequency of inter-ethnic contact was the single biggest predictor of positive attitude change (ibid., p. 240). However, the contact is only likely to be successful if it takes place under certain conditions. Miles Hewstone has been a major force in the development of 'contact theory' and the practice of inter-group contact, over many years. In a range of contributions to academic journals and books, he has dealt with very specific subjects, such as inter-group contact to help resolve 'the troubles' in Northern Ireland (Hewstone *et al.*, 2006), to a much more general analysis of the role of inter-group contact in the promotion of inter-group harmony (Hewstone *et al.*, 2006a). Social psychologists are now developing new approaches and with much clearer and positive results:

> The causal sequence traditionally implied in most contact research is that lack of or biased knowledge about the outgroup (i.e., stereotypes) promotes prejudice ... Intergroup contact cannot, however, be considered only in terms of its cognitive processes; a deeper understanding requires recognition of the role of affective processes ... and shows that affect plays an equally important role in changing intergroup judgements. We aim ... to point out the existence of a growing body of evidence about intergroup contact that is compatible with a new process of prejudice reduction, a process that we call 'affect generalization'. (Ibid, p. 3)

'Contact theory' is therefore a cornerstone of community cohesion practice, though the nature of that contact is clearly critical and this is examined further in Chapter 6.

The notion that we identify with, or even prefer, 'people like us' is very prevalent in the thinking of a range of diverse opinion from the extreme right wing racists, like Griffin (BNP website, 2004), to liberal commentators like Goodhart (2004). It also seems embedded into academic studies, such as Putnam's *Bowling Alone*, which distinguishes 'bonding' and 'bridging' social capital in which the latter 'requires that we transcend our social and political identities to connect with people unlike ourselves' (Putnam, 2000, p. 411). But who are people 'like ourselves'? Perhaps they are no more than the people we already know and feel comfortable with because of regular contact – our circle of friends, acquaintances and colleagues, in other words, our various 'in-groups'. This would suggest that people 'like ourselves' are defined by social circumstance and familiarity, rather than some idea about common identity. Of course, we will tend to associate with people with whom we have something in common, such as a religious affiliation or a particular social or cultural activity and, in turn, such associations determine the bonding of the group through repeated contact. However, changing our associations would appear to change our ideas about who is 'like ourselves'.

The idea of multiple identities is, in any event, now taken for granted – it is possible to be, say, white, Muslim, middle class and a Londoner – and many more things at the same time. From this range of overlapping identities, it appears to be difficult to say what will constitute 'us' and what will constitute 'them' on anything more than an individual basis. Ethnic identity, for many it seems, will often trump the other identities to determine who is really 'like us'. However, this is a judgement, often implied rather than explicitly stated, by commentators who are working in the context of traditionally racist society, and assuming such differences as 'natural'. What would be a 'natural' affinity for a white middle-aged man, wearing a suit, stepping out of his BMW and walking up the steps to his office, if confronted on one side by a young white man in a torn leather jacket, adorned in chains, with 'love' and 'hate' tattooed on either knuckle and accompanied by a dog attached by a string? Would his 'natural' affinity to this fellow white person be stronger than that which he feels towards a man similarly dressed to himself, middle aged and apparently also a professional person, who just happened to be black or Asian? Surely our ideas about who are people like us are complex and the extent to which we place a premium on ethnicity is a learned and socially defined identity, rather than innate tendency?

One may ask, however, as in this example, if the apparent affinity to another man who appears to be a similar professional person, in preference to another who is of the same ethnicity, but appears very different, is just conforming to another equally unacceptable stereotype? This is inevitably the case, as we all make instant judgements about others, but those judgements are based on pre-existing information which has helped to inform our categorisation. They can, however, change and, again, studies suggest that contact and 'disconfirming' information can dispel the stereotypical views (Brown, 1995, p. 113).

It is not possible to demonstrate that people have an innate distrust of others who are visibly not 'like them' and that therefore we are inherently racist or sexist, given that so much of our reactions are inevitably 'learnt' from our immediate associates and from the wider society in which we live. Some studies have used young children as subjects, in an attempt to demonstrate preferences for others that have the same ethnicity and gender and this does appear to have some basis. However, even with very young children, it is difficult to be sure that they have had no contact with others, nor have learned responses and even if this were the case, it may only demonstrate that this 'visible' barrier was one waiting to be broken down by subsequent interaction – in other words, that young children are both curious about differences and wary of them, but as they explore difference they may, just as likely, prefer the company of people not visibly like themselves. Just as a child may be concerned about a new food, a strange looking toy or an alarming sound, so they may also be wary of another child that looks different and of whom he or she has no experience. Their initial reticence may be dealt with either by reassurance or by reinforcement and the subtle process of 'socialisation' can soon begin to determine future attitudes and values.

Indeed, our identities and perceptions of others' identities are dynamic, constantly changing, responding to individual and societal events and developments. For example, the awareness of the Muslim faith and the subsequent development of Islamophobia in the Western world after September 11, has nothing to do with a 'natural' instinct based on religious differences, and can only be explained by the new fears and prejudices provoked by political events and the response to them in the mass media. Ansari argues that the emerging Muslim identity in Britain pre-dates 9/11 and was generally subsumed within ethnic identifications until the 1980s. It now transcends ethnic differences and is evolving as an identity of ' "unbelonging in a culture of resistance" in contest with hegemonic British identity' (Ansari, 2004, p. 9). The in-group and out-group theory also has difficulty in explaining how and why demonisation and hatred is generated on the basis of such simple affinities. If it does help to explain group loyalties and perhaps even differential treatment, why would such differences necessarily develop into more extreme rivalries, violent conflicts and genocide? This is especially hard to understand when different groups can just as easily be seen to find common cause and co-operate together in pursuit of a wider cause; many protest movements are an example of such inter-group co-operation. Ethnic conflicts are not the norm, despite the 'exaggerated impression of the power of ethnic violence' given in the press and media – the reality is that ethnic violence is rare and ethnic peace is much more the norm (Varshney, 2002, p. 297). This view may be at odds with what often seems a general belief that humans – and human groups – are naturally competitive. However, the attitude and behaviour of groups towards each other is more likely to be determined by social circumstance, than any natural disposition.

There is also an unsatisfactory element in psychological explanations of racism and racist behaviour, in that they often appear to depend upon rather deterministic and fixed views of group motivation and individual personality types, rather than dynamic relationships. The 'authoritarian personality', for example, is presented as one which is set in early years and with the attitudes and motivation fixed from that time on. Both the identity of individuals and the social categorisation of individuals into groups, also seem to underestimate our ability to reason and to change our affections and affiliations constantly over time. The suddenness in which mass anxieties and the demonisation of one group by another group arise cannot be overestimated and both our affections and our disaffections, are very susceptible to mass manipulation and even hysteria – the concerns about Muslims in general or the way in which East European 'gypsies' have been whipped up by the British press and media have been recent examples of this.

Sociological models

Rex and Moore sought to explain the behaviour of the majority community towards black and ethnic minorities in sociological terms. They argued that it was not a minority of citizens, harbouring the prejudice borne of a disturbed authoritarian personality, but rather the protectionist attitudes of the majority of the host community (Rex and Moore, 1967, p. 12). In their pioneering study of Sparkbrook, part of the inner city of Birmingham, Rex and Moore sought:

> not merely to classify behaviour as prejudiced but to understand the part which customs, beliefs, norms, and expectations, play in a larger social structure, be it the structure of an ethnic minority group or that of the overall urban society, marked as it is by diverse intergroup conflicts. Once we understand urban society as a structure of social interaction and conflict, prejudiced behaviour may be shown to fit naturally into, or even required, by that structure. Prejudice may be seen as a social as well as psychological phenomenon. Moreover, once it is so understood, 'discrimination' in according rights to an outgroup might be seen to follow as a logical consequence given the beliefs that are held.

A member of a more powerful and privileged majority group is therefore, behaving rationally, if unfairly, by participating in systems that discriminate against members of less powerful and minority groups: sharing out opportunities between a larger number on an equal basis will clearly reduce the advantages and opportunities available, compared to retaining them within the more limited number. But such 'protectionism' is clearly unacceptable in modern multicultural societies, at least in terms of the values and rights which they claim and extol. A tension is therefore created between that which is fair and just on the one hand, and self and group interest on the other.

The unacceptable nature of self-interest is deflected by the myths and demonisation which they have been created to characterise other groups. These other groups are then presented as not deserving equal treatment and consideration, because they are less well educated, less skilled, less capable, or simply too lazy, feckless and untrustworthy. However, the presence of minorities, which have rapidly grown in most multicultural societies, also raise questions of identity. This may again lead to not only spurious justifications of differential treatment – they are not truly French, British, American, etc., – but also more complex notions of who are 'our' people, who we trust and with whom we share a common bond and a common cause.

At the same time, the decline of traditional manual labour, in both the primary sector and in manufacturing has brought a decline in 'working class' occupations and numbers. The middle class has become the predominant class in developed nations. The working class has not disappeared and working class occupations and activities have simply been exported to the poorer countries of the South. The gulf between the living standards of the rich and poor nations has, at the same time, widened enormously. 'Class' may now be starting to reflect the differences between nations rather than those within them. This has had a number of particular effects. In the first place, the perception of the poorer nations is one of even greater poverty and backwardness. They remain more firmly at the bottom of the 'pecking order' and both the richer nations as a whole and their citizens inevitably regard them as inferior. This perception is not helped by the fact that people from poorer nations will be prepared to undertake work at lower rates of pay, whether as immigrants, or as providers of goods and services from within their own nations.

This, again, creates a perception of inferiority, which is based on nothing more than economic circumstance. Nevertheless, the white nations' perception of poverty and inferiority is quite closely aligned with non-white nations, irrespective of whether those same white nations have contributed to their continuing deprivation (see previous chapter).

Within modern multicultural societies, these economic realities and the consequent perceptions are carried over, with the host community generally being prepared to use immigrant labour to fill the gaps in labour supply. This is sometimes in direct competition with the poorer sections of their own communities and becomes one of the key drivers of racism, as those poorer communities seek to protect whatever slim advantages they may have over other groups, whether distinguished by ethnic, faith or national characteristics. This protectionism is usually reinforced by stereotypes and myths about the minority group or groups, which is then used to justify that protectionism. Race in this sense, is autonomous of class and creates divisions in order to both reinforce and justify social and economic advantage and which, in turn, creates prejudice and bigotry which is 'racist'.

The 'competition model' is now often advanced to explain poor race relations, particularly with respect to the arrival of new immigrants into existing areas, which are generally the poorest and most disadvantaged. The attitudes of middle class people towards immigrants has also been contrasted with that of working class people, simply as a result of their economic and social position and the function that migrants perform in relation to their own class position:

> We recognise that inward migration does create tensions and that these do not necessarily revolve around race. It is easier for the more affluent communities to be tolerant towards newcomers, as they do not perceive them to be a threat. Many immigrants will not, initially at least, be able to afford homes in the more affluent areas, will not be sending their children to schools in those areas and will not have the skills to compete for the higher level of jobs. Indeed, they will often be providing services to middle class families, keeping petrol stations open 24 hours a day, working in restaurants and providing au pairs and cleaners.

By contrast, many disadvantaged communities will perceive that newcomers are in competition for scarce resources and public services, such as housing and school places. The pressure on resources in those areas is often intense and local services are often insufficient to meet the needs of the existing community, let alone newcomers. These fears cannot be disregarded (Cantle, 2004, p. 15).

The attitude of the host community to minorities will often be ambiguous, depend upon class and other factors and change as social and economic factors also change. The economic function that minorities perform will be welcomed initially by, at least some of the host community, when additional labour is required and certain skills are in short supply. If the position of the minorities remains as one of an 'underclass' the poorer sections of the host community may also feel that their privileged position is not substantially threatened. This may be the case where citizenship rights are limited and the seasonal or 'guest workers' are expected to return to their home countries. An economic downturn can soon transform economic positions – and community relations, however. If the economic position remains strong and a gradual integration of the host and new minority communities develops, then tensions may be limited. But if the minorities remain separate from the host community, both physically and socially, they will continue to be seen as the 'other', and not regarded as equals with equal rights, their position will remain tenuous and become even more so, as the economy declines.

Fear and conflict can therefore be evident at a number of levels – within neighbourhoods, within societies as a whole and between nations – and is often linked to social and economic position. Where one nation, or one group or class of people, believe that they are so clearly superior to another and therefore do not perceive them to be a threat, competition and potential conflict will be at a minimum level. This rises, however, as the perceived threat to their advantageous position becomes more real. But perceptions of the 'other' do not simply develop as each migrant group emerges, and are generally overlaid by a long history in which inter-group relations have been determined and have become part of our socialisation processes. For example, the history of imperialism and colonialism has had an important effect on the way in which we conceptualise race, as has the development of racist ideologies and practices (Solomos and Back, 1996, p. 45). So, whilst a significant component of the 'degree of difference' is the objective social and economic position of the minority and majority groups, including the relationship between minorities, this also depends upon the perception of one group as being superior to the other as a consequence of their heritage nation being at a more advanced stage of economic development. If a nation state is in an inferior economic position and placed lower in the economic order of nations, usually measured by GDP and average income per capita, then it is likely that its people will be seen in the same way and regarded as an inferior group. Such a crude view of 'worth' depends, of course, upon a Western value system that places real importance on wealth and economic circumstance to define position.

The conception of the 'other' therefore assumes a degree of independence, which can precede and even condition economic and social relations and is embedded in our common language and images, our humour – and our most venomous of views.

The 'fear of difference'

Uncertainty, anxiety and fear are all instinctive reactions by which we, and the whole animal kingdom, protect ourselves. The circumstances that arouse such fears are, at least in part, however, learnt. For example, we learn that walking down an unlit alleyway in certain areas is a risky business, or that cutting an apple with a knife in a certain way could give rise to an accidental injury. Gradually we learn to distinguish the real risks from the remote possibilities. So too, we learn about people. We may be anxious about people that appear to be different from ourselves, in terms of social class, ethnicity, age, gender and other factors. Even then, in certain settings, such as when we meet a doctor from a different ethnicity to ourselves, any learnt prejudices may be overcome by the trust of the medical profession which we have also learnt. In the same way, we learn that our differences are not as important as our similarities and even if they are significant, we learn how to relate to each other and develop trust and understanding.

Overcoming the 'fear of difference' is fundamental to community cohesion, though this is difficult enough in itself, given the way in which many societies have separated themselves physically, economically and socially into different groups, often with little contact and positive interaction between them. In more extreme circumstances, where rivalry has developed into conflict, and differences have been compounded by the use of long-standing myths to demonise different communities, then such divisions may have become so volatile that they are sufficient in themselves to become the cause of further conflict.

Tackling the fear of difference can only be done by exploring that difference, and by understanding and coming to terms with it. The opportunity to do so, however, has become severely curtailed, partly by the many, very worthy, attempts to control discrimination and racist and other unacceptable behaviour. The focus of social policy has been very much on controlling behaviour, through legislation, with very limited emphasis on tackling underlying values and attitudes (despite a similar statutory duty upon some agencies to proactively promote 'good race relations' – see Chapter 2). Legislation may well have some impact, however, if people internalise their behaviour, accepting it as the right thing to do. There is also some survey evidence to suggest that prejudice, based on ethnic and gender stereotypes, has reduced over the past thirty or forty years or so, at least in the United States (Brown, 1995). On the other hand, Brown (1995) also suggests that the form of prejudice may simply have changed, becoming expressed in new forms or developing into 'aversive' techniques, based on avoidance and coolness to others.

Legislation has, to some extent, made the discussion of difference very difficult, as any such discussion would entail examining the myths and irrational fears and prejudice expressed about the 'other'. A number of countries have criminalised any public expression of hatred for particular groups, especially where it might be expected to lead to violence against them, as in the 'incitement of racial hatred' in Britain, or the laws against 'religious and racist vilification' in Australia. This sort of restriction can, however, appear to create a 'catch 22' situation in which it is illegal to express fears about difference, but without open discussion the difference and the fears can never be fully understood and answered. In the meantime, right wing extremists can avoid prosecution and continue to promote such views through informal networks or by carefully coding their prejudices, for example, by attacking religious groups rather than ethnic groups.

The opportunity to explore differences does not just relate to the majority and minority relationships. Some of the differences between minorities are even more profound, long-standing and potentially violent, than between black and white communities. Again, it has been difficult to explore and discuss them in a climate in which prejudices are difficult to admit to and potentially illegal. Further, at an informal level, the culture of race relations in Britain at least, made it difficult to recognise that minorities could hold racist views. During the various attempts at 'race awareness' training in the 1980s, it was often asserted that black and ethnic minority people could not be racist as they had experienced racism every day. There is still a real reluctance to recognise and discuss such divisions even though fundamental differences, for example, between Hindus and Muslims, have long been apparent in minority communities. Darcus Howe was one of the first to openly expose such divisions in a television documentary and in complementary article, 'Turning on Each Other', in *The Guardian* (Howe, 2004), when he described the enmity between some sections of the Asian and West Indian community and, also, where 'the Caribbean community is most unwelcoming – some visit on the Somalis the kind of racial abuse we suffered in the period of early migration'. In the same article, Howe, nevertheless, went on to express his fear that his honesty would result in his detractors charging that his views in the TV documentary, in particular, 'will strengthen the cause of the BNP'. The most recent riot in Britain, in Lozells in Birmingham, was between Asian and black community members, resulting in the loss of two lives – and a wider recognition of the tensions that can arise between minority communities.

It is as though admitting to prejudices and even being willing to discuss them, will somehow give the upper hand to the racists. For example, even though the British Government formally agreed 'to take on board the need to generate a widespread and open debate about identity, shared values and common citizenship', demanded by the Cantle Report (Denham, 2001), three years later the consultation paper on the Government's new Community Cohesion and Race Equality Strategy was still expressing concern about how such a debate could take place 'which doesn't fuel the prejudice against Black and minority ethnic communities' (Home Office, 2004, p. 18). Three years later a Government report has indicated that it will now initiate a series of public debates to establish shared British values (SoSJLC, 2007). There is no alternative to confronting the prejudices and fears – community cohesion is (to coin a phrase) about 'being tough on the prejudice and the causes of prejudice', however painful and possibly regressive, the first steps appear to be. Driving such prejudices into the background will not answer them, nor give people the confidence that they can be answered, and will mean that they can be inflamed at any future point.

There is also a danger in making the 'incitement to religious hatred' illegal, even though it is clearly necessary to protect religious minorities, especially when religious beliefs have been used as proxy by the extreme right as a means of attacking those ethnic minorities that coincide with a religious identity. The British Government, therefore, committed itself to introducing legal protection for faith communities so that 'people cannot use religious differences to create hate' (Blunkett, 2004, p. 12). It is at least theoretically possible, however, to introduce legislation which allows robust discussion about religion, but prevents the incitement of hatred against those people who practice a particular religion.

Nevertheless, the balance between the need for open discussion and the use of the subsequent hijacking of that debate to create intolerance remains difficult and the present tendency is to 'tiptoe around the sensitive issues of race, religion and culture' and:

> Unless our society can move at least to a position where we can respect our neighbours as fellow human beings, we shall fail in our attempts to create a harmonious society in which conditions have changed so radically in the last 40 years. Such respect depends, in part at least, on being open with one another about differences of belief tradition and culture. In our anxiety to eliminate the forms of insulting behaviour and language we have created a situation in which most people are unwilling to open any subject which possibly lead to uncomfortable differences of opinion. In this lies a big danger. If neighbours are unable to discuss differences, they have no hope of understanding them. Those who wish to cause trouble have a fruitful field in which to operate. (Cantle, 2001, p. 20)

The 'fear of difference' is central to the community cohesion agenda which seeks to recognise the need for openness in its attempt to 'establish a common vision and sense of belonging for all communities' and in allowing 'different backgrounds and circumstances (to be) appreciated and positively valued'. This is seen to spring from the 'positive relationships being developed between people from different backgrounds' as much as from the creation of 'similar life opportunities' (for full definition of community cohesion see Figure 2.1). In other words, communities have to find what they have in common – and agree upon it – by dialogue and interaction, not seek to avoid contact because of the risk that it might be unlawful, unacceptable or difficult.

Race and religion are, in any case, only a part of what constitutes 'difference'. A number of other areas have been struggling to come to terms with the stereotyping of groups, based on real or ascribed general character- istics and the subsequent conditioning responses to individuals of that group. The lessons from these other areas are not, however, often discussed in relation to ethnic divisions, despite appearing to be very pertinent. Many societies have sought to keep apart those groups that have exhibited behav- iours that they have not understood or been able to rationalise. The mentally ill, for example, were often kept in institutions in geographically isolated areas, often creating and reinforcing irrational fears. Even as we have come to recognise the medical conditions and to be able to offer effective treat- ment, the various attempts to provide 'care in the community' have met with resistance and hostility. Gradually integration has, however, now helped to break down the barriers and to understand the differences.

Similarly, people with learning difficulties have also been institutionalised and hidden from the rest of the community for fear of offending their sensi- bilities. Children, in particular, have been segregated simply because of their mental incapacity or their physical disability. Again, progressive education authorities have begun to break this down with a policy of inclusion. This is recognised as a vital part of societal education and requires that all children learn first-hand about such differences and that, despite those differences, everyone is entitled to respect. The Centre for Studies on Inclusive Education (2004) developed an 'Inclusion Charter' which stated that:

> segregated education is a major cause of society's widespread prejudice against disabled adults and those experiencing learning difficulties in learning and that efforts to increase their participation in community life will be seriously jeopardised unless segregated education is reduced and ultimately ended. Desegregating special education is therefore a crucial first step in helping to change discriminatory attitudes, in creating under- standing and in developing a fairer society.

The 'parallel lives' in schools, based on disability has, therefore, hopefully had its day, at least in the British education system, with separation limited to very few areas where mainstream education is simply impractical. Educationalists, however, in general are yet to apply the same philosophy to other forms of stereotypes, based on ethnicity, faith and gender. And, for physically disabled people in general, the 'does he take sugar' syndrome is far from ended, with disabled people constantly facing discrimination as a result of ignorance and prejudice – including the inability of others to engage directly with the person with the disability, rather than the person that they happen to be with.

It is not surprising then, that the extent of discrimination cited in a number of European countries was considerable and wide-ranging, including age, ethnic origin, religion and beliefs, physical disability, learning difficulties or mental illness and sexual orientation (EUMC, 2003).

Each area of difference may create barriers between different groups. These differences may be psychological, practical or structural. For example, 'visible differences' based on physical appearance may provoke a number of reactions from simple curiosity to outright hostility and ridicule. Such differences might be thought to be the subject of less reaction as time moves on, given that modern communications enable most differences to be observed, indirectly at least, and that such differences will be more commonplace, even in the most traditional of mono-cultural areas. Nevertheless, visible differences are often enough in themselves to provoke abuse, harassment and even attack. Visible differences simply reinforce our own prejudices and fears, which are not limited to 'ethnic' difference, nor based on evidence of different behaviours. These 'parallel lives' do not allow for the exploration and gradual understanding and acceptance of difference. They reinforce the separation allowing politically motivated and divisive forces to capitalise on the ignorance of others and to spread misinformation, ensuring that their bigoted views will fester and grow.

5
Identity, Values and Citizenship

The terms 'citizenship' and 'nationality' and 'national identity' have been interpreted in different ways and are quite often conflated. The contribution that they each make towards shaping individual identity and the way in which they help to create a value system for individuals and groups is also less than clear and sometimes disputed.

Nationality is a matter of fact for virtually everybody. It simply describes the country to which one belongs, as is evident from the contract between the individual and the state, whether written or unwritten, setting out some rudiments of allegiance by the individual on the one side, and the protection and rights granted by the state, on the other. Nationality can be won or lost, as allegiances change, though generally only in exceptional circumstances, or through marriage and by adoption in respect of children. Nationality does not depend upon feelings of belonging, or even upon a set of criteria created to bind people together and there are no predetermined levels of unity, dependent upon common language, culture, faith or ethnicity. However, each state provides real and tangible manifestations of nationhood by controlling its borders and by imposing internal order through a panoply of laws and regulations and also, by planning and prioritising governmental programmes, which inevitably rely upon a heavy burden of fiscal measures. Each nation state is also supported by a range of socialisation measures, most of which are very informal and subtle processes, which bear more heavily on the behaviour of individuals than is generally recognised by those that are subject to them. These burdens, not only constrain action in the public realm, but also challenge faith, beliefs and personal values, in the private sphere. To exist, a nation has to be real and visible to its own people, but also has to pass the international test – to be recognised by others, in the sufficient use of the instruments of power and authority.

The nation state also creates a political framework for individuals, in which people can debate, discuss and decide upon collective priorities and the use of the pooled and shared resources. The nation state is the vehicle by which we each trade our rights for responsibilities and vice versa, we can negotiate support for others, in return for protection and support for ourselves. It is the basis by which we can create public services, constrain and contribute to private enterprise and assist or inhibit international activities. This will inevitably create a bonding of sort, simply as a result of the dialogue and participatory process involved, though not necessarily, one based on consensus. Cultural affinities, however strong, cannot achieve the collective action that nation states rely upon to build a 'society' – or a society of interests. In this sense, nationality may be seen to create a political identity, an affiliation and contractual loyalty, based on mutual self-interest.

Nationality is, therefore, in essence a contractual relationship, but one that seldom remains so simple. It will have a considerable impact on our identity and our values, but it is not the only influence and it is not necessarily the strongest. Of course, for some people identity is defined by nationality and there is a coincidence of national, cultural and personal perspectives. But for many, the picture is more complex, with national identity supplemented, or even supplanted, by other identities. For example, people may describe themselves as British and Catholic, French and European or Black and American. Such loyalties may well transcend national boundaries and mean that, whilst they are aware of the contract with their nation state and generally abide by its laws, they have other allegiances which can be at odds with particular, or even the prevailing, norms of that state, for some or all of the time. By contrast, some nationals may only identify with a part of the state in which they live, especially where separatist movements have felt oppressed by the wider interests which they feel do not represent their views, nor give them the rights to run their own affairs, for example, in the Basque region. More than 30 countries also allow dual nationality (UNDP, 2004, p. 12), which is often maintained following marriage or adoption. Dual nationality may, of course, imply a degree of dual identity with both the nations concerned, but as it is not possible to live in two places at the same time, it does not necessarily undermine the 'nationality contract' in the country of present domicile, as the individual can simply live by the rules applicable in that case and it will not in itself prevent strong emotional attachments to the other country from continuing or an additional one from forming.

'Citizenship' has also been a changing and developing concept though still drawing upon the work of classic scholars, such as Aristotle and Plato, and the relationship of the individual to the state which was the central concern of political philosophers like Hobbes and Locke, through to the more contemporary analysis of T. H. Marshall (1950). Marshall traced its development through three periods: the 'civil' period in the eighteenth century, with the focus on equal and civil rights; the 'political' period in the nineteenth century; and the 'social' period in the twentieth century – though not universally accepted as a linear process (Pattie *et al.*, 2004, p. 10). Marquand (1991) adds an 'active' period which he suggests developed during the latter part of the twentieth century and it is this concept of 'active citizenship' which is of greatest relevance to this debate. It has only recently begun to shape policy in Britain and aims to build a greater sense of affinity between nationals and the state.

Citizenship was first linked to nationality in the *1948 British Nationality Act*, but then simply as an adjunct to the historical term of 'British subject', becoming more generally used in the *1981 British Nationality Act*. However, in the Government's White Paper *Secure Borders, Safe Haven* they felt it necessary to explain that the emerging value laden concept of citizenship, which they described as necessary to 'uphold common values so that people understood how they could play a part in our society' (Home Office, 2002, p. 29), was not at odds with the previous descriptors of nationality.

The government went further down this route, in *The Nationality, Immigration and Asylum Act 2002*, and made the granting of naturalisation dependent upon the individuals taking an oath and pledge at a citizenship ceremony. Similarly, in Canada, the conversion of foreigners to Canadian nationals (in other words, 'naturalising') requires more than simply living in Canada for a period of time; it also requires agreement to a positive statement of allegiance. It is also about both rights and responsibilities:

> Becoming a citizen of Canada requires knowing one of our official languages, knowing our history and geography, and knowing the rights and responsibilities of citizenship. It is also about identifying with the character of Canada. Becoming a citizen is about participating in Canada's governmental, social and economic life and accepting with enthusiasm, your share of responsibility for what Canada will be in the future. (Ministry of Public Works and Government Services Canada, 2001)

'Citizenship' therefore implies more than simply bearing the status of a 'national' and, first, places greater emphasis and value on the idea of social responsibility. This aspect of citizenship was particularly emphasised by the British Government with the introduction of the citizenship curriculum in schools in 2002. This was introduced by the then Secretary of State with responsibility for education on the basis that it was 'not just about formal knowledge of the political, constitutional and economic system (but) also offers young people the opportunity to take social responsibility ... to engage in wider community life' (Blunkett, 2001, p. 65). The development of citizenship in this way had, no doubt, been primarily aimed at engendering social responsibility and civic-minded behaviour, with a view to reducing what was seen as the rising tide of criminal and anti-social behaviour amongst young people.

The idea of a citizen as a 'socially responsible' national is not, in itself, difficult. It may still imply little in terms of identity or emotional attachment. It places more emphasis on responsibilities, particularly in behavioural terms, rather than on the exercise of rights. This is often expressed in activity, particularly by contributing to society through volunteering. However, Marquand (1991, p. 340) reminds us that citizenship is fundamentally about 'government' and about citizens governing themselves. Marquand also suggests that:

> politics is the most civilised and civilising activity in which human beings can take part. (Ibid., p. 343)

In a multicultural context, this second aspect of citizenship is potentially the most significant element, though sometimes overlooked. It creates membership of the state as a political entity, in which interaction is based upon mutuality and governed by clear rules and legitimising process. It is the basis upon which trust is built, and whilst it does not depend upon vague notions of cultural identity, it will inevitably help to develop a common bond and purpose.

The state as a political entity provides the opportunity to debate the introduction of new laws and regulations, or to propose that the existing ones should be dispensed with; that taxes should be increased or reduced; that spending priorities should favour this scheme or some other cause; and even that action should be taken against another state and that conflict should ensue. These rights will also include the right to espouse widely different views, to argue and disagree with others, though such debate generally remains within the agreed democratic framework and with a view to building consensus around a particular decision. In this sense, 'citizenship' is about being part of a political entity and inevitably creates a political affinity, irrespective of the internal disagreements and disputes and the cultural differences between different groups and between individuals.

The distinction between 'nationality' and 'citizenship' can be more than a little blurred in some instances, for example, where nationals are domiciled outside the state's boundary. Whilst they can generally take little active part in the running of that state, they are expected to take on at least some of the responsibilities of citizenship and this is recognised by their classification as 'denizens'. Denizens enjoy certain rights under the laws of the land and will be expected to obey those laws and to behave responsibly – or to act as good citizens. They will generally be protected against criminal acts, and are often able to buy and sell assets, sometimes with restrictions, or to drive a car or other vehicle based on their home country's test. They may even enjoy certain limited voting rights, for example, as an EU national of one country, living in another. As long as a foreign national has a right to enter and live in another country, or has 'leave to remain', he or she will suffer relatively little detriment, at least in terms of day to day activities as compared to a citizen of that country. Many countries assume that foreign nationals will live as denizens in that country for several years, prior to even applying for naturalisation.

The Foreign Policy Centre (2005) has used the term 'civic citizenship' to cover this grey area. Civic citizenship would guarantee a number of core rights to third country nationals who are long-term residents in the European Union, such that they are treated in a comparable way to nationals of their host state. Civic citizenship uses EU citizenship as benchmark for rights and apart from basic non-discrimination principles, civic citizenship includes the right of residence, protection against expulsion, access to employment, education and social security and some political rights. The Foreign Policy Centre believes that 'civic citizenship' fits with the aims of the Tampere European Council (October 1999), to grant long-term residents' rights which are as near as possible to those enjoyed by EU citizens, and has supported its analysis with an index which compares the performance of EU members in this regard.

'National identity', has proved to be one of the more contentious aspects of the multicultural debate. This is largely because there is no single view of what 'Britishness' (or 'Frenchness', or other national characters) actually represent. 'National Identity' also goes well beyond the common bonds of democratic engagement and the acceptance and observance of the various laws and regulations imposed by the state and is suggestive of an emotional attachment to the nation – as in 'identifying with the character of Canada'. But the concept can encompass a very wide range of different ideas, most of which are subjective, value-laden and potentially homogenising. These conceptions are generally about various aspects of 'culture', which are similarly subjective, with little common agreement about what is shared. For example, the teaching of historical 'facts', to engender national pride and to emphasise shared experiences, will generally conflate many different understandings about past events, even those of long-standing inhabitants, let alone migrant communities who find it hard to identify with an idea of history which does not include them.

'Identity' is a complex mixture, based entirely on subjective views about affinity to a nation, ethnic, faith or other group, and to individual personal values, both of which can often change and develop over time. It may relate closely to the national story, or hardly at all. Our personal beliefs and values, which help to determine our own individuality, and generally seen as part of the private realm, may overlap with, public realm affinities, for example, in respect of faith and religion. On the other hand, affinities that are ascribed to us, such as ethnicity, may not be valued or recognised as part of our own individual identity at all. The boundaries of our own identities are also inextricably tied to those of others – we can only determine who we are by reference to who we are not – and are socially constructed, rather than biologically determined.

The lack of agreement about the use of terms and the subjective nature of identity and culture has created a number of problems in conceptual and practical terms. It reflects the confusion over 'difference' more generally and the way in which all forms of difference (see Figure 3.3) have often been described by the generic term 'cultural'. Similarly, nations are often referred to as 'multicultural', but this encompasses a wide variety of cultural dimensions which may be completely overshadowed by much more fundamental

Table 5.1   Components of identity and values

Component	Impact on identity and values
Nationality	Creates contractual principles of membership, based on societal rules (laws), and rights of individuals, which are largely universal and non-negotiable; focusses on behaviour, not values
Citizenship	Similar to nationality, but with overtones of 'social responsibility' and duty – i.e. being a 'good' citizen
Active citizenship	Similar to nationality and citizenship but with emphasis upon 'contributing', e.g. through volunteering and also through membership of the political entity, involvement in democratic debate and engaging in the decision-making processes (which inevitably increases affinity to both the democratic process and the state)
National identity	Emotional attachment to nation, highly variable based upon many different conceptions of what is accepted and what is acceptable. But supported by pervasive and common symbols, with some state support, forming part of ongoing socialisation. Focusses on values (generally public realm, with impact on private realm); may allow heterogeneous view of the nation but generally homogensing
Cultural identity	Characteristics of distinct cultural communities usually defined by faith and ethnicity, or by common beliefs and behaviours. May be supported by diaspora or transnational communities, or by national systems (see national identity) Focus on private realm, with impact on public realm. Again, may present homogenous or heterogeneous view of a particular culture
Personal identity	Belief and value system, which may be underpinned by faith or based upon heritage and life experience to form cultural identity, but essentially individual and private realm
Linguistic identity	Common language(s) essential for effective participation as a 'citizen' – i.e. to understand obligations and to claim rights – and to contribute to ongoing debate and change; not a 'value', but contributes to their development through engagement. However, the language of majority and minorities, also underpins national and/or cultural identity and heritage

differences in political identity and beliefs – irrespective of what our neighbours may look like, or even whether they speak the same language – do we trust them, do they value the same principles and, when it matters, will they be on our side? The significance of each aspect of difference depends upon how they have been instrumentalised to create divisions that favour or disfavour particular communities or sections of communities.

The terminology is therefore crucial and many of the above terms have been used in different ways, sometimes interchangeably by different commentators. Table 5.1 therefore attempts to provide a conceptual framework and forms the basis for the discussion in the remainder of this chapter.

Identity and nationality

As a result of invasion or settlement over many years, 'foreigners' may well have become the dominant, controlling community, possibly riding roughshod over the rights of the then indigenous communities, perhaps most notably in the United States and Australia and other countries where an indigenous community was displaced by colonial expansion. The 'host' community may therefore not necessarily be the indigenous community and with some countries experiencing a number of such changes over the centuries, the bona fides of the indigenous community will not always be clear. As the settlement and nature of the host community of countries change, so do the prevailing norms and values. Such change has often been imposed against the will of the weaker community, with little tolerance of difference and even with the violent suppression of other faiths and cultural characteristics. Whilst sudden violent and dramatic change, by way of invasion and occupation, is now generally in the past, the dynamic nature of nationality and identity is no less real in modern democracies (although, inter-ethnic conflict, rather than international conflicts have become far more prevalent in the developing world).

The general experience of foreigners, however, prior to the Second World War, was that over time, they would gradually be assimilated into the prevailing culture, having lacked a critical mass of their community to sustain their own beliefs, language and norms – and without the means of communication to maintain regular contact with their homeland, heritage and values. The impact of minorities upon the host community was limited, but over the generations, they will have changed, gradually adopted different foods and culinary techniques, dress and fashion, music and arts and responded to the minority community in many other ways. The relatively slow pace of change, together with the emphasis on the host community's pre-eminence, meant that migrant minorities had little alternative than to accept the prevailing norms, maintaining what they could from their cultural heritage.

In the period immediately after the Second World War, immigrants also felt obliged to downplay their own cultural identity and with some groups showing a great willingness and determination to even 'feel British' before they came and to try to 'fit in' – an accommodation that was not reciprocated by the host community (Winder, 2004, p. 275). Whilst in the 1960s the world was beginning to be thought of as a 'global village' in intellectual circles, Rex and Moore described a very different experience of people in the inner city community in Birmingham, as one in which the immigrant is 'simply cut off from his native culture (and) we may speak of the minimum situation when the immigrant is not in effective contact with the society of his home country' (Rex and Moore, 1967, p. 14).

It is only really in the last 20 years or so, that globalisation has become a reality for ordinary people. International transport and communication costs have become widely affordable, including to the immigrant groups who are often at the bottom of the socio-economic ladder. For example, in 1973 only 43 per cent of all British households even possessed a telephone (Central Statistical Service, 1974, p. 131); international telephone calls were expensive and only around 10 per cent of the population took a foreign holiday, of which around 90 per cent were in Europe (ibid., p. 109). Access to the Internet was, of course, not even part of enquiries made by the Central Statistical Service and neither was access to satellite TV. Whilst over 90 per cent of households possessed a television, most programmes were home grown, or of American origin. This contrasts with the position just 30 years later, when the possession of television and home telephones were almost universal and 75 per cent of adults also possessed a mobile phone. Further, around 50 per cent of households had Internet access, with Internet facilities also widely available outside the home (National Statistics, 2004).

The experience of newer groups of migrant is, therefore, very different and they are far more able to maintain regular contact with their heritage nation from the outset. This new ability to build and maintain links with the heritage country has also meant that people who immigrated many years ago are able to reconnect with their heritage in ways that were simply not possible just a generation or so ago. The temptation to do so will be particularly great where immigrant groups feel that they have not been accepted or valued by the host community and now have the ability and means to find external frames of reference – and the most obvious place will often be where their roots are. As Ouseley noted, this may apply to long-standing migrant communities who simply turn in on themselves:

> There are many minority ethnic people who are British to the core. Their children are immersed in British culture. They participate as much as they are able to in British institutional life. They speak English. They are law-abiding and pay their taxes. Yet they experience discrimination and exclusion. That is why they form their own organisations, businesses, places of worship, restaurants, newspapers and leisure facilities. (Ouseley, 2004)

All communities are now subject to daily exposure of all parts of the world, including some of the most distant and previously inaccessible countries and even from the safe distance of television screens or the pages of newspapers, the customs and practices of others can still offer some level of challenge to home-based norms and values. Why then should we continue to accept the frame of reference of our own nation state, when we now have so many others on offer? Might we actually choose to adopt another set of values and cultural experiences, possibly by moving from country to country as European Union and other nation states expand common rights of domicile? Will we get to the point of having sequential identities, in the same way that the idea of 'jobs for life' have been replaced by time-limited and episodic careers and that many marriages have also become a series of part-life partnerships?

The nation state's influence, however, should not be underestimated and constantly reaffirms its bonds, not simply by emotional attachments, which can vary in strength, but also by constitutional and practical means and by maintaining the integrity of national borders. The clash of political ideologies has weakened since the end of the cold war in which the West lived in fear of the Soviet dominated Eastern European nations and vice versa, and in which many far flung nation states were pressed into alignment with one side or the other and wars between the blocks of nations were fought by proxy in all continents. Huntingdon (2002) suggests that 'in this post-Cold War period, the most important distinctions are not ideological, political, or economic – they are cultural', advancing his view of a 'clash of civilisations' between the West and the 'Muslim world'. However, the politicisation of cultural identities, both within and between nation states has become a far more potent force and, potentially at least, creating much greater emphasis on the 'us and them' distinctions based largely on visible differences, rather than that of competing ideologies. The creation and heightening of cultural differences to secure political and economic advantage has now become commonplace, perpetuating the myth of a natural order and giving legitimacy to the idea that ethnicity is more than a social construct.

Although the United Nations was created over 50 years ago and with the noblest of aims to maintain 'peace and tolerance' throughout the world, – broader international perspectives have not yet prevailed. Indeed, the United Nations itself now notes that the 'global clash of cultures is resonating so powerfully – and worryingly – around the world' (UNDP, 2004, p. v) and cultural differences are often politicised with the intention of fuelling divisions and animosities, rather than finding common ground and encouraging collaboration. The growth of international communications has not, it seems, automatically created a greater sense of internationalism and it would be possible to argue, though difficult to demonstrate, that the loss of the more rigid national boundaries and nationalistic identities upon which they were based, have led to greater feelings of anomie, which encourages even stronger ethnic and faith identities.

At least part of this confusion seems to stem from the way in which the concepts of 'nationality' (more latterly transposed into citizenship) and cultural identity have been conflated. It is essential to recognise that, whilst identity may be derived, to a greater or lesser extent, from whatever national cultural characteristics are evident, nationality is not in any way dependent on these subjective feelings of belonging – it essentially denotes membership of a political entity, in which the individual is endowed with rights and burdened with responsibilities. Those burdens include paying taxes, observing the laws of the land and even, being prepared to defend its territory(ies). Such responsibilities, for the most part, cannot be easily legally evaded, even though they may have been determined by representatives of other opinions and interests and opposed by the individual in question. However, the same individual has the right, in a democracy at least, to argue against such provisions and to propose alternatives. In fact, it is worth reflecting that, in most modern democracies, like the United States and Great Britain, the government is regularly elected by a minority and that many laws and regulations are created by governments that were not supported by a popular majority.

The Parekh Report (2002) consistently presents 'Britishness' as a matter of *cultural* identity, and one that is swirling around, with boundaries constantly changing. Some elements of the popular press also confused the conception of British identity with the bonds of nationality, and severely criticised the Report for suggesting that 'Britishness is racially coded'. The lack of recognition of the requirements of nationality, was, however, redressed by Parekh, to some extent, in a subsequent article (2002, p. 1), in which he made clear that:

> membership of a political community entails rights and entitlements as well as obligations and sacrifices. We pay taxes that benefit others, defer our demands in order that the more urgent ones can be met first, obey laws that sometimes go against our deeply held beliefs and die for our country.

and

> mutual trust and consequent confidence that no member will be a free rider; and that they can count on each other to obey the laws, respect the rules and in general discharge their share of the burden of collective life. (Ibid., p. 2)

A common sense of belonging makes the acceptance and enforcement of the obligations of nationality much easier, but the order it imposes, should not be underestimated. The bond of political allegiance – that fellow nationals will support you and you them, even though you may never have met or have anything in common, other than your nationality – is very real. This does not depend upon feelings of identity and cultural affiliation, it is much more basic mutual obligation – ensuring personal security by making a common bond with others. This common bond operates at every level, from the mundane example of the way in which we assume we will receive support from a fellow countryman if we need help in a foreign country, to the harsh treatment of those that they spy for another country. Even conscientious objectors have found that their principled stance is not respected and that the basis of their objections were either not believed, or rejected out of hand, and were treated very unsympathetically as a result (Taylor, 1965, p. 87). Similarly, if the state fails in its duty to its individual citizens, for example, by failing to protect them against discrimination, or by wrongfully depriving them of their liberty, action can be taken by those individuals to seek a remedy, or compensation, though not always easily or successfully. In the context of British Muslim identity, Hussain points out that without being able to 'psychologically take up the identity of being British' and not being able to 'feel at home' Muslims would forever 'be condemned to remain as migrants, never really putting down roots' (Hussain, 2004).

Baubock (2002, p. 67) agrees that all political systems are, to some extent, coercive and all citizens are required to accept the legitimacy of government. Further, the state is able to 'define the limits of tolerance', for example, by outlawing acts of discrimination. Immigrants and members of minority groups are therefore no different from the host community in the sense that all members of a nation state will be at odds with the political, economic and social direction of that state at some time. Many will also have cultural, religious and other identities, which are not entirely in tune with the prevailing cultural norms within that state. Nevertheless, Baubock (2003, p. 25) seems to reject the idea of any particular obligation of nationality and prefers the idea that national identities should allow for divided loyalties. He suggests that to hyphenate an ethnic identity with a national one by, for example, becoming a British, French or German Muslim, is a 'profoundly illiberal idea'. National identity should not, according to Baubock override all other affiliations; national and ethnic identities should be allowed to overlap. This confusion of national identity and nationality, in which all forms of identity seem to be regarded as equal and in which cultural identity is equated with the freedom and responsibilities of nationhood, seems to be tantamount to advocating that people should be allowed to enjoy the rights of nationality without commensurate responsibilities; they would be under no particular obligation to their nation, as their obligations would also be owed to other nations and groups. The freedom and order of societies, however, depends upon mutual trust and reciprocity within those societies.

In the present discourse over race and diversity, there is an assumption that xenophobia and distrust of others, is essentially 'racist' and based upon the lack of acceptance of cultural differentiation. This may well be a strong component but, perhaps, some of the resentment towards identifiable groups, whether or not based upon ethno-national characteristics – is more about whether people living in the same land, sharing the same public services and governance, have the option of choosing an alternative *political* allegiance when it suits them, undermining the very trust and reciprocity that political allegiance is meant to convey. The focus on 'cultural identity', which can be separated from nationality and political allegiance, has been unhelpful in this respect.

From a completely different political perspective, Norman Tebbit also made the same mistake with his famous 'cricket test' which he advocated in 1990. Tebbit suggested that immigrants should prove their loyalty and be required to support the host nation's cricket team (he was referring to the English team, as there is no British cricket team which rather undermined his own position). However, there is nothing in the 'nationality contract' which would require any individual to support the host nation's teams and such support depends entirely upon emotional attachment to a nation (and to the sport). Cultural identity is, or should be, separable from the fact of membership of a particular nation and can indeed overlap, and such overlaps would be encouraged by any state which embodies freedom from discrimination and promotes tolerance and respect for such differences.

Nationality can, therefore, be coupled with cultural identity, as whilst they may overlap they are not fundamentally in conflict and express two separable concepts, one based on contractual requirements and the other upon emotional attachment. That is not to say, however, that many people will not experience tension between the two – and tension which nation states have been slow to recognise and to codify in any meaningful way.

The conflict between 'nationality' and cultural and religious values is put particularly strongly by Modood (2003, p. 101) in relation to the Muslim community who have borne the brunt of a new wave of suspicion and hostility, since September 11.

> There has been widespread questioning about whether Muslims can be and are willing to be integrated into European society and its political values. In particular, whether Muslims are committed to what are taken to be the core European values of freedom, tolerance, democracy, sexual equality and secularism. Across Europe, multiculturalism – a policy suitable where communities want to maintain some level of distinction – is in retreat and 'integration' is once again the watchword. These doubts have been raised across the political spectrum.

These conflicts are therefore real and tangible and not simply a question of developing more liberal and tolerant 'values'. Modood is of course right to focus on the present dominant issue of multiculturalism, Islamophobia. But whilst diaspora identities are now easier to maintain they are not new (Soysal, 2000, p. 2) and western democracies have regarded them as a threat to national affinities in the past, for example, in respect of the transnational Jewish community in the 1920s, and the Black African-Caribbeans in the 1960s and 1970s. These transnational identities remain evident with a number of faith and ethno-national groups retaining meaningful associations in different countries and across continents. However, the key question is how these transnational cultural identities and affiliations are combined with the requirements of nationality in each case and whether a homogenising national identity inevitably becomes associated with that nationality. Emigrant groups may even be conceptualised as 'diaspora' even when, as in the case of the Italian migrants, they are largely assimilated (Brubaker, 2005, p. 3) and the boundaries of any diaspora are not, in any event, fixed but are in a state of constant flux (Soysal, 2000, p. 12).

The British Government has begun to redefine the relationship between the individual and the state through its new 'civil renewal' agenda. This presents nationality as more than a passive contract, in which rights are traded for responsibilities, with active engagement of the individual expected:

> we have to assert that our identity as members of a political community is a positive thing. Democracy is not just an association of individuals determined to protect the private sphere, but a realm of active freedom in which citizens come together to shape the world around them. We contribute and we become entitled. (Blunkett, 2003, p. 1)

The distinction of a 'political community' is, useful, for the reasons discussed earlier, but it is not yet clear how this relates to the idea of a 'civil society', whether or not 'renewed'. Blunkett's enthusiasm was underpinned by the development of an Active Communities Unit and a Civil Renewal Unit in the Home Office at the time, both eager to build participation in every sphere of community life. But the notion of a 'civil society' also lacks clarity with no commonly accepted meaning (Keane, 1998, p. 36) and with the danger that it becomes no more than a 'political buzzword' and difficult to separate form terms like 'community' (McGhee, 2003). According to Pahl (1995, p. 346), who describes the term as 'elusive', civil society is seen by some as 'embracing everything except the state and others limit it to family and voluntary areas'. Keane (1998, p. 36) distinguishes three approaches: the relationship between social and political forces and institutions; a pragmatic guide to social and political action; and as a means of maintaining the ethical superiority of a political regime in comparison to others.

With such divergent views of civil society, it would appear that the concept of a political community, espoused by Blunkett, is the more straightforward and does suggest a means by which mutuality and trust can be established, without an over reliance on more ephemeral ideas about identity.

Nevertheless, it will depend upon an acceptance of 'democratic values' and even this can impact, in challenging forms, on those groups that do not have egalitarian traditions in the public realm, such as those with traditions of paternalism and deference which prevent robust challenge and debate, and where gender inequality, caste divisions and strong familial and kinship loyalties limit rational and objective choices in the public realm. In particular, the 'democratic values' may conflict with cultural norms which may be in 'a form of social control for women and young people' (Castles and Miller, 1993, p. 287).

This 'active' model of nationality or citizenship, in the sense that it encourages engagement with political and social processes on the basis of mutuality and equality, is an essential component of community cohesion. The interaction with other members of the community, particularly on a cross-cultural basis, will help to break down barriers between groups and build mutual trust and common purpose. The involvement will also begin to create a stake in society and engender a sense of belonging – which is where some form of legitimate national identity begins to emerge.

National identity

National identity is often assumed to tend towards homogenisation. Generalisations and stereotypes become self-fulfilling as the common character deepens. The modern multicultural state, together with its various agencies and with the support of the community and voluntary sector, can, however, counter these stereotypes and ensure that a more diverse picture is presented. This can ensure that a multicultural picture of daily life is portrayed and that diversity is presented positively, as, for example, through the 'One Scotland – Many Cultures' campaign in Scotland or the 'We all Belong to Canada' approach – see Chapter 6 for further details. The informal and subtle process of socialisation will nevertheless tend to reflect majority interests and views and some sort of national picture is likely to emerge, even though it is constantly changing and adapting to both internal and external influences.

The focus on 'culture' develops from the unfortunate fusion of identity and nationality, where the former is simply defined by the latter. Nationalism then develops and takes on an ideological aura and embraces a complex set of themes, in which the world is divided into 'ours' and 'theirs' and assumes a morality of duty and honour (Billig, 1995, p. 4). To be, for example, British, American, French, does not, of course, require such ideological passion, though the two have sometimes gone hand in hand, especially at times of international tension and hostility. Nationalism is often evoked by powerful nation states, who are preparing to take up arms and need mass popular support of their people in pursuit of territorial ambitions and is not, by any means, the preserve of peripheral extreme right wing groups, or separatists. Rather, it can rouse 'dangerous and powerful passions, outlining a psychology of extraordinary emotions' (ibid., p. 5).

 This same 'overwhelming strength of patriotism and national loyalty' was recognised nearly 50 years ago by George Orwell:

> there is nothing to set beside it. Christianity and international Socialism are as weak as straw in comparison with it. Hitler and Mussolini rose to power in their own countries very largely because they could grasp this fact and their opponents could not. (Orwell, 1957, p. 63)

Recent conflicts, whether in the Balkans, the former Soviet Union or the Falklands, have produced outbursts of nationalistic sentiment, but nationalism is not created at times of crisis, it is always under the surface in a 'banal' form:

> nationhood provides a continual background for political discourses, for cultural products, and even for the structuring of newspapers. In so many little ways, the citizen is daily reminded of their national place in a world of nations. However, this reminding is so familiar, so continual, that it is not consciously registered as reminding. The metonymic image of the banal nationalism is not a flag which is being consciously waved with fervent passion; it is the flag hanging unnoticed on the public building.

and

> National habits embrace [sic] all these forgotten reminders. Consequently, an identity is to be found in the embodied habits of a social life. Such habits include those of thinking and using language. To have a national identity is to possess ways of talking about nationhood ... it should involve the detailed study of discourse ... Having a national identity also involves being situated within a homeland, which itself is situated within the world of nations. And, only if people believe that they have such national identities, will such homelands, and the world of national homelands be reproduced. (Billig, 1995, p. 8)

One of Billig's key points is, therefore, that identity will not be found within the body or the mind of the individual, but within the 'embodied habits of a social life'. Feeling a real sense of national identity is unlikely until, over a period of time, we gradually and unknowingly, acquire the trappings of belonging through day to day discourse, interaction and the recognition of symbols and symbolic acts. In such circumstances, how will immigrants begin to feel that they have a new national identity to accompany their new nationality? Over time, perhaps over generations, immigrants also begin to take on the national identity through the subtle process of socialisation, whilst at the same time enriching and redefining it. However, the 'embodied habits of social life' are perhaps beginning to take on a different character and are less dependent upon the national institutions and formal and informal communications systems. The power of new transnational and global communications, such as satellite television and the internet, mean that there is a higher level of exposure to a broader range of influences which all contribute to subtle socialisation processes. National governments increasingly feel the need to reinforce their nation's sense of belonging, recognising the increasing competitive nature of the process of identity formulation.

The acquisition of a national identity will, then, depend upon a range of factors, including the 'degree of difference' between the new and old identities, how compatible they are and the extent to which the new socialisation process is facilitated and encouraged. It will also depend upon the migrants desire to embrace the new identity and their ability to maintain and reinforce their previous values, contacts and lifestyle – and whether there is any conflict inherent in the two. In any event, regional, class, faith and cultural variation within a nation state, may mean that a newcomer finds it easier to identify with aspects of the new national identity, rather than with the prevailing norms as a whole. Parekh underlines the difficulty of cultural identity and believes that, as it is not uniform, it simply cannot exist in any meaningful form:

> there has never been a single 'British way of life' ... there have always been many, often contested, ways of being British ... a sense of national identity is based on generalisations and involves a selective and simplified account of a complex history. Much that is important is ignored, disavowed or simply forgotten. Many complicated strands are reduced to a simple tale of essential and enduring national unity. (Parekh, 2000, p. 22)

In the context of Britain, 'national identity' is particularly complex, and become more so with the further devolution of government to Scotland and Wales. This has also led to a reassertion of 'Englishness' (Blunkett, 2005), once simply taken for granted as the pre-eminent and dominant culture. However, pinning down any sense of national identity, even one based on a more limited national conception, like Blunkett's Englishness, appears very bland and imprecise – 'we can find it in our traditions of fairness and civic duty and in our spirit of imagination and invention' (ibid., p. 11).

The inability to set out the tenets of a national identity, however, and the generalisations that it conveys, which tend to leave out those groups or individuals who have no place in the dominant national story and find it difficult to understand how they could properly belong, should not lead us to dismiss it too lightly. Even Parekh does finally agree that it is 'no less real simply because much of it is invented or distorted' (ibid., p. 16).

National identity must not therefore be underestimated: it becomes real and potent for the host community, which includes the long-standing BME residents, who unknowingly have had their identity 'flagged' and symbolised in many ways over many years. A new diversity with many different images and symbols will challenge those conceptions. Some societies may be open to those changes and see 'difference' as an opportunity to enrich their community, others may resist those differences or take a long time to adjust to them. However, the resistance to such changes cannot simply be regarded as irrational or 'racist' (see Chapter 4). As diversity grows and spreads, the symbols of modern national identity will change: mosques, churches and temples will be seen alongside each other, different musical rhythms will be heard on the airwaves and new tastes will excite our palates. New national symbols will appear apparently overnight, for example, Robin Cook, the former British foreign secretary was able to suggest that chicken tikka masala, rather than fish and chips, had become Britain's favourite meal. Almost unknowingly, the conception of our nation and ourselves will change until the unfamiliar becomes the familiar and is embedded into the national story, without any sudden or noticeable change taking place.

Baubock (2003, p. 27) describes such changes in the conception of nations as the 'catalyst model' in which we trigger

> a chemical reaction that changes the substance to which it is added (and) we should not expect that immigrants will simply melt into national identities that have been constructed for native populations ... instead we should see a process that sets into motion a process of self-transformation of collective identities towards a more pluralistic and maybe even cosmopolitan outlook.

In a similar way, Bragg (2003) illustrates the constant change and adaptation in the English language, which has taken many thousands of words from other languages over hundreds of years of conflict, colonialism, trade and immigration. Language is a fundamental part of culture, defining the way in which we construct the world around us. Our values and our identity will be constantly changing and be enriched by ongoing social processes, including inward migration, broadening our view of ourselves and our global position, but such catalytic effects are not instantaneous and changing our image of the nation and ourselves may take more than a little time. Community cohesion programmes may succeed in speeding up the acceptance of such changes if they are pursued positively and proactively (see Chapter 6) and recognise that past attempts to build positive community relations have failed to address the social and psychological needs of both the host and immigrant communities.

The concept of the 'host community' is, however, becoming somewhat outdated and can no longer be thought of as a largely white and homogeneous whole. Many members of previous waves of black and Asian immigrants have become part of the host community, assuming varied conceptions of national identity and, at the same time, changing and redefining it. However, in some cases they have also maintained, or developed, hostilities to other ethnic minorities within the community or towards new migrant groups. The identity of older and newer migrant groups therefore changes in relationship to each other, as well as between them and the (white) host community. In Britain, the rivalries between different immigrant groups have also occasionally led to conflict and resulted in sporadic violent incidents over the years. Much of this stems from the long-standing enmity between ethnic, faith and national groups in the heritage countries. This has been carried over into the new nation states despite an expectation that those different groups will have developed a common bond as outsiders to the national story. Again, however, this is a somewhat mixed and complex picture. Gilroy (1992, p. 204) draws attention to the 'contingent and partial belonging to Britain which blacks enjoy, their ambiguous association' and their development of a process of 'cultural syncretism':

> Accordingly, their self-definitions and cultural expressions draw on a plurality of black histories and politics. In the context of modern Britain this has produced a diaspora dimension to black life. Here, non-European traditional elements, mediated by the histories of Afro-America and the Caribbean, have contributed to the formation of new and distinct black cultures amidst the decadent peculiarities of the Welsh, Irish, Scots and English.

'Black' identity has always covered a range of values and perspectives. It was, perhaps, most simply understood as an expression of common experience in heavily racialised and divided nations and as a means of developing a common cause. In reality, there is as much difference between the many black cultures as there is between them and white cultures. In Britain, the pretence of a universal black culture began to break down as the experience of different ethnic minorities diverged and international reference points became more distinct and stronger. Modood (1988, p. 399) referred to the idea of an inclusive black identity as a 'meaningless chimera' and suggested that Asian culture was separate and distinct and that religion was as powerful a factor in identity as class or race.

The focus has, perhaps, been on 'black' identity and 'white' identity, which is similarly diverse, and has been taken for granted and assumed to be homogeneous. The long-standing friction between some white national groups, in Europe and further afield has led to some extremely bloody conflicts over the years. The definition of 'white' is, in any case, problematic with clear divisions emerging along cultural lines, or based upon faith or national differences in Europe, as in the Balkans, Russia and elsewhere in recent years. A significant proportion of the Jewish community may well describe themselves as 'white' but their faith defines them as an ethnic group in many systems of categorisation. People of Middle-Eastern origin may also describe themselves as 'white' when faced with crude categories. In Britain, the Irish are regarded as a separate ethnic group, within the 'white' category. There is no white diaspora, little attempt has been made to 'universalise' white identity, but equally no common definition or assumption lies behind it – it remains culturally defined – and constantly changing and adapting as does 'culture' itself.

People of mixed race, a growing number, may also feel as if they count for very little in such a debate. They fit into neither category, nor, to a universal identity of 'mixed race people'. As their race is 'mixed' so the underlying assumption is that their identity will also be 'mixed' or possibly even confused between however many strands of 'pure' identity in their make-up. At the same time, in predominantly white nations, white people do not see themselves as an ethnic group and simply take their 'whiteness' for granted. Similarly, in black nations 'blackness' is also taken for granted and not used to define identity. Ethnicity therefore appears to emerge as the principal means of identification for minorities, a statement about who we are not, rather than a statement about who we are, which probably reflects both the degree of difference between communities and the degree of acceptance of diversity within the nation state. Multiculturalists have tended to present identity as 'hybridity', a sort of 'pick and mix' approach to the way people conceptualise themselves. There is undoubtedly some strength in this argument and people will label themselves in many different ways, using social class, faith, nationality, gender, sexual orientation, age, ethnicity and other descriptors. However, others appear to infer from this that establishing a common conception of identity is a pointless exercise and that all of the descriptors have an equal weight, or that none should have any particular weight. 'Nationality' is not determined by identity, however, and will depend more upon the contractual relationship between the individual and the state, with less focus on cultural and personal values and more on political and social behaviour.

Multiculturalists also appear to fear that the label of 'British', 'American', 'French' and other national terms, even if hyphenated with a cultural identity, implies an acceptance of everything done in the name of that country. However, it would almost be a denial of democratic values, if such a level of political agreement were to be assumed. Similarly, the adoption of a 'national' label does not imply acceptance of all aspects of the prevailing norms or culture. In cultural terms, a conception like 'Britishness' is inevitably difficult to define and can include so many aspects of our daily lives, such as dress, language, cuisine, faith, music, art, kinship, customs and certain behavioural norms. It would be all too easy then to construct an identity built around stereotypes – 'Britishness' means wearing a flat cap, drinking tea, eating fish and chips (or chicken tikka masala), displaying little emotion (with exceptions for football hooligans), morris dancing and orderly queues! Such stereotypes are almost laughable, but yet, there is a danger that they are dismissed too lightly. We all conceptualise others and ourselves through stereotypes, we think of foreigners in particular ways and foreigners, equally, hold stereotypical views of us. We each of course, have different conceptions and stereotypes, depending upon our experiences and socialisation, but a certain body of this may well cohere into an identity which can be described as 'national', even if far from universally accepted and adopted.

This view may be contrasted with what some commentators see as the transition 'from modernity to postmodernity', in which the old politics of nationhood are giving way to the politics of identity. This trend is expertly dissected by Billig (1995), who recognises that globalisation has had a profound impact on our lives and that global brands and icons now compete with national symbols – 'banal globalism' rather than 'banal nationalism' is flagging our daily lives. He also recognises the growth in international communications and that the movement of capital, finance and labour around the globe has resulted in a stronger economic interrelationship of nation states. On one level, he says, 'the logic of late capitalism is dictating a homogenized culture, rather than a patchwork of bounded national cultures, which claim to be uniquely different' (ibid., p. 131). This may also suggest that the forces of globalisation are producing cultural homogeneity, diminishing differences between nations and fragmenting their imagined internal unity. At the same time economic pressures are forcing nation states to combine and collaborate in ways which require a partial diminution of their sovereignty, for example, through the European Union. In addition, both supranational and subnational identities challenge the pre-eminence of nationhood.

Yet, the vitality of nations remains as a 'mobilising point against the uncertainties of the future' and whilst conceding some functions to transnational and localised bodies they are strengthening others (Hutchinson, 2000, p. 667). National identity appears, then, to defy the apparent logic of these globalising trends. Perhaps, argues Billig, the postmodern psyche is not yet fully understood and that it has tended to be analysed in rather academic terms and without the benefit and understanding of the thoughts and feelings of ordinary people – 'the subjects of postmodernity'. The assumption of the growth of the identity of 'tribalism' – or caste, colour or religion – has not been proven and Billig then questions the way in which reactions to this 'pastiche personality' have been presented. It is assumed that some people may either be driven towards authoritarianism as they seek the security of a strong single-minded and exclusive affiliation or, at the other extreme, enjoy a mind-expanding journey through different identities with unemotional detachment. Billig recognises these extremes, but reasserts the importance of the middle ground, in which the state is not in fact withering away. Despite the possible attractions of the extremes, the importance of the nation remains daily 'flagged' and politicians continue to address the nation as the nation. The daily ordinariness of the nation also continues to exert subtle but powerful influence and if identity politics is based on a vision of the 'multicultural society' then it should not be forgotten that 'this politics takes for granted that there is a "society" which is to be multicultural' (Billig, 1995, p. 148).

This 'middle ground' will presumably cover a considerable variation in national and other identities. Some modern states have only just formed, whilst a number of longer-standing nations still lack any real coherence and their boundaries remain contested. The United States illustrates the conundrum of national identity – one of the world's most multi-ethnic nations, scarred by ghettoes and with every form of identity – from strong gay and lesbian areas to the 'redneck' communities – making their presence felt. Yet, the 'flagging' of identity is nowhere more evident than in the United States and, as a nation, it remains strong, presently absorbing about 800 000 immigrants each year with its coherence not seriously contested, from either internal or external pressures.

A British survey, published by the Office of National Statistics (2004) suggested that identity is increasingly being influenced by national, rather than ethnic, dimensions and that feelings of Britishness among people of mixed race and ethnic minority were growing as a result. Of those of mixed race, 87 per cent identified themselves as British, with other ethnic minorities ranging from 75 per cent to 81 per cent, with feelings of Britishness particularly strong among the young and in groups where the majority of people had been born in Britain.

The power of national identity, then, remains strong, particularly in the hearts and minds of those citizens that have had any sort of long-standing association with their nation. This is very evident in so many ways, from the following of international sporting competitions, for example, during the Olympics, to the neighbourhood level where local communities feel challenged by the presence of newcomers. This psyche appears to be better understood on the political right than on the left, with nationalistic, xenophobic and racist sentiment exploited by politicians who readily capitalise on the anxieties and fears of people, especially those who are economically or socially vulnerable. The growth of right wing political parties in Europe, the incitement of ethnic conflict in Britain and elsewhere, and the groundswell of Islamophobia across the world, is recent testament to this.

The focus of the extreme right is often thought to be the minority communities and people of 'difference'. This is the case in the sense that they are often the targets of their prejudice, but their aim is to build support in the majority population. The nature of their appeal will change but their aim remains the same, to win power by appealing to the concerns of the majority, even if this is by strongly disadvantaging the interests of the minority. They have developed support by drawing attention to the conflict over resources and services, particularly in respect of housing and employment. However, the focus of their attention has increasingly been on identity and what they present as unacceptable cultural differences and belief systems. They exploit this 'identity challenge' by recognising that the majority host community (including long-standing migrants and ethnic minorities) take time to adjust to newcomers with different frames of reference and different behavioural patterns and beliefs. They take advantage of the failure to invest in support to the host community:

> We do not believe that concerns about migration should be simply dismissed as 'racist'. Nor do we see them as resulting from 'ignorance about the facts'. It is of course true that racists try to use immigration and the fear of people who appear to be different for their own ends. We recognise that inward migration does create tensions ... . Many disadvantaged communities will perceive that newcomers are in competition for scarce resources and public services ... housing, education, health and other services all take time to expand. But people also take time to adjust. The identity of the host community will be challenged and they need sufficient time to come to terms with, and accommodate, incoming groups, regardless of ethnic origin. The pace of change (for a variety of reasons) is simply too great in some areas at present. (Cantle, 2004, p. 15)

A Report which examined the resettlement of asylum seekers in Scotland made a similar point about 'the rapid pace' which had created demands upon different agencies with little time for 'coherent strategic planning' (Scottish Centre for Research on Social Justice, 2004, p. 74).

Both reports went on to advocate a much more proactive approach to 'manage settlement'. Further, the need to tackle 'the social and psychological needs of existing communities', to supplement the government's policy of 'managed migration', based on economic interests, was identified (Cantle, 2004, p. 15). The 'need to support existing communities' was subsequently accepted by government in their Community Cohesion and Race Equality Strategy (Home Office, 2004), and has been reinforced recently by the Commission on Integration and Cohesion who have advocated a new Government Agency to oversee the process of settlement (CIC, 2007), though it remains to be seen how these recommendations will be responded to.

Multiculturalism and identity

The various models of multiculturalism (see Chapter 3) are founded on very different ideas about nationality and national identity. For example, the multiculturalism derived from the guest-worker scheme model in countries like Germany, Austria and Switzerland, provided for economic immigration in a one-dimensional way – immigrants were simply temporary workers to fulfil a role in the employment market, housed in separate enclaves, with little attempt at integration. It was expected that they would retain their own identity and nationality and return home in due course, with 'no real need to incorporate them into the receiving society' (Entzinger, 1994, p. 19). However, over time, this arrangement broke down, 'home' became the host nation, especially for the children of guest workers. Meanwhile, the socialisation process would remain limited until the status of the guest workers, in this example, as 'Germans' or 'Austrians', was resolved – something which could take many years and may even remain unresolved indefinitely.

This can be contrasted with the approach of nations, such as France, which tended more towards the 'assimilation model', in which naturalisation is relatively quick and easy and there is little differentiation between newcomers and the host population in French law (Entzinger, 1994, p. 20). The assimilation model assumes that the immigrant community will have little opportunity for the preservation of their own cultural background and that they will become bonded to French society. Ethnic, regional or religious categorisations are ignored (Bertossi, 2002, p. 73) and the emphasis has been on the assimilation of people as individuals, rather than through the medium of distinctive communities, although this is not a universally accepted policy (Rachedi, 1994, p. 68). The process of 'assimilation', however, has not resulted in equality for immigrants and their children, nor the creation of homogenised neighbourhoods dominated by French national culture. Rachedi (1994, p. 69) noted that Algerians were to be found in 'depersonalized suburbs of larger cities' and over-represented in 'special' schools and had higher rates of unemployment. In fact, the level of ethnic minority unemployment in France was one of the highest in Europe (Leonard and Griffith, 2003, p. 19) and much of the success of the extreme right in France has been built upon opposition to immigration and the development of racist sentiment. More recently, the controversy over the banning of the Muslim headscarves (and other religious symbols), in state-run schools, demonstrated that at least some of the 5 million Muslims in France are far from assimilated into French society.

In countries like Britain and the Netherlands, immigrants have not been expected to forego their cultural identity and, in terms of official policy at least, pluralism was endorsed and accepted. Nevertheless, an acceptance of national identity and a shared sense of belonging have also proved elusive. In Britain, in 2001, the race riots led to a description of the 'parallel lives' of different communities and that some immigrants felt like 'foreigners in their own land' (Cantle, 2001). In the Netherlands, Entzinger (1994) tells a similar story in respect of the 2.4 million residents of the Netherlands who were either immigrants themselves or had at least one parent born abroad. In this case, the largest group were Surinamese, closely followed by Turks and Moroccans, who, with significant populations of southern Europeans and other groups, were highly concentrated in the four major cities of Amsterdam, Rotterdam,

The Hague and Utrecht. Compared to the host population, they experienced very high unemployment rates and a 'considerable number' did not speak Dutch after 20 years or more of residence. Many had 'hardly ever met a Dutch person' and withdrawn into their own communities.

Britain's attempts to promote 'good race relations' have also had a mixed impact, although the resources committed to it have been limited and not equal to that of the Netherlands (Husband, 1994, p. 85). The objective position of ethnic minorities in socio-economic terms is also well below the host community in almost all respects. Further, whilst it was expected that second generation immigrants would become more integrated and develop similar patterns of educational and occupational achievement, this has not been the reality for many ethnic minority people. Some of the first generation immigrants tended to cluster geographically and occupationally by sector and, for example, to support the textile industry, and when these sectors subsequently declined, housing market and skill constraints made it difficult for integration, dispersal and progression to take place (Saggar, 2002, p. 81).

The United States is one of the most diverse nations in the world and is presently experiencing one of the largest and longest waves of immigration in its history. Its model of multiculturalism is founded on the principle of the rapid acclimatisation of immigrants, who would quickly become American (Martin, 2003, p. 134). It is a distinctive model, based on a strong belief in individualism and, therefore, with a reluctance to embrace group identities and to monitor ethnicity. The very evident investment in civic culture through the 'flagging' of the American identity has emphasised unity and proclaimed the American ideal, which to outsiders and in a different national context, would be held to be oppressive and jingoistic. Perhaps, however, this has succeeded in generating a common sense of belonging and explains, to some extent, the solidarity of the nation and acceptance of 'Americanness'. Nevertheless, the United States is also a divided society, with many black, Hispanic and other ethnically dominated ghettoes and separate experiences:

> On the shared national experience African Americans and whites live separate lives. Take TV ratings. If you look at the top ten TV shows in the US there is only one programme in common between black viewers and white viewers – Monday Night Football. Everything else is different.
>
> On mixed communities: American cities are still effectively segregated and the racial zoning of American cities has, if anything become more entrenched. Even where the educational and economic fortunes of African Americans have improved, the races still live separately – witness the gated ghettoes for black millionaires in every city. (Phillips, 2004c)

The impact of the various multicultural models – and they are, in reality, more likely to represent a continuum of different approaches rather than distinct types, with variation in approach within each 'domain of difference' – has not suggested a common pattern of shaping national identity and generating a national sense of belonging. To a greater or lesser extent, the 'parallel lives' of ethnic minorities and the host community can be found throughout Europe under all types of policy regimes (Bloomfield and Bianchini, 2004, p. 29) as well as in the United States and in some parts of every continent, almost irrespective of the multicultural model employed.

Kymlicka sets out the present dilemma:

> Some commentators argue that in a world of migration, we must recognise that the whole idea of 'national citizenship' is increasingly obsolete. On this view we need to develop a new way of assigning rights and responsibilities, perhaps based on international law and human rights norms, that does not presuppose that immigrants will, or should, become 'national citizens'.
>
> Others argue, on the contrary, that the increasing ethnic and religious diversity within modern states requires a more active effort by the state to construct and sustain a sense of common national citizenship. Feelings of solidarity and common values, which could perhaps be taken for granted in a period of greater ethnic and religious homogeneity, must now be actively promoted by the state, in part emphasising the centrality of common citizenship. On this view, learning to live with diversity requires a 'revaluation of citizenship'. (Kymlicka, 2003, p. 195)

One of the most significant debates was been generated by David Goodhart's article in *Prospect* magazine (2004), which posed the question 'are we too diverse?' This suggested that it may not be possible in countries like Britain to generate and maintain the required 'solidarity and common values', even if they are actively promoted, beyond a certain level of multiculturalism.

Goodhart was of course right to raise such a fundamental question – and it is one that must be answered – and it is unfortunate that some of the responses to Goodhart's article were, to say the least, intemperate, denouncing it as 'racist' (Goodhart, 2004a). The more considered responses were also generally critical, but did begin to bring out and question the key issue identified by Goodhart – his reliance on the concept of 'people like us' which he appeared to present as some form of genetically determined identity, rather than simply a product of social and psychological construct (*The Guardian*, 26 February 2004). Gary Younge (ibid.), in particular, noted that, Goodhart's article was:

> littered with assumptions about 'us' and 'them' and peppered with references to a 'common culture' and 'homogeneity' as though such terms are universally agreed but eternally static. No wonder he concludes that 'National Citizenship' is 'inherently exclusionary'. Of course it is, if defined by race and frozen in time.

Goodhart is indeed free with his assumptions and assertions, for example, that 'evolutionary psychology stresses both the universality of most human traits and – through the notion of kin selection and reciprocal altruism – the instinct to favour our own'. He also suggests that 'in a developed country such as Britain ... we not only live amongst stranger citizens but we must share with them' and 'therein lies one of the central dilemmas of political life: sharing and solidarity can conflict with diversity' (Goodhart, 2004).

Given that no society, whether or not 'developed', can consist entirely of one's kin, in which they are literally – and genetically – 'like us', all of the remainder must be 'strangers' and 'not like us'. However, Goodhart's assumption is that only those that do not look and talk like us are real strangers. To underline this, Goodhart also suggests that the welfare state, and the solidarity that it generates, is also imperilled by diversity supporting the idea that we can only extract money from people in the form of taxation, if the sums are paid out to recipients who are like themselves and facing the same sort of difficulties. Taxation, however, has always been used to fund 'strangers', people who may include, but never limited to, our kith and kin and with a wide variety of backgrounds and circumstances. 'Strangers' are now it seems, people from ethnic and national backgrounds different from our own.

Goodhart's views do, ironically, appear to resonate with at least some of his critics, who also see 'identity' as much more than a political and social construct – when applied to minorities. 'Culture' is then apparently something that we are each born with and is fixed deep in our psyche. Our ethnicity, our faith, our history, our art and more besides, all have to be preserved and protected as of right, as though they are unchanging and immutable.

Our culture, however, we choose to describe it, may well help to define us, but it is constructed by the world around us, not by us. This even seems to apply to our most personal and deep-seated beliefs:

> religious identity is largely determined by, and always dependent upon, factors of time and place. ... the likelihood that a child born this morning in Sakakah, Saudi Arabia, will be Muslim is far, far, far greater than the likelihood that she or he will be Episcopalian or a worshipper of the Aztec mother-goddess Tonantzin. The truth is that the overwhelming majority of people who are Muslim or some other religion today aren't Muslim or some other religion because of brain chemistry or even some individual/ personal choice or life event. While there are always notable exceptions, most people who are Muslim or some other religion today are not such because of genetics or even personal preference. Rather, they were born at a specific time in human history and in a particular place that made such a religious identity possible or, rather inevitable – if not downright imperative.

And similarly:

> between 80 and 90 percent of Costa Ricans are Catholic. Why? After all they could just as easily be Buddhist or Jewish or worshippers of Odin. So why Catholic? Do they have certain Catholic brain structures? Of course not. Do they all just 'like' or 'prefer' Catholicism better than all the other religious options out there – that is so most people in Costa Rica periodically compare and contrast the costs and benefits of all existing religions and then consistently and nearly unanimously agree that Catholicism is simply the best choice? There are simply too many problems with such an egregiously simplistic, insufficiently sociological 'rational choice' explanation. (Zuckerman, 2003, p. 37)

Religious identity is not, of course, determined by the culture we are born into, however pervasive that may be. We can redefine it, as many people choose to do. The probability of such cultural determinism nevertheless remains high.

The same is, of course true of ethnic culture or ethnic identity. There is no 'natural', white, black, Asian or any other skin colour-dependent culture. A white person born and brought up in a black African village will adopt the language, dress, culture, religion and beliefs of that village if totally immersed within it. So too, will a black African child born and 'socialised' in a city in the West – again providing that no countervailing cultural pressures are apparent. Later they may chose to accept and adopt cultural dimensions from the white, black, or other diaspora and international frames of reference – or they may not – probably dependent upon their degree of exposure to them and the extent of domination within their early socialisation. Nevertheless, ethnic and other identities are often held to be 'natural', rather than socially determined. This emerges implicitly in many forms, for example, the controversy over the adoption of children by parents who are not of the same ethnicity as the child. Some argued that this confused the child's identity, even though many children are born of mixed parentage and are visibly dissimilar to one or both of their natural parents. Children may well suffer, in some cases, a 'crisis of identity', whether as a result of adoption or mixed parentage, but this is again socially determined and generally the result of ethno-centric views, or racism, in which the child may simply reflect the antipathy that the different communities have towards each other and have internalised those conflicts.

Some of the arguments about mixed marriages also seem to be partly about preserving the notion of 'purity' of culture, if not of 'race' itself. The cultural embargo on mixed marriages of some groups reflects this (see, for example, Modood et al., 1994, p. 115, with regard to Caribbean and Asian groups), as does the stigma attaching to them. Mixed marriages might otherwise be seen as a positive sign of integration and that cultural differences have been set aside or overcome, but the cause of mixed marriages is rarely championed, nor celebrated in this way and, rather, it has been seen as almost a betrayal of one's culture and stigmatised, or even forcibly prevented, within many majority and minority communities.

There is also a pretence about the solidity of particular cultures and identities from within and a belief in homogeneity which can be even more oppressive than the pressure from other cultures. Again, odd alliances can be made which undermine rational debate and try to turn 'culture' into an immutable homogeneity, in which the similarities are diminished and regarded as 'unnatural' and the differences emphasised and presented as 'natural'. This is true in respect of the present debate about Muslim faith and culture. Right wing extremists have relished the task of stereotyping Muslims, as fundamentalists, or as terrorists and have sought to demonise them by spreading myths about their characters and beliefs. The defensive response can, however, reinforce the idea of cultural homogeneity and present an idealized and unchanging view of itself. It can become trapped in this mode and in responding to those attacks, may simply reinforce characteristics, which are by no means universal, nor internally accepted. The controversy about the banning of the headscarf, or hijab, in French schools, for example, resulted in its use being presented as a birthright, whereas it is only a relatively recent form of dress in some Muslim countries and not used at all in others. It is also far from universally accepted within the Muslim community leading Yasmin Alibhai-Brown to complain: 'millions of us Muslims ... do not cover our heads; our mothers only do so when praying. But now they castigate us the hijab devotees' (Alibhai-Brown, 2004).

In a similar way, and on a broader set of issues, Sardar (2004) illustrates the variety of social circumstances in Muslim dominated societies, which result from different interpretations of Islamic law. For example, the expectations about what Muslim women will wear, what if any job they will do, or whether they can drive a car or be seen alone socially, varies enormously, even within Muslim dominated countries, such as Saudi Arabia and Indonesia. Within Britain, Ansari, who has traced the development of the Muslim community since 1800, is well placed to warn against the tendency to develop an 'equally homogeneous imaginings of the Muslim community' (Ansari, 2004, p. 1) rather than recognise the difference and variety within it, even with regard to the extent of identification with and attachment to the notion of 'Britishness'. The Muslim faith is not unusual in this respect and the same variety can, of course, be found within all religions and in all secular and non-secular states. However, there seems to be an underlying assumption in the work of some multiculturalists that there is more stability and uniformity in an 'ethnic culture' than in any form of national identity. For example, Parekh (2000) grapples with the concept of identity under a 'national culture' – in this case 'Britishness' – and suggests that it is so diverse as to have no real meaning, whilst the 'culture' of particular groups or communities is substantial and meaningful.

The ephemeral nature of 'culture' is evidenced by the attitudes of younger people who have been exposed to multicultural experiences. Most young Britons, for example, for example, who have a close friend from a different race or colour, would marry someone from a different race (88 per cent) and most also agreed that 'all races are equally trustworthy' (84 per cent). Moreover, whilst 77 per cent of 28–30-year-olds had friends from mixed backgrounds, this rose to 88 per cent for the 18–20-year-olds. This contrasted with another recent poll, across all age groups, which showed that nine out of ten white Britons had no, or hardly any, ethnic minority friends (*The Times*, 14 September 2004).

Yet, even if so much of our identity is shaped by accident of birth and subsequent socialisation, it does not mean that it can easily be deconstructed or simply removed to another environment, without distress and difficulty. Our identity, in whatever way it is derived, gives meaning to our lives, and change will often be regarded as a threat rather than an opportunity, at least until we have explored that change – over time – and decided to the contrary. But Goodhart (2004) appears to believe in the 'glue of ethnicity', which he describes as 'people who look and talk like us'. It is not 'ethnicity' itself that provides the glue, but the common understandings, familiarity and mutual respect acquired over time and through interaction. He is therefore also wrong to deride the idea of the replacement of the glue of ethnicity with the 'glue of values', as this 'glue' is simply borne out of interaction, whether that interaction is within or between different groups. The essence of Goodhart's view appears to be that the more diverse we become, the more the solidarity of the nation becomes threatened, presumably on the basis that the nation will have to accommodate a wider range of values, which are each ascribed to particular ethnic groups. In a more recent publication, Goodhart argues for a 'refashioned civic nationalism' in which 'British citizenship, membership of the British national community, remains valued and protected by mainstream politics' (Goodhart, 2006, p. 55).

The 'glue of values', both within and between different groups, is important at least in so far as it means the development of a common understanding, and the ability to interact, to build trust and to reach an accommodation based on co-operation rather than conflict. This is nowhere more evident than in Northern Ireland, where communities are not divided by 'ethnicity', nor by fundamental differences in values – both communities are Christian, share a common language, democratic traditions and so on – but where differences stem from structural divisions and political aspirations. Many conflicts around the world have similarly been based on conflicts over the distribution of resources and ethnic and faith divisions have been created, or instrumentalised, in support of one power block or another. Solidarity therefore depends on common aims and aspirations (or the 'values' which underpin them), rather than adherence to a particular faith or similar ethnicity, even if they are used as a convenient label to distinguish and justify the protection or promotion of the interests of one group and limiting the resource distribution to another.

Values, identity and nationality

Nationality is not, therefore, the same as an 'identity', nor does it automatically create a set of values (though it may contribute more than is generally supposed to both the identity and values of nationals). Nationality is a contractual relationship, bestowing rights and obligations and whilst it may trump cultural affiliations in certain situations, it need not undermine them in all circumstances. Identity is subjective, it creates emotional attachments, possibly to the nation – and for patriots this is certainly the case – though nationality does not require a particular level of identity and may mean no more than a simple honouring of the contractual arrangement entered into by the individual. 'Citizenship' has developed in such a way as to imply a more active assertion of nationality and it is hard to see how this would be developed without at least some emotional attachment to what the nation represents. It also implies an honouring of the contract on both sides, so that it is unlikely that the individual will become a more active citizen, if he or she feels that the state has failed to deliver its obligations, for example, through ensuring equal opportunities and preventing discrimination. This again illustrates the need to tackle the 'equalities agenda' alongside cohesion.

Baubock (2003, p. 21), however, doubts whether common values are essential for cohesion. He draws upon the 'venerable tradition' of Emile Durkheim, one of the founding fathers of sociology, to suggest that shared values have a limited role to play and that 'social cohesion is provided by a functional division of labour in which individuals occupy different and complementary roles, rather than by a "mechanic solidarity" that relies on similarity'. Baubock appears to take such a view because of the way in which values might be constructed and used:

> Immigrants don't have to support the particular cultural traditions of the host society or to assimilate into a national identity defined by history that is not theirs. All that is required is that they subscribe to those political values that are at the core of democratic constitutions .... They can be asked to do so because they are universalistic ... their content is culturally neutral and ought to be shared by all groups and traditions.

The problem, then, for Baubock is that these apparently 'universalistic' values are interpreted in definite and particular ways by western democracies creating 'a dilemma for immigrants who have to choose between these western values and their identities of origin'. He believes that this is 'exclusionary' and that 'immigrants should be allowed to retain a previous citizenship when they naturalise.' He would simply prefer that the choice did not have to be made and that the contractual relationship is sufficient.

The report of the 'Life in the United Kingdom' Advisory Group sees no such conflict and endorses the contractual relationship stressing that to be British means respect for the law, the parliamentary and democratic political structures and the giving of allegiance to the state in return for its protection (Crick, 2003, p. 11). However, the Report also proposes that 'over-arching beliefs, values and traditions' would bind the nation together and that this does not involve defining 'Britishness' too precisely, nor redefining it – 'a common culture does not mean that original identities are lost'. But what are these common values and if we cannot specify them or define them in such a way that they challenge both migrant and host communities, are they in any way meaningful?

The laws of the land are, of course, already codified and for the most part, even the 'democratic principles' referred to in the British pledge, which accompanies the Oath of Allegiance, are also enshrined in law – the right of free speech, the right of association, the equality of individuals, regardless of race, gender, etc., the right to vote and the panoply of rules and regulations which govern the way decisions are taken in modern representative democracies. The duties of 'citizenship' are also sometimes formalised, for example, the Canadian Government sets them out in a booklet to all citizens in terms of the responsibilities to vote, to help others, to care for and protect the environment, to obey the law, to eliminate discrimination and injustice and to express opinions freely whilst respecting the rights of others (Ministry of Public Works and Government Services, Canada, 2001, p. 31) These are also circumscribed by legal process, but the extent to which they are observed depends upon whether citizens adopt, the minimum passive role, or develop a more active engagement.

What may appear to be very modest requirements of nationality and 'culturally neutral' values are actually much more prescriptive than generally supposed. Baubock (2003, p. 22) acknowledges this, when he points out that immigrants 'from countries considerably less democratic than the receiving country' find themselves confronted by the new values. These present a very real conflict over concepts of religious tolerance, often well established in democratic societies, where different faiths coexist and compete and where agnosticism and atheism are respectable positions. In the West, religion has generally been pushed further into the private realm. In some cases, it is almost completely separated. In France, for example, the principle of *laïcité* has been enshrined in French law for about 100 years underpinned by the establishment of a secular state with complete separation from the church. In Britain some remnants of the connectivity of the church and state remain, for example, in the choice of public holidays, which were founded on the Christian diary. However, this is all very different from those societies where religious law and state law amounts to much the same thing, other faiths are by definition heretical (and often forbidden), and religious observance is very much part of the public realm, governing all aspects of behaviour.

Similarly, the role of women in some societies may be very different from that of western democracies, with their ability to move freely in the public realm, let alone take an active role in citizenship, often being heavily proscribed. The open decision-making process, dependent upon free speech and the equality of 'one person one vote' is also in contrast to those societies where great deference is shown to community elders, or familial and kinship leaders.

These are more than differences of 'culture' and amount to a conflict of values, which will affect many aspects of the public and private realms and daily activity. Other ethical differences, based on fundamental principles have also emerged, for example, whether 'ritual slaughter' is consistent with the laws and codes of practice dealing with animal welfare. But such ethical conflicts are not confined to the immigrant communities and are not necessarily aligned with an ethnic minority identity. For example, hotly contested debates have continued over the use of animals for the testing of drugs and animal welfare. The British Government banned fox hunting on the grounds of unnecessary cruelty, in 2005 (having been previously banned in Scotland by the devolved administration). The opposition to this ban came almost exclusively from the white rural areas of Britain which were hostile and vociferous in their opposition. Such differences are the result of different values, but may only be seen as a 'clash of cultures' if aligned with a particular ethnic group or identifiable culture. In the case of fox hunting the rural community has learnt from this and actually positioned itself as a separate 'culture', which they claim is apart from, and misunderstood by, their urban oppressors.

The conflict over values also cuts in both directions, as migrant communities have often found that the equal opportunities and freedom from discrimination have been denied to them, with the consequence that they face much higher levels of unemployment, poor housing and poverty. Further, they are often portrayed in the press and media in a poor light and even demonised, used as the butt of racist jokes and stereotypes and made to feel unwelcome. This even applies to very long-standing migrant communities, who have not enjoyed a sense of belonging and made to feel like 'foreigners in their own land' (Cantle, 2001). This alienation means that they then look elsewhere, perhaps to their former homeland, or to an international frame of reference, for support and identity.

Some concepts of 'multiculturalism' actually cast doubt on any meaningful definition of 'core values' and perhaps even the more tangible requirements of 'nationality'. Parekh (2000, p. 56), for example, proposes an admirable mixture of rights, responsibilities and values: equality and fairness; dialogue and consultation; toleration, compromise and accommodation; recognition of and respect for diversity; and – the determination to confront and eliminate racism and xenophobia. At the same time, he salutes the traditional 'British virtues' of 'tolerance, moderation, readiness to compromise, fair play, individualism, love of freedom, eccentricity, ironic detachment, emotional reticence', but these are to be understood and 'related to in different ways' (ibid., p. 23) – undermining the very principles he espouses.

The relationship between 'values' and 'identity' is therefore complex and whilst some values may be associated with a particular ethnic or cultural identity, they may be challenged where the core requirements of nationality are at odds with them. In fact, failure to do so may not only result in the tendency to 'reproduce separatism', but also to 'marginalize (communities) as minority, unconsciously reinforcing the dominant ethnic conception of the majority as white, rather than the political conception of a democratic majority' (Bloomfield and Bianchini, 2004, p. 28). Failure to do so may allow a variety of interpretations to continue and this has the advantage, in the short term, of avoiding a painful dialogue, but generally results in a continued coexistence and separation and subsequent misunderstandings between different communities.

To this (limited) extent the common values could be homogenising, such a process could also include defining those 'cultural' matters which should be respected and protected within a multicultural framework (and it should not be supposed that the values within different cultural groups are either fixed or uniform). From this starting point, communities can begin to develop a greater shared understanding and mutual trust, as well as a greater sense of belonging and, possibly, a new national identity.

Community cohesion and shared values

Behaviour is shaped by both the rights and responsibilities we bear and the values we hold – and those that we hold in common. The stronger the bond of rights and responsibilities and the more that we hold in common, the more likely that our behaviour will harmonise with that of others and the less likely that it will lead to disagreement and conflict. Cohesion will depend upon the observance of basic principles of fairness, justice and mutuality, to ensure that we can work together in a political entity. Having common ground and mutual understanding is, in fact, a prerequisite for any relationship and is more important than a shared history or culture (although this might be expected to make the common ground easier to attain). It is also essential that part of this understanding is to respect and nurture each other's cultural, linguistic and other differences, rather than to regard them as a threat. By actively seeking to maintain different traditions and views, we make it clear that one 'value' that we hold in common is to respect what we do not have in common. This must clearly be within a formal context of the law and established principles and rights, such as the right to free speech or to democratic participation and can provide significant reassurance about the basis upon which the engagement takes place.

The concept of 'community cohesion' recognises, first, that equality of opportunity is central to a cohesive society and that the very existence of a substantial disaffected and disadvantaged group will militate against any real sense of community harmony. As community cohesion is based on 'a common vision and sense of belonging' where the 'diversity of people's backgrounds and circumstances is appreciated and positively valued' (see Figure 2.1) the very existence of such wide disparities in life chances would illustrate that, even if a 'vision' was shared, it had not yet impacted upon outcomes and cohesion was therefore unlikely. Second, common ground and any form of meaningful understanding will be very difficult to establish if inequalities, whether based on ethnicity, faith, social class or other divisions, are so pronounced and widespread.

In practical terms, differences in lifestyles, where of a profound nature, can also make common ground difficult to attain. This is not just in respect of ethnicity and faith; for example, differences between older and younger people, those in town and country locations and between students and longer-standing residents, can all find it difficult to establish mutually accept-able meeting places, or any form of communication with which both sides feel comfortable. Community cohesion nevertheless attempts to emphasise what we hold in common rather than what divides us and to build a greater sense of clarity about rights and responsibilities and a shared set of values. In other words, rather than simply attempting to legislate to prevent conflict, discrimination and hate crime and to enforce equal rights, community cohe-sion relies upon changing the very attitudes and values that give rise to the 'fear of difference' by building mutual understanding and trust.

The practice of building common values and resolving conflicts between majority and minority values is still developing, but new approaches have begun to emerge from the practice of community cohesion (discussed in the next chapter) and have been evident for some time in the development of cit-izenship in Canada and elsewhere. Any imposition, by government and its agencies, however, is likely to be discounted and 'common experiences' and 'dialogues about the commonalities' are far more likely to generate a greater sense of ownership. Nevertheless, government has to take the lead and accept a policy shift towards the centrality of attitudinal change. The need to develop a greater sense of common purpose has gradually gathered pace over the last few years. In Britain, the government launched a Community Cohesion and Race Equality Strategy (Home Office, 2005) and this reflected concerns, which were wider than the integration or segregation of ethnic and faith groups – and wider than the continuing debate about immigration:

creating a shared national purpose also reflects a deeper need: to redis-cover a clear confident sense of who we are as a country. I believe that just about every central question about our national future – from the constitution to our role in Europe, from citizenship to the challenges of multiculturalism – even the question of how we deliver our public services in the manner we do – can only be fully answered if we are clear about what we value about being British and what gives us purpose and direction as a country. (Brown, 2004)

Community cohesion therefore has a much broader role in more clearly establishing what we should hold in common, as core principles of nationality, and what we should support and value, both in terms of the national characteristics or national identity, and what we should value and embrace as cultural difference. The dangers of engineering such a debate are well understood by governments, however, and even in this instance a question constantly looms large in the mind of policymakers – 'How can we ensure that we have an open debate around how to manage migration and prevent abuse of asylum which doesn't fuel prejudice against Black and minority ethnic communities?' (Home Office, 2004, p. 18).

There are some doubts, however, about this development, or at least the context in which it is unfolding. For example, Blunkett's (and at the time, the government's) approach has been seen by some 'as the road to assimilation' (Rattansi, 2002). Rattansi draws a link between the Government White Paper on asylum and immigration, 'Secure Borders, Safe Haven' in 2002 and a number of statements made by Blunkett, which Rattansi sees as 'defining Britishness by counterposing it to forced marriages and genital mutilation' (ibid., p. 98).

Others support Rattansi's fears that the present 'shared values' agenda is really moving towards assimilation, with Blunkett putting too much emphasis on 'the norms of acceptability (Lewis, 2005, p. 543). It has been suggested that other European countries are taking a similar direction (towards assimilation) and that the language classes and induction programmes of the type developed in the United Kingdom are too focussed on certain (mostly Muslim) minorities rather than on majority populations (Baubock, 2002). This approach to multiculturalism, it is feared, would create a requirement that ethnic minorities change their identity, without a similar accommodation by the mainstream native population.

On the other hand, Kymlicka (2003, p. 206) has no doubt about shared values and, 'from a North American perspective, sees little that is unfamiliar or surprising'. But he also casts doubt on the motives of British politicians, who have noted the success of extreme right wing parties across Europe and may have taken the view that, they can limit the political damage in some way by recognising and assuaging some of the fears and concerns that the far right have stirred up – 'there is a fine line' he says, 'between acknowledging public fears and reinforcing them'. Ouseley (2004) is also concerned about the political context and that New Labour, like the Thatcher Government before them, are perceived as 'striking a blow against the BNP by stealing its thunder'. However, despite the suspicion, Ouseley believes that the ground is shifting and 'it is becoming more common for liberals as well as the right' to argue in favour of more integration of migrant populations as long as this 'reasonable' process does not 'divert much- needed attention from the actions necessary to tackle deep-seated racism'.

Nevertheless, modern multicultural societies have failed to develop processes for mediating conflicts over conceptions of nationality, defining national identity and developing a consensus over the boundaries of cultural affiliations. The process of government and the tools of governance have failed to keep pace with the development of multiculturalism. We are therefore faced with very reasonable proposals for 'over-arching' values, 'core principles', 'overlapping identities' and the like, without any agreement about what the terms actually mean, let alone how to build a consensus about the values themselves.

Further, such debates are always seen within a political context and a highly charged arena in which virtually every player is viewed with suspicion. However, approaching the issue through everyday activities, which bring different cultures together and learning through experience on a more localised basis, has proved less controversial. This would imply a sustained and rigorous approach in all localities and, at the same time, relating them to some form of national or 'over-arching' values. But a locally focussed agenda has its limitations and, for some countries at least, the development of the citizenship has been seen as complementary, or even more important.

The citizenship agenda

The granting of nationality, or naturalisation, is increasingly used as a means of attempting to engender allegiance and create common values but, despite the philosophical basis behind much of the historical conception of citizenship, most of the developments adopted in recent years are rather more prosaic and have been from a limited range of practical measures.

These generally revolve around the use of citizen and language tests, citizenship ceremonies and oaths, celebrations, such as citizenship days or events, and are well established in a number of countries, for example, in the United States and Canada (Kymlicka, 2003, p. 196). The British Government, in attempting to introduce a similar regime in Britain, sought to give reassurance about the nature of such practices by demonstrating that, these measures were widespread and embedded and provided an international table for comparative purposes (see Table 5.2).

Table 5.2   Naturalisation requirements and provisions in selected countries, November 2001

	Australia	Austria	Canada	France	Germany	Netherlands	USA
First generation							
Min residence period	Min. 1 or 2 years	6 years	3 or 4 years	5 years	8 years	5 years before application	5 years
Knowledge of society	Yes	—	Yes	No, but integration must be demonst-rated	—	Yes	Yes
Language skills	Yes	Yes	Yes	Yes	Yes	Yes	Yes
Good character	Yes	—	—	Yes	—	—	Yes
Absence of criminal record	Yes	Yes	Yes	Yes	Yes	Yes	Possibly
Dual Citizenship formally accepted	Yes	No	Yes	Yes	No	No	No
Oath	Yes	No	Yes	No	Yes	No	Yes
Language classes							
Classes	Yes	No	Yes	Proposed	Proposed	Yes	Yes
Compulsory attendance	No	Yes	No	n.a.	Yes	Yes	No
Citizenship classes							
Separate from language classes	No	No	No		Yes	No	n.a.
Compulsory classes	No	Yes	No		Yes	Yes	n.a.
Areas covered	History, culture, accessing public services	History, culture	History, culture, accessing public services		Legal order, culture and history	Culture and heritage, accessing public services	n.a.
Run by	Local service providers – government funded	n.a.	Local service providers – government funded		n.a.	Local service providers – government funded	
Citizenship ceremonies							
Provision	Yes	Yes	Yes	Yes	No, but held in some towns	No	Yes
Compulsory attendance	Yes	No	Yes	No,but yes, in practice	No		Yes
Individual or group ceremony	Group	Both	Group	Both	Group		Group

Source: Home Office (2002).

Most of these measures are modest and practical, with limited scope for linking them to the notion of values. Ironically, the restrictive process of specifying a minimum residence period will probably contribute most by way of attachment, simply because the applicant will have begun a long process of naturalisation, finding out about customs and norms and presumably feeling comfortable enough with them to want to remain. Similarly, it is an opportunity to discover whether they are 'of good character' and have not fallen foul of the law, at least in the period of around 5 years average minimum residence used by countries. The tests for 'knowledge of the society' are a little more proactive, although they tend to revolve around fairly practical matters and historical facts. Canada's 'citizen test' is relatively demanding and sets out 197 potential questions (Minister of Public Works and Government Services Canada, 2001), covering Canada's history and geography, the indigenous minorities, constitutional provisions, electoral and democratic arrangements and local and regional government. Britain has recently established a citizen test and so too, has Australia, dubbed in the popular press as the 'mateship test'. Generally, however, the tests of citizenship are not particularly onerous and the language skill requirement is relatively low, or even rudimentary. Citizenship and language classes are now provided by most of the countries highlighted in the table, but with varying degrees of provision and not all are free or freely available.

The arrangements for citizenship might be seen as a means of either encouraging naturalisation, or as a means of restricting it. For example, the arrangements in Austria have, since 2000, been based upon the establishment of mandatory classes, where German is taught and potential citizens also learn about the Austrian political system and European values, with participants expected to meet half the cost (Baubock, 2002). In Europe, however, the most restrictive approach to citizenship is that of the Swiss, who have a residence period of 12 years and will not even grant automatic citizenship to the grandchildren of migrants born in Switzerland. Those applying for naturalisation must also be approved by local committees, who judge whether applicants are 'Swiss enough'. Not surprisingly, Switzerland has the highest proportion of 'foreign' residents in Europe – 1.5 million out of the total of 7 million (*The Times*, 2004).

Britain's citizenship agenda has gradually been stepped up and now covers the above measures, together with a number of new approaches to 'active citizenship'. The introduction of 'citizenship ceremonies' provides for a *public* declaration of what all citizens would have previously signed up to in private and have been adopted on a widespread basis and proved to be very popular with new citizens. The oath remains what Crick (2003, p. 30) described as the 'long established and unchanged Oath of Allegiance to the crown', however, and as required by *The Nationality and Immigration Act*

2002, in itself does little to promote common values:

> *I – name – (swear by almighty God) (do solemnly and sincerely affirm) that, on becoming a British citizen, I will be faithful and bear true allegiance to Her Majesty, Queen Elizabeth the Second, her heirs and successors according to law.*

Crick (ibid.) recognised this deficiency and suggested that a 'fuller view that citizens are signing up to a modern constitutional democracy' would be served by the addition of a pledge inserted via the same Act:

> *I will give my loyalty to the United Kingdom and respect its rights and freedoms. I will uphold its democratic values. I will observe its laws faithfully and fulfil my duties and obligations as a British Citizen.*

However, whilst this refers specifically to 'loyalty' and to 'upholding democratic values', it adds relatively little, dealing with values in only the most general of terms. The brief given to the Crick's Advisory Group was to 'advise the Home Secretary on the method, conduct and implementation of a "Life in the United Kingdom" naturalisation test' (ibid., p. 3), and it therefore went on to recommend and produce a 'Living in Britain' handbook, to be given free to people applying for naturalisation; a basic English language test (or Welsh or Scottish Gaelic); a programme of studies, involving language development (if required); and 'civic support' for all immigrants, including some historic content, knowledge of the law, how to get a job and everyday needs.

The motivation of migrants to become citizens may, however, have relatively little to do with buying into a set of national values or being persuaded by an attractive version of national identity. The background research to Crick's Report (2003, p. 53), indicated that the 'key triggers for different nationalities' influencing their decisions to apply for naturalisation was generally related to the practicality of travelling abroad. All of the foreign nationals asked – Bangladeshis, Pakistanis, Nigerians, Indians, Poles and Somalis – saw the freedom and ease of international travel as the most important benefit of British citizenship.

From the perspective of the foreign national, in Britain at least, adjusting to new values and even acquiring new rights and responsibilities, may simply not be on the agenda. Being able to speak a little English, acquiring a little knowledge of British history and current affairs and taking an oath of allegiance is all the adaptation that is required. This is not surprising since these values and rights and responsibilities are not clearly explained to, nor understood by, the host community, let alone presented to naturalising citizens. The Home Office Citizenship Survey (Home Office, 2003b) reported that when people were asked what they thought their rights were, the most frequently mentioned were:

Rights	%
Right to freedom of expression	35
Right to fair, equal, respectful treatment	13
Right to protection from crime, attack, threat	13
Right to health care 12 Right to education	8
Right to free elections	8
Right to freedom of thought, conscience, religion	6
Right to state provision of services	6

This hardly represented a consensus and a similar pattern emerged with regard to the most frequently mentioned responsibilities:

Responsibilities	%
Obeying and respecting the law	36
Being good or following moral/ethical/religious code	12
Looking after and protecting family	12
Helping others/being good neighbour	11
Treating others fairly and with respect	10
Civic duties	8
Behaving responsibly	7
Duty to work	6

The concept of a 'citizen culture', expounded in another context by Crick (2001), is also very far from the reality of the other components tested in the above survey. The survey found that only 24 per cent of people felt that they could influence decisions affecting Britain (43 per cent felt they could influence decisions about their local area) and there was a low level of trust of politicians and Parliament.

Not surprisingly then, the government has embarked on a range of initiatives to develop the culture of citizenship, with some of these only now beginning to emerge. The most significant of these was the inclusion of 'citizenship' within the national curriculum for schools in 2002, developing the idea of the broader engagement of the individual as a social being and as a means of renewing democracy.

The use of the curriculum, however, failed to make an impact, perhaps because schools are continually under pressure to meet very specific performance attainment targets and social objectives tend to receive a lower priority. The Community Cohesion Panel's Report (Cantle, 2004, p. 13) reflected that citizenship education in schools had had 'limited impact' on the race and community relations agenda and called for it to be 'fundamentally reviewed so that it concentrates on real priorities, rather than attempt to deal with such a wide ranging agenda'. Like many citizenship initiatives, it was also seen as rather remote from the real world in which 'young people had the opportunity to engage with all sections of the community'. The Community Services Volunteers (CSV, 2004) subsequently confirmed that when pupils were asked what citizenship meant to them, two years after the introduction of the subject into the curriculum, 22 per cent said it was about rights and responsibilities, with only 9 per cent suggesting 'tolerance and respect' (CSV, 2004). A Review Group was set up in 2005, headed by Sir Keith Ajegbo, to consider why the uptake and quality of citizenship education had been so limited. The subsequent report, *Diversity and Citizenship* (Ajegbo, 2007) put forward a number of proposals to ensure a much more thoroughgoing approach and provided a clear sense of direction:

> ... we passionately believe that it is the duty of all schools to address issues of 'how we live together' and 'dealing with difference' however controversial and difficult they might sometimes seem.

In a related, but very much supportive and complementary development, a new duty to promote community cohesion in schools was introduced with effect from September 2007, for which guidance has been issued (DCSF, 2007) and this incorporates much of the Ajegbo thinking.

The government has pinned a lot of its hopes for citizenship on the young – although in the reports following the riots, younger people were often found to be more willing to engage with people of different backgrounds and were less resistant to change (Cantle, 2001; Ouseley, 2001). Indeed, young people often felt under pressure to succumb to the prejudice of their parents and elders. This was, perhaps, most graphically illustrated when a video was made by the Government's Children and Young Persons Unit (CYPU, 2002), entitled *Colour Blind*. Designed to showcase cross-cultural activity between Asian and White young people, the video captures the local (white) elders throwing stones at the Asian youngsters when visiting the white area for the first time.

A series of further initiatives have been developed. For example, the Department for Education and Science (DfES) have attempted to move beyond the citizenship curriculum for schools and piloted citizenship training for 16–19-year-olds. This covered how society works and how people can get involved and develop through participation and active citizenship. However, it was initially limited to 11 small-scale pilot schemes for a two-year period. The Department of Health (DoH) also developed a 'Learning Pathway', which aimed to ensure that all citizens had a basic understanding of their rights and responsibilities within the NHS. This was also limited to four regional pilot schemes in Salford, Lambeth and Lewisham, Birmingham and Cornwall. The Government's Neighbourhood Renewal Unit (NRU) has also developed projects based upon community participation and citizenship, particularly to deal with conflict resolution. The government has also created a 'Civic Pioneer' initiative, with wider aims 'to encourage local authorities to commit themselves to apply the ethos of community engagement to everything they do and help develop the skills and capacity of local people and community organisations in learning to work together' (Blunkett, 2004). Launched in 2004, as part of the government's 'civil renewal' agenda, it will engage 10–15 local authority areas.

The government set up the Russell Commission to evaluate services to young people, with a view to providing the opportunity to develop a new community spirit among young people and envisage something along the lines of the community service in other countries:

> If America has its Peace Corps and now its Americorps, South Africa its National Youth Service, France its 'Unis-Cite', the Netherlands its 'Groundbreakers Initiative', Canada its 'Katimavik' programme, should not Britain ... engage a new generation of young people in service to their communities. (Brown, 2004)

A number of proposals have recently emerged from a range of politicians, expounding the benefits of some form of national community service, or a more formalised programme of volunteering in support of community based causes. These ideas about how to develop 'citizenship' are particularly intended to distinguish and champion the cause of 'active citizenship'. However, the schemes are, as yet, relatively minor and tentative and unlikely to engage with the real and pressing issue of 'over-arching' values and will remain more focussed on the safe territory of democratic engagement, volunteering and 'working with the needy'. It remains to be seen whether the latest Green Paper proposal (SoSJLC, 2007) to establish a statement of British national values will result in anything meaningful. The government's initiatives are, however, complemented by the work of local authorities and the voluntary sector, though this again is often patchy and on a small scale. It can be contrasted to the sheer weight of mainstream government programmes and services which continue to be provided on a silo basis, generally designed to meet only one objective at a time.

In the meantime, the government has had to face the growth in public concern about immigration and asylum, which 'has soared since the 1990s (and) is consistently seen as one of the top three issues facing Britain ... a remarkable change that cannot be ignored by anyone, even if it is uncomfortable' (Page, 2004). However, the issue of migration and the attitudes and values that surround it, whilst being fundamental to citizenship, remains to be addressed. The government continues to see migration as an economic issue to be managed, although it has been urged to complement this with 'managing settlement' (Cantle, 2004), in which a new agency would be created, dedicated to the task of promoting the values associated with nationality and national identity, supporting both newcomers and the host community in the process. This has been taken up more recently by the Commission on Integration and Cohesion (CIC, 2007). The Commission proposed a new agency to manage migration, along with 'a new model of rights and responsibilities' and a campaign to promote 'shared futures'.

The fact that the focus of some specific citizenship activities are seen to be focussed on the migrant communities has also heightened some concerns that they are thought to be the least 'citizen-like'. The new citizenship ceremonies, for example, are not extended to all citizens as a 'rite of passage' and whilst the citizenship oath sets out the commitment of the individual, there is no reciprocal undertaking by the host community to defend their rights, nor to ensure equality of opportunity and to involve and value them as part of their new society. Some attempts at providing mentoring or 'buddying' of new arrivals and prospective citizens have emerged (Crick, 2003), but despite their potential, are of a limited and patchy nature and do not yet convey a real genuine warmth of welcome.

The British experience is not unique, with similar and even more limited attempts in many nations, to take citizenship seriously. The exceptions are, perhaps, the nations that have sought to build a nation from immigrants without a dominant host community, particularly Canada and Australia, where citizenship days and other activities are well established, though still being extended in the light of their own tensions between communities. The reluctance in the UK to take this agenda forward with the urgency it deserves, is at least in part, due to the very idea that citizenship values may develop into American style flag waving jingoism. Yet Page (2004), who is Director of the MORI Social Research Institute presents a choice – 'how far do we encourage diversity in needs and wants, based on ethnic and cultural differences, and how far do we encourage mixing and a simple set of basic standards and ways of living that we all agree to?'

A response is provided by Prof. Putnam (MORI is working with Putnam's University – Harvard):

> while Europeans sneer at many aspects of the US, we will need to become more like them as we become more diverse. The very things that liberal Europeans sneer at are some of the things that hold America together. The question for us is what will bring us together in Britain. Doing nothing is not an option any more. (Ibid.)

The very idea of 'Americanising' British (or even European) citizenship is not likely to be greeted with enthusiasm, though in this context in particular, it would be ironic if such an approach were rejected simply because it was American.

Community cohesion offers something of a way forward, in that it is based on active 'mixing', and sees this as a way of fundamentally challenging and changing underlying attitudes and values. Many aspects of citizenship also imply interaction, taking part in voluntary and community activities, rather than in the home-centred world of television and family networks. Active citizenship is therefore, likely to contribute to cohesion simply by creating the shared space for activities that can bring people of different backgrounds together.

Community cohesion also challenges the assumption that a shared set of over-arching national values can be created and constantly developed and reinforced, without the creation of shared life experiences. Shared values will depend upon some degree of interaction between people of different backgrounds, whereas separate development will almost certainly entail a continuing divergence of values. 'Solidarity' comes from people interacting, collaborating – and disagreeing – but most of all, by developing a *political* identity, through active membership of the nation state, which regulates individual behaviour, and provides for collective action. This 'regulated' mutuality and reciprocity is more likely, over time, to form our identity, rather than any built around the spurious idea of people that 'look and talk like us'.

6
Developing a Programme for Community Cohesion

The recent fractures in western democracies have generally been along ethnic and faith fault lines. However, the aim of community cohesion is to tackle the 'fear of difference' more generally and to enable people to be more comfortable with all areas of difference, including those based on sexual orientation, disability, social class and age. The community cohesion agenda can also be applied to all types of communities whether in towns and cities, or in suburban and rural areas, where ethnic minority and faith communities are very small. Indeed, the host community in monocultural areas may be far more intimidating for minorities, who feel that they are treated with suspicion and believe that they are unwelcome and even unsafe in such areas. This can also apply to people moving to them on a temporary basis, for example, as students or for holiday purposes, and will certainly inhibit their wider freedom to live, work or even visit, them wherever they chose.

Community cohesion programmes must clearly, therefore, embrace all parts of the country and not just those with high proportions of ethnic or other minority populations. Indeed, in a modern multicultural community which is attempting to come to terms with its diversity, and in which people inevitably move to different areas for education, work and leisure purposes and communicate in so many different ways, no part can be successfully isolated from the other. And the implication of being part of a national democratic framework, in which priorities are decided, resources are allocated and where measures to maintain security are created, is that each individual will make a real effort to understand the needs and aspirations of fellow citizens.

Community cohesion (and democracy itself) therefore also depends upon the use of a common language, or languages. This will generally be confined to just one language unless all information is available and accessible on an equal basis in more than one language with translation and interpretation facilities so advanced as to ensure that meaningful dialogues can take place across the language divides. Most modern multicultural societies, however, now have a wide range of minority languages, with no real ability to maintain a regular dialogue in those languages outside each of those minority communities. There are of course exceptions to this, such as the use of French in Canada, but this represents an historic bi-polar development, which is not extended to new minorities. In general, the acceptance of the dominant language, together with the active pursuit of the development of good language skills, will be necessary to ensure that the democratic dialogue and interaction can take place. This should not imply, however, that the use of minority languages will not be supported within those communities, nor that they cannot be maintained and used together with the dominant language or languages.

Dialogue is a prerequisite for common understanding and citizenship and may also lead to the development of common values. This was recently recognised by the Commission on Integration and Cohesion (CIC, 2007). But 'dialogue' does not necessarily imply a generalised and societal-wide debate, or large-scale re-education programme. Information is imparted, understanding and trust developed and attitudes and values are shaped – possibly all the more easily – by direct involvement in everyday activities and events. However, local-level engagement is much more likely to create a common understanding if it is reinforced by an overall value system.

Community cohesion, therefore, asserts a new model of multiculturalism, one in which a common vision and sense of belonging is built, with justice and fairness at its heart and where diversity is seen as an enriching and positive experience for all faiths and cultures, including for the majority community. This will depend, to a large extent, upon whether people have created meaningful relationships and mutual respect, as a result of positive interaction, across cultural boundaries.

Constructing a programme

With the development of any new programme, there is always the temptation to create a special series of initiatives. This will inevitably be necessary to some extent in the first instance when new techniques and approaches are being considered and developed. However, special initiative programmes do not always succeed in generating widespread and sustained change and they often remain as marginal to the main business or service. In terms of monetary value, the resources employed are generally minor compared to the mainstream programmes and invariably wither on the vine once the additional special resources come to an end and the 'newness' loses its shine. Community cohesion programmes should, therefore, be quickly turned into part of the everyday way of doing things and put into the mainstream activity of public service, private enterprise and voluntary effort.

This means being able to use 'initiatives' to reshape mainstream services and to ensure that those providers change practice, accept responsibility for anticipating trends and consider future needs and how service changes will be perceived. In particular, it means questioning how they will contribute to heightening or lowering the tensions between different groups – and the fear and acceptance of difference. For example, public sector regeneration schemes have often been designed on the basis of addressing the housing and other needs of a given community on an objective basis. Nevertheless, such schemes were perceived as providing an unfair advantage to a particular group who received that support, in contrast to other communities who received little or nothing – this was in fact one of the most commonly held views in the towns in Northern England who were subject to the 'race riots' in 2001. However, such programmes should not be constructed simply to avoid the raising of tension and can be used much more positively to create dialogue between different groups and to develop mutual understanding again a failing of recent regeneration schemes. In other words, community cohesion must concern itself with the way things are done, as well as what is actually done.

Community cohesion programmes are also not confined to any particular level or sector and should apply equally to national, regional and local activity – any layer of government, private sector or voluntary service. The private sector can contribute to the agenda, for example, by remodelling its training and development programmes, revising its sports and social provision and, of course, by reviewing the way in which its goods and services are delivered. Again it should ask how such activities can reduce or heighten intercommunity tensions and how they might contribute to building mutual understanding and respect. Such reviews may result in changes to the way in which companies advertise their products, recruit their staff and create opportunities for dialogue and understanding within and beyond the workplace. Businesses also have collective interests. For example, in Oldham, one of the towns affected by the riots in 2001, the private sector has led an 'Oldham United' campaign to help bring sections of the community together and to encourage business development (CRE, 2004a, p. 14) and in Blackburn, private employers have been given a 'toolkit' to encourage cross-cultural contact within the workplace (Blackburn with Darwen Strategic Partnership, 2004).

The voluntary sector too, has a role to play. Voluntary organisations generally fall into two blocks – advocacy groups and service providers, although they can also be a mixture of the two. Advocacy groups are established to represent a particular, or single interest, group. Some do seek common cause, across cultural and other boundaries, or they may even be constructed on the basis of interconnected interests, as in the example of inter-faith networks. However, far too many focus on differences rather than similarities. Those that provide services may again do so in ways that reinforce separate interests rather than cross divides. Given that such groups are often established in order to fill in particular gaps in the public services, their single-minded approach is hardly surprising, but it often results in further separation and represents something of a missed opportunity to work across boundaries. The role of voluntary organisations therefore needs to be considered in relation to their ability to support cohesion, rather than simply provide advocacy and services to particular groups, valuable though this may be.

Community cohesion should also work on the basis that it can be measured, with a baseline established and developments and progress mapped over time. The existing measures of community cohesion are a mixture of objective indicators, such as the number of racist incidents in a given area, and subjective indicators, such as the perceptions of local people about whether race relations are improving. These are set out in *Building a Picture of Community Cohesion* (Home Office *et al.*, 2004a) and will no doubt, be developed and refined in the light of experience and they were, in any event, also conceived on the basis that they would be subject to local adaptation. However, the very idea of attempting to measure the dynamics of community relations again sets it apart from the 'equalities agenda' which is generally limited to constraining behaviour, rather than developing and promoting a more positive and forward looking programme which addresses underlying attitudes and values.

Creating a baseline position is clearly essential as any programme needs a starting point and this should represent the present state of community relations in a given area, region or country. There may be a history of long-standing divisions, misunderstanding and conflict, or relatively minor differences in lifestyle and mutual suspicion borne out of the newness of the relationship. The British expertise in community cohesion has rapidly developed over the last five years or so and around one hundred local authorities now have dedicated community cohesion officers, or teams, and have produced community cohesion strategies and plans. Nearly all of these plans will be accompanied by a performance framework. This developing practice will be considered below, together with the potential links to the much more difficult interethnic and inter-faith conflicts, some of which have been subject to attempts at 'forgiveness and reconciliation' work, in different parts of the world.

Measures to promote equality and prevent discrimination

The human race has had many thousands of years to think up ways in which it can divide itself and for one group to create the most spurious of grounds to achieve superior economic and social position over another group. These include grounds of nationality, ethnicity, faith, age, gender, sexual orientation, health and disability. When viewed historically, some of these divisions now appear ludicrous – did we really believe that women were not capable of using a vote only 80 years ago; and was the Eugenics movement respectable only 60 years ago? Were landlords really allowed to display 'no blacks, no dogs' signs, only 40 years ago? Whilst remnants of these divisions, of course, still continue, and many new ones are being devised, perhaps we can anticipate a time when rationality and reason overcomes ignorance and prejudice.

One glance at the unevenness of life chances across the world, however, will soon dispel any sense of complacency: 1,200 million live on less than $1 per day; 828 million go to bed hungry; 114 million children of primary school age are not in school; and 11 million children die each year of preventable causes (UNDP, 2004, p. 30). The inequalities within modern democratic nations are rarely quite so acute but our notion of the 'worth' of others will inevitably be shaped by the inequalities on our television screens and in our newspapers. And as has already been noted, cohesion is difficult, if not impossible, to achieve where one or more sections of a society are so relatively disadvantaged that they are unlikely to be convinced that they are valued in that society, and nor will they have any real stake in it.

Many modern democracies, such as the UK, have well established, if not wholly effective, programmes for tackling inequalities, and the history of some of these were discussed in Chapter 2. They are integral to the community cohesion agenda and must be developed and implemented contemporaneously. The key equality measures, which might be expected to form part of the overall community cohesion agenda, are summarised below.

- *Anti-discrimination measures* – based on legislation stretching back over 40 years, largely in respect of race, to prevent discrimination in respect of employment, housing and other services. Gradually extended by a tougher regulatory regime and in scope to gender, age, sexual orientation and disability – though measures are not on a comprehensive basis and not yet applicable in all circumstances. For example, protection against discrimination on religious grounds is presently limited to employment and training.
- *Prohibition of incitement to racial hatred* – also based on legislation, it has had some effect on controlling the advocates of conflict and violence, particularly by the extreme right. However, their activities have become more covert and, possibly, as a result, more difficult to openly discuss and defeat by rational argument. In addition, their targets have changed to enable them to get round the law, for example, by targeting Muslims on a faith basis, rather than Asian or ethnic minority people on the basis of their ethnicity or race.
- *Ethnicity monitoring* – access to goods and services, and to employment, is monitored by ethnicity (and also by gender, disability and other measures) to provide a means of checking whether services are provided, or applicants are attracted for employment, on a proportionate basis and whether the outcomes in each case have any particular bias. This practice is now widespread in the public and voluntary sectors and with a considerable take-up by private employers, particularly larger organisations, and is probably the only effective means by which a charge of discrimination can be effectively countered.

- *Equality targets* – have been developed as a management tool, in association with ethnicity monitoring, for example, in respect of social housing allocations and recruitment and selection for employment. The targets usually compare the application and success rates for each group in relation to applicants overall. So, if a town or city comprised people of different ethnic origins; 85 per cent white, 3 per cent Irish, 4 per cent African-Caribbean, 5 per cent Pakistani, 2 per cent Indian and 1 per cent other; and by gender 51 per cent female, 49 per cent male; with a further 12 per cent considered to have a disability, targets might be established to attract applicants in a similar proportion, with the success rate monitored on the same basis. The targets are generally refined to take account of age and need profiles, rather than their proportion the population as a whole. Many organisations have also developed more sophisticated targets to focus on qualitative aspects, such as the number of disadvantaged groups represented in their managerial positions and whether disadvantaged groups are more likely to be offered poorer quality housing.
- *Positive action measures* – these include a wide variety of measures which are designed to equip members of disadvantaged groups with the skills to compete on an equal basis for employment, social housing and in other areas, and have been used to support equality targets. At the most limited level, they may include ensuring that the advertisements for jobs are placed in areas where under-represented groups are more likely to see them and in ways that they can relate to them, for example, by using images of those same groups in the advertisements. However, the measures may also include more interventionist actions, such as the provision of training for underrepresented groups to give them the skills required to apply for jobs on an equal basis. More generally, measures have also been used to develop the confidence of under-represented groups to apply for representative positions, such as school governors and councillors.
- *Positive discrimination* – this is generally unlawful in countries like Britain, although there are some very limited exceptions, for example, where a 'genuine occupational requirement' can be demonstrated. This could include stipulating that a fashion model should be male, where male clothing is to be modelled. These are very minor provisions, though not without precedent – it is often forgotten that employment quotas were introduced after the First World War in respect of disabled servicemen. Other nations, most notably the United States, have had 'affirmative action' where discrimination is allowed in order to ensure that people from disadvantaged groups can meet certain quotas. Positive discrimination and positive action are often confused and sometimes deliberately so in order to make a political point. However, any form of action targeted at one group, rather than at others, is in one sense discriminatory and is often seen as 'special treatment' even if it is only intended to create a more level playing field for all groups to participate.

- *Processes to prevent indirect or institutional discrimination* – this recognises that overt direct discrimination has become increasingly rare. The Macpherson Report of 1999, following the death of a black teenager, Stephen Lawrence, in Eltham, London, created a renewed emphasis on the ways in which organisations could create rules, processes and ways of working, both at a formal and informal level, which would effectively prevent discrimination against a particular group. One of the more common measures adopted by employers, for example, has been to remove higher levels of language skills from job requirements, where they are unnecessary to perform the duties associated with that role. Institutional barriers can, of course, also disadvantage people on the basis of their gender, faith, disability, sexual orientation and age, as much as on grounds of race and ethnicity. A common measure to promote more equal opportunities for women to work, for example, has been to restructure working hours and to introduce workplace nurseries.
- *Awareness training* – generally aimed at employers and decision takers to ensure that they are fully aware of the different needs, customs and practices of other groups, so that they are better able to both avoid inadvertent discrimination and take appropriate positive action measures. This has also included some attempts to persuade people to come to recognise their prejudices, sometimes in very challenging and confrontational sessions, though these techniques are now generally out of favour. Newer style 'diversity training' is much more widely based on all aspects of difference, is less focussed on race and consequently has a much more inclusive approach. It is often a formal requirement in respect of participation in a number of processes such as recruitment and selection for employment.
- *The role of public sector agencies* – measures have been introduced to ensure that public sector agencies operate in a proactive manner. For example, local authorities were given a duty under section 71 of the Race Relations Act 1976 to promote equality of opportunity between persons of different racial groups. The extent to which these duties have been taken up has varied enormously, but many did attempt to improve communications with minority groups by translating documents, setting up special forums and by providing resources to representative voluntary bodies for those groups. Central Government has also developed many special initiatives, often delivered through local government and other agencies, to direct resources to those areas with concentrations of disadvantaged ethnic minorities. Resources have been distributed in various ways since the Urban Programme in the 1960s, and from many different guises of 'inner area programmes' – including responses to race riots at various times – to less obviously targeted programmes of 'City Challenge' and regeneration initiatives in the 1990s. This was supplemented by schemes set up to help local agencies to meet the educational and social welfare needs of ethnic

minorities, largely emanating from Section 11 of the Local Government Act 1966. These measures were significantly strengthened by the Race Relations (Amendment) Act 2000, which developed the 'general duty' to promote racial equality to a wide range of public authorities, backed by a 'specific duty' with regard to their own functions and action planning.

One of the unfortunate, but understandable, effects of the equalities agenda has been the way in which differences and separate identities have been instrumentalised, through statutory and voluntary sector programmes. These programmes respond to 'difference' by attempting to build the capacity of a particular group, or more specifically, their leaders and then make good comparative deficits in social and economic performance. Whilst the focus on disadvantage can be justified, the separate programmes tend to undermine the possibilities for building a shared identity and common cause has tended to be neglected.

However, the equalities agenda is of crucial importance to community cohesion in many different respects. The moral case for individuals to be treated equally, without reference to some spurious categorisation of their worth, should clearly drive the agenda. From a wider community perspective, any identifiable group which is discriminated against is likely to become disaffected and threaten the solidarity of that society. Further, discrimination will lead to separation and segregation of different communities, reducing the possibility of day to day contact and the development of mutual trust and understanding. So, for example, if different communities have some semblance of equal representation in council chambers, trade unions, the criminal justice system, chambers of commerce and all of the principal institutions and associations, then not only is the principle of fairness seen to be upheld, but the opportunities for cross-cultural contact and understanding are also greatly enhanced.

A common vision and sense of belonging

There are several interrelated aspects of the community cohesion agenda (see Figure 2.1 for the formal definition). These include the creation of a common vision and sense of belonging, positively valuing the diversity of people's backgrounds, creating similar life opportunities and developing strong cross-cultural contact and engagement. The equalities agenda, or 'similar life opportunities' has already been discussed and the other components are considered below. However, all of the different components are interrelated and the creation of similar life opportunities is central to them all.

Programmes to develop a common vision are now becoming more widely adopted by local authorities and their partners and these have moved beyond the rather limited attempts to counter the negative views of multiculturalism and have begun to promote a meaningful expression of common interest.

As discussed in earlier chapters, the establishment of 'over-arching' goals or 'core values' is crucially important and can transcend cultural differences, foster political identity and create a union or bond between disparate interests. This can be achieved by the production of very worthy and 'wordy' statements, but can also be presented more imaginatively through visual imagery, celebratory events and symbolic acts.

At a national level, some nation states have made more progress than others, at least in terms of trying to create an acceptance of diversity as a positive attribute. For example, Canada, like some other newly constructed nations, has had to focus much more on nation building and has invested in its programme of 'We All Belong to Canada'. The way in which this is presented – emphasising multiculturalism, together with the clear set of values and pride associated with Canadian citizenship (Ministry of Public Works and Government Services Canada, 2001), is certainly suggestive of a clear sense of direction and common purpose, though that does not necessarily mean universal acceptance of that approach. Scotland has developed a public awareness type campaign under the slogan of 'One Scotland, Many Cultures' which is designed to try to help the host community to be more comfortable with higher levels of inward migration.

Across Europe whilst some political support for multiculturalism and the acceptance of diversity more generally, has been evident, there has been little by way of an active campaign to engage all sections of the community in developing a common vision. However, the community cohesion programmes in many local areas are now beginning to address this more directly (a number of these are mentioned below).

Some countries remain in denial about the evident nature of their multiculturalism and the support for the extreme right who continue to argue for an end to immigration, or even repatriation, dominate the debate. Given, that in some European countries, the extreme right can attract over 20 per cent of the popular vote, some politicians may shy away from open support for anti-racist and pro-multicultural policies, for fear of becoming unelectable. The political sensitivities are also evident in Britain where the call for, and government agreement to, a widespread public debate to establish clear and progressive values in 2001 (Cantle, 2001; Denham, 2001) has not yet been taken up, for fear of giving a platform to those intent on 'fuelling prejudice against black and minority ethnic communities' (Home Office, 2004, p. 18). There are now signs that this particular nettle is about to be grasped (SoSJLC, 2007).

This may, however, also reflect the personal ambivalence of some politicians towards multiculturalism, across the political spectrum and whilst some have been prepared to defend anti-discrimination measures, far fewer have actively campaigned to recognise and promote the reality of multiculturalism. This may reflect electoral realities, or their own prejudices. It may also demonstrate, however, that community cohesion places new demands upon their role and that, as yet, few political leaders see it as their function to actively engage with different communities of interest, develop a longer-term vision of the future, seek to create a consensus on the basis of agreed over-arching values and areas of retained differences. The nature of the societal change may have changed faster than the ability of political leaders to cope with it (and, also in wider terms, as evidenced by declining electoral activity and disenchantment with the political parties that reflect outdated class and other societal divisions). Multicultural societies can cut across many of the established political boundaries and redefine them in ever reducing periods of time. Whereas, it may have been assumed, only 50 years or so ago, that political ideologies and national and political identities would change very slowly, from one generation to another and by degrees, modern communications are global, with many more competing ideas and cultural and other affiliations forming and re-forming on a continual basis.

The same political ambivalence and difficulties has been found at a local level:

A significant component of the breakdown of community cohesion appears to be the extent to which a clear and consistent message has been evident from the principal political and community leaders, at a local level over a substantial period of time. In our view the lack of leadership in some areas has undoubtedly led to the growth of racist and extremist groups.

and

We have seen examples of a clear determination to tackle racism and discrimination at the highest level, right down to ensuring that racist graffiti is immediately removed from every area. Leadership has, therefore, to pervade every level of each organisation ... should underpin community plans, regeneration and other key strategies, as well as policies for education, policing and service delivery and must be constantly updated to keep abreast of changing needs. (Cantle, 2001, p. 21)

The various reports into the riots in northern English towns in 2001 all highlighted the lack of a clear vision. For example, Ritchie (2001, p. 14) referred to the 'lack of strategic direction and a vision for the way Oldham should develop'. Ouseley (2001) in the foreword to his report on Bradford (commissioned prior to the riots in 2001) drew attention to the need for 'leadership to promote and carry forward the mission, vision and values'. The Local Government Association (LGA), the commission for Racial Equality (CRE) and two government departments, subsequently published guidance (LGA *et al.*, 2002, p. 13) which urged political leaders 'to develop a vision of the type of place that their constituents want their locality to be' noting that 'people moving towards a commonly agreed goal are more likely to interact, understand and value differences positively'. The very process of creating a vision can also have another beneficial effect in that, if it is done on the basis of participation and interaction of people from different backgrounds, it helps to reinforce the membership of the political entity which the nation state, or local state, can provide, irrespective of cultural affiliation and identity.

The LGA Guidance (ibid.) went on to propose a series of further components of the vision which could be developed at a local level, including creating pride in the local area, welcoming newcomers, tackling deprivation and disaffection and working across cultures to ask 'what each community can do for others as well as what others can do for them'. This begins to move the concept of vision-making forward to the point where, rather than focussing on differences and past conflicts, there is an attempt to build common agreement about the future nature of society. The priorities which people from disparate groups have are often very much the same – a safe and secure area free from crime, an attractive and clean environment and good prospects in education and employment – and the revelation that people actually share common aspirations, may well be a turning point in community relations.

Since 2001, a number of local authority areas have constructed rudimentary vision statements, often as a result of wide-ranging consultation exercises. In addition, these vision statements have explicitly cut across political party lines and made it clear that the support of one community will not be sought by appearing to criticise or disfavour another. For example, the London Borough of Hounslow's *Vision and Political Leadership – Statement of Commitment* states:

> We will not, in our campaigning materials or in our dealings with constituents and other members of the community, seek to create or exacerbate divisions between different groups within the community. (London Borough of Hounslow, 2003)

The Statement was signed by Conservative, Labour and Liberal Democrat politicians. Many similar protocols have been agreed upon by a range of local authorities in England, assisted by a draft protocol in template form, in circulation on an informal basis, by representative local government organisations and has been presented in popular terms as agreement 'not to play the race card'.

The City of Stoke on Trent used the government's £6 million 'Pathfinder' programme, which was set up to explore new 'cutting edge' policies to promote community cohesion and to develop a 'charter' for a range of local agencies to sign up to (Home Office and Vantagepoint, 2003). The government's Beacon Council Scheme, which was established in 1999 to allow local government to learn from the best practice of other authorities, was also used subsequently as a means of emphasising the importance to cohesion of clear vision and committed leadership. Councils, such as Leicester, Rochdale and the London Boroughs of Barnet and Tower Hamlets all developed such approaches and were awarded 'Beacon' status as a result (ODPM and IDeA, 2003).

In many areas, the leaders of the wider community have also been a party to agreements and, significantly, many inter-faith organisations have drawn up similar protocols in which they aim to promote a sense of belonging for people of all faiths and backgrounds, tackle discrimination and inequality, promote pride in and commitment to the local area – as well as seeking to develop unity rather than exacerbate divisions. Some local areas have taken a more public and campaigning role. For example, Blackburn with Darwen Council has promoted a 'belonging' message, using bus and poster advertising to feature people of different backgrounds who all 'belong to Blackburn'. The 'belonging' message has also been used as a means of providing reassurance and to bring the community together following an incident or extremist violence which might otherwise lead to reprisals against a section of the community who are blamed for what is thought to have been carried out in their name. For example, after the London bombings in 2005, the Greater London Authority developed a highly visible, but quite subtle campaign on the basis of 'Seven Million Londoners; One London' which has been developed into a more broad ranging 'One London' campaign, supported by a range of public and private sector partners and proudly featuring the multicultural nature of the city. Similarly, the London Borough of Waltham Forest developed '225,000 people – One Community' following the arrest of alleged Muslim extremists in the Borough in 2006.

Local authorities are required to prepare plans and respond to many initiatives on a wide range of issues. There is a danger, that despite broad political commitments (which in any event will only apply in areas intent on best practice), community cohesion will be seen as a separate initiative and not part of a coherent and integrated strategy for the area. Authorities have therefore been urged to develop cohesion on an integrated basis as part of the overall community plan and related to statutory equality programmes:

> Leadership and ownership needs to be backed up by action and we believe that each area should now develop a Community Cohesion Strategy, as a significant component of the Community Plan. Indeed, we would expect this to be part of a more broadly based vision for the area which, on the one hand, challenged the negative and, sometimes racist, views whenever expressed and, on the other, promoted a positive and supportive approach to diversity (for local authorities this could also be a means of discharging their new duty under the Race Relations (Amendment) Act 2000). The strategy will need to be based upon a comprehensive mapping

of community needs and provide a means of addressing them with specific and over-arching strategies. (Cantle, 2001, p. 21)

A new vision is beginning to emerge in some local areas, though a clear set of national over-arching values, which are capable of shaping and constraining behaviour is still some way off. True, the vision statements usefully talk about a sense of belonging, tackling discrimination and inequality and valuing diversity, but the everyday differences that divide people of different faiths, cultures and ethnicities are still evident. At one level, differences seem to have become tolerated or even welcomed, over time. For example, the wearing of traditional costumes and religious dress and symbols, such as skullcaps, turbans and headscarves are generally supported. There is less clarity about support for other differences, for example, in respect of arranged marriages (as distinct from forced marriages) and the choosing of marriage partners from heritage countries rather than from the indigenous heritage communities. There has been little attempt to codify these values and the rights and responsibilities that stem from them and they remain at a level of generality and ambiguity, which defies proper debate and consensus building.

As suggested earlier, however, national cohesiveness may depend as much, if not more, upon the development of a forward looking *vision* or set of over-arching goals, which transcend ethnic, faith and cultural divisions. Wider debate and agreement, about common aims, such as the protection of the environment and guarding against climate change may be more powerful unifiers, than cultural divisions. – if they can be shared and jointly owned. *Vision* should not, therefore, be simply seen as an ephemeral concept to promote inter-cultural relations, but rather as a means of transcending them and through dialogue and debate to establish goals, which are shared within a broader political identity.

In the absence of informed and open national debate, a heavy responsibility falls upon local political and community leaders. They must be prepared to promote a positive vision of diversity and attempt to tackle prejudice and intolerance whenever it emerges at a community level. Leaders have also been urged to develop a programme of myth busting to counter the traditional stereotypes which often lead to the demonising of minority communities (LGA *et al.*, 2002). This requires a proactive approach, working with a wide range of partners, using existing channels, such as the youth service and parish councils to challenge negative views and to promote more positive ones and to try to get the press and media on side to help with this endeavour. The ability to work in this way is not necessarily part of the traditional skill set of politicians, and some may feel that they have no political interest in building bridges between communities when they can profit electorally from divisions between groups.

Politicians and the local government officials and civil servants that support them, also receive little or no training in the nature and engagement of their communities. The qualities required to be selected by a political party and elected by the electorate are not necessarily those required to build community cohesion. *The Councillor's Guide 2003/4*, published by the Improvement and Development Agency for Local Government (IDeA) in 2003 urged councillors to make the links, between local authorities' community leadership role, enshrined by the Local Government Act 2000 and community cohesion. The IDeA believes that 'councillors have a key role to play in building cohesive communities at ward level' and helping to 'address conflicts and misunderstandings between different groups within a local community'. The IDeA offers training programmes to fill the gaps in knowledge and skills, but there is no compulsion and take-up is inevitably patchy.

The leadership role is, of course, in no way confined to politicians and there are a wide range of community leaders in responsible positions in the statutory and voluntary sectors, from business and education and faith institutions. The plethora of partnerships in all local areas means that a much wider range of people have the potential – and the responsibility – to influence local attitudes and values. This is particularly crucial in the way that they take decisions about priorities and communicate those decisions, ensuring that they are focussed on needs and not offering unfair advantage to any one section of the community. Not surprisingly therefore, training across this spectrum has been suggested. However, a more specific issue was also raised in the Ouseley and Cantle reports of 2001 – that of probity. Ouseley (2001, p. 10) referred to the culture of doing deals between 'establishment key people' and the various self-styled community leaders to retain power and 'maintain the segregated status quo'. Cantle (2001, p. 23) also suggested the need 'to address concerns such as "sweetheart deals" and back-home politics, in which votes were solicited by political parties in return for community projects, irrespective of genuine need'. Vidal-Hall (2003, p. 140) referred to the 'bribery' of different BME groups in Leicester's early multicultural days, something that could be applied to more recent experience in other cities.

This gives rise to a more general concern about the nature and role of community leaders, who often hold quite powerful positions, with the seeming ability to garner support for a political party or a particular project without any real debate or challenge within their community. This is due, in some cases at least, to the deference given to leaders of some communities, for example through the *biraderi* system in the Pakistani community, but is also due to the way that some statutory agencies have found it expedient to confer such power and status on certain individuals as a way of creating power blocks which can be more easily harnessed. In this way, some community leaders adopt a 'gatekeeper' model of leadership in which all decisions are filtered though them, they control the finances for the group and generally impart little information, preferring to keep their communities in a dependency relationship. This can be contrasted with a 'gateway' style of community leadership, in which the leader does his or her best to empower the community, provide information, devolve power and influence and has an open and democratic style. Generally, communal politics goes hand in hand with the 'gatekeeper' model, helping to keep the leader in their position of power and making it easier for statutory authorities to appear to discharge their responsibility to consult and engage with the community.

In a different context – inter-ethnic conflict in India – Varshney (2002, p. 37) refers to the more general problem of politicians who cannot obtain power without appealing to one group at the expense of another. He supports the view that political systems should have a structure which prevents political parties from winning power unless they can make appeals across ethnic boundaries.

The same point has been made with regard to Northern Ireland:

> As Northern Ireland can testify, a culture of blame appears to make community cohesion difficult, if not impossible, to achieve. Local and national political leadership is a very important element in developing a shared vision that can translate into a shared and peaceful society. If politics is presented as a 'zero-sum game' – if their side wins, our side loses – then the scenario of a diverse and tolerant environment in which everyone wins becomes unachievable. There needs not only to be voices speaking out in favour of intercultural dialogue and living, but also there needs to be a picture painted in the public mind of how this will be. In the absence of such a vision, it becomes all too easy to paint the pictures of resentment, unfair shares and claim and counter-claim by those who would exploit division and difference. In Northern Ireland, there is no consensus on cultural pluralism or what a shared society would look like. The latest Northern Ireland, Life and Times Survey data show that numbers of people believing that relationships between Protestants and Catholics are better now than five years ago have fallen from almost 60% in 1995 to below 30% in 2001. (Northern Ireland Council for Voluntary Action (NICVA), (2004), ev 200)

The social and economic conditions of the whole community and the various sections of it, is also a key consideration. Whilst, it may be possible to construct a vision of the future which embraces all groups, it seems unlikely that it will be sustained, unless those groups really believe that they will have an equal stake in its future and that their deprivation and disadvantage will be relieved in some way. Nevertheless, the power of a common vision, as a unifying force, should not be underestimated. In Northern Ireland, in many ways a hopelessly divided society, NICVA felt able to assert that:

> it is naïve to think that economic solutions, full employment or a better environment is the whole solution. The first step in creating a cohesive

community is to build an agreed vision that a community or a wider society can and must be shared by those who inhabit it. (Ibid., ev 199)

This may be a false dichotomy, however, as any meaningful vision would indicate how the needs and aspirations of all groups would be accommodated in future arrangements.

The ability to build and develop a common vision and set of values on a national or local level is, therefore, inevitably constrained by structural and practical issues, as well as relying on an understanding of how such messages will resonate with the local community. However, this work should not proceed in isolation from the other elements of the community cohesion programme and would be part of an ongoing and dynamic process, in which all sections of the community should be engaged and in which new challenges will almost always be evident.

Valuing diversity

The second principle of the definition of community cohesion is that the 'diversity of people's backgrounds and circumstances are appreciated and positively valued'. This should be taken at two levels, first, it stems directly from the common vision which necessarily depends upon the building of an inclusive society and is an expression of the need for much more openness in which the fear of difference is minimised and relationships with new cultures and different backgrounds are seen to be an opportunity, rather than a threat. But how do we encourage people to seek out new experiences and to explore wider horizons, rather than to remain within their own comfort zones? Some cultures are more inward looking than others, more hostile to foreigners and internal deviance from cultural norms. There is, presently, little by way of monitoring and measurement of the tolerance and respect of others and the propensity to welcome, or resist, difference. This is an area where the community cohesion agenda remains to be developed and the significance of societal openness to change, in cultural terms at least, is yet to be understood.

It is possible to contend, however, that the extent to which societies are divided and segregated by faith, ethnicity, class, caste and other factors, is to some degree, an expression of their ability to adapt and to integrate cultural and subcultural differences and that this is partly the result of the lack of contact and continuing separation and insularity of different groups. It is also possible to approach this problem from a second level, through localised and shared activities and experiences. Many towns and cities now have programmes to 'celebrate diversity', with civic backing for different religious and cultural festivals, awards for successful minority businesses, the use of multicultural images on websites and posters to promote the area and the development of specialist ethnic minority music and artistic events – all with the intent of creating a positive view of diversity and the contribution that it can make to the local area. However, some of the celebratory events are only designed for the purposes of boosting the confidence of the particular community and, perhaps, reinforcing their traditions, history and culture, rather than reaching a wider audience. For example, a 'Black History Week' may have a limited appeal to people from other than a black heritage and be simply seen as a means of reinforcing and celebrating black culture. With relatively minor changes, it could also be designed to attain a wider appreciation and understanding. Many local authorities are now trying to broaden the appeal of their carnivals and celebrations. The Notting Hill Carnival has attracted support and interest from a wide range of communities over many years, whilst others like Middlesbrough have just developed their first 'getting to know you' event in 2007 and brought together people of different faiths, cultures and backgrounds through music, food and dance (Middlesbrough BME Network, 2007).

Introducing people to new experiences in non-threatening environment and trying to make it a pleasant and exciting encounter will, it is hoped, have a positive effect and generally encourage people to engage with new experiences and different cultures. This also encourages the idea that 'difference' is something to be regarded as interesting and worth exploring, rather than recoiling from out of fear and apprehension. Further, activities that help people to reflect on their own experiences and develop experiential learning are more likely to have a lasting impact than presenting generalised information about racism and multiculturalism (Lemos, 2004a, p. 57).

There has also been a tendency in the past, to criticise, or even condemn as 'racist', people who had little experience of difference and, as a result of this ignorance, were apt to show their apprehension or even make ill-informed and prejudiced remarks. There is, of course, always a need to be vigilant and speak out against committed racists, but in order to value diversity, we first have to ensure that everyone really does have the opportunity to meet with, and learn about, others in non-threatening and interesting environments. The concept of valuing diversity has to be owned and promoted at all levels. Perhaps the most obvious starting point is in schools and the new focus on 'diversity in the curriculum' (Ajegbo, 2007) and the new 'duty to promote community cohesion' in all schools as from September 2007 (DCSF, 2007) will certainly help that educative process to develop. However, it needs to be supported at a community level, in the workplace and in the media and other communications. Employers perhaps, have been slow to support the moral case, but have also generally not recognised the business case for widening their labour market and broadening their expertise so that they are better able to interact with customers and understand their needs.

Cross-cultural contact

One of the principal tenets of community cohesion is that 'strong and positive relationships are being developed between people from different backgrounds in the workplace, in schools and within neighbourhoods' and that
the 'diversity of people's backgrounds are appreciated and valued' (LGA
et al., 2002). This approach was proposed as a means of countering the
growth of 'parallel lives' in which there was no contact between different
groups and a real ignorance and lack of understanding between them.
Moreover, the ignorance was easily exploited by racists and extremists who
were then able to spread false information, develop myths and demonise
minority communities. The terminology employed by community cohesion, however, implies more than the avoidance of conflict, and suggests
more supportive and active engagement of people and the development of
helpful and co-operative interaction. (The concepts of *parallel lives*, segregation and separateness was discussed in Chapter 3.)

Parallel lives are hard to break down and it will take some time for communities to establish *positive relationships* where there has been no contact
with each other at any meaningful level in the past. The concept of parallel
lives was born out of experience in the northern English towns where the
2001 riots took place, but its more general applicability is now being recognised and is applied to relationships between communities in many parts of
the country. Whilst there are many towns and cities which do not have a
high level of physical and geographic segregation, there are many areas and
pockets within them that are very much dominated by one community or
another, and where meaningful contact is extremely limited. Further, whilst
the spatial segregation may be less acute, parallel lives can still be evident
because of separation in other ways – for example, in education, employment, faith, and in cultural and leisure pursuits. Apparently mixed communities may therefore offer very little in terms of meaningful interaction, in
which fears and prejudice are broken down and positive relationships, based
on mutual trust and tolerance, are developed.

There is also a tendency to assume that the principal difficulties are
between white and minority communities. Whilst this is often a common
factor, there are some very long-standing tensions between sections of the
minority communities themselves, and communal tensions in the British
Asian communities are also apparently on the rise (Kundnami, 2002) – the
'fear of difference' is not confined to the white community. Similarly, the
white community can also be just as easily divided, as in Northern Ireland:

> People separate out at different times. Particularly in 1968 and 1969 there
> was a big movement of people … . There are areas which are predomi-
> nantly Catholic and predominantly Protestant and it is easy to grow up in

those areas and not really know the other side; certainly if you are below 40. What happens is that the community organisations will come forward and they will be almost exclusively one side or another, simply by the area that they are in. ... . We have a system of faith schools, which has failed entirely to promote any form of social cohesion. We have almost entirely separate housing. Our workplaces have become increasingly seg-regated, so it is impossible to meet in neutral venues and to live any kind of lives which are integrated in any way. (McCandless, 2004)

The 'fear of difference' is also not limited to race and faith and plays a part in inter-generational conflict, hostility to the gay and lesbian people and to those who suffer from mental illness and physical disability. The 'does he take sugar?' syndrome illustrates how unwilling individuals can be to inter-act with others that they have limited, or no, knowledge about – and how inappropriate that interaction might be. The breaking down of stereotypical views is key to the change required, as illustrated in respect of elderly people:

> Another barrier can be the stereotypical view of older people that sees them as passive members of the community in need of services and sup-port, rather than as active members who contribute to their communities and, given the opportunity, might choose to do more. ... older people can be the 'glue' in the community. Projects that bring older and younger people together can be particularly beneficial in breaking down barriers and mistrust. Age Concern has been involved in a number of projects that do this. For example, 'LifeLink' projects set up in North Shields to combat the fear of crime within communities by bringing together social groups who mistrust each other. (Age Concern, 2004, ev 195)

The hostility to various 'care in the community' projects over the years also illustrates the way in which both adults and children who are different, or 'special', in some way can easily be demonised, simply because their charac-teristics – and their 'normality' – are unknown to most people. The integra-tion of children with special needs into mainstream schools has, more than many other initiatives, helped to break down the irrational fears of others and to promote understanding and tolerance. However, as in cross-cultural contact, there are some essential *ground rules* to be followed and some pitfalls to be avoided, if such contact is to be successful.

Cross-cultural contact takes a number of different forms and the process will also depend upon the local context. The 'science' of cross-cultural con-tact is, however, only now developing. The guidance issued to local authori-ties in 2002 (LGA *et al.*, 2002) is of a general nature, such as 'use the networks of statutory and voluntary agencies to develop cross-cultural contact at all levels' or phrased in the form of questions, such as 'do youth activities help to build understanding and tolerance between different groups?' Gradually the practice of community cohesion in this area is being developed, the vast majority of which is apparently having positive results.

A body of international practice and experience is also beginning to emerge which is based on cross-cultural contact, often as a response to violent conflicts between different ethnic and faith communities. Varshney (2002), for example, in his study of *Ethnic Conflict and Civic Life* has usefully distinguished 'associational' and 'everyday' forms of cross-cultural engagements. The former, he suggests are formed in organisational settings as part of civic life, whereas the latter requires no organisation and occurs at an individual level. His study also suggested that associational engagement was 'a sturdier bulwark of peace' than everyday contact. Civic networks were a precondition for associational engagement, not only because of the communication that they created between members of the different religious communities, but also because of the shared interests in business, cultural and other activities. Varshney suggests that in rural settings, the everyday form of contact would be likely to be sufficient to maintain contact between groups, whereas in an urban setting strong associational forms would be required.

In support of his argument, Varshney seeks to explain why the conflict between Hindus and Muslims was highly localised, despite similar social and economic conditions and proportions of each group, for example, between the cities of Aligarh and Calicut, and points out that:

> though not anticipated when the project began, the pre-existing local networks of civic engagement between the two communities stand out as the single most important *proximate* cause (his italics). Where such networks of engagement exist, tensions and conflicts were regulated and managed; where they are missing, communal identities led to endemic and ghastly violence ... (and the pre-existence of) civic networks often make neighbourhood-level peace possible. Routine engagement allows people to come together and form temporary organisations in times of tension. Such organisations ... turned out to be highly significant ... these organisations policed neighbourhoods, killed rumours, provided information to the local administration and facilitated communication. ... sustained prior interaction or cordiality allowed appropriate crisis managing organisations to emerge. (Varshney, 2002, p. 9)

Varshney also turns his attention to Northern Ireland and suggests that certain communities, such as Dunville, have remained peaceful, in contrast to other areas, like Kileen/Banduff and Upper Ashbourne Estates, because of the civic interconnections between Protestant and Catholic communities, which did not exist in the latter areas. He also suggests that attempts at 'instrumentalism' where political elites have used faith and ethnic divisions for political purposes has been thwarted by the 'winning coalitions' which refuse their divisive overtures. To understand ethnic violence and conflict, therefore, Varshney believes it is essential to analyse regional and local factors, rather than follow a traditional approach of enquiry along national and global lines.

Varshney's distinction of 'associational' and 'everyday' forms of cross-cultural contact is very helpful. However, still further distinctions might usefully be made. Associational forms may be divided into those that are created by networks of single identity groups and those that are integrated. In Western democracies, most civic bodies will be constitutionally integrated, for example, local councils, will have representatives from each area who serve on an equal basis. Other forms of association, most notably faith groups, are constructed on an exclusive basis, but may be networked by 'umbrella' bodies such as inter-faith organisations. Everyday, or social, forms of cross-cultural contact may be thought of in terms of incidental contact where it occurs naturally without any organisation and also in communal settings which do not constitute part of civic life, for example, through arts, music and sporting arrangements. Further, cross-cultural contact also has to be thought of on a structural level, where the form of provision and market conditions, for housing, education and employment, shape the nature of cross-cultural engagement.

Cross-cultural contact and engagement might therefore be developed in at least five separate ways – see Table 6.1.

Table 6.1   Forms of cross-cultural contact and engagement

Associational

Intra-associational – integrated and multiple identity
   Associations are open to people of different backgrounds and facilitate interchange and co-operation within the organisation
Inter-associational – networked single identity bodies
   Associations represent separate and distinct interests on an exclusive and single identity basis, with associations formed by networks of separate bodies

Social

Social Incidental – arising from everyday activity
   Interaction by individuals meeting through shopping, travelling or leisure activities, at an individual level, without organisation
Social Organisational – arising from planned and organised activity
   Interaction by participating in sporting, music, drama and arts, which involves group activities, generally organised through clubs and societies.

Structural

Structural Cross-cultural Contact
   This will depend upon the extent to which schools and housing are segregated, employment opportunities are linked to particular groups and market factors create divisions, which militate against cross-cultural engagement

---

In practice, many of these forms of engagement will overlap and be, in part at least, interdependent. For example, a common form of 'social incidental' contact is through parents meeting at the school gate when collecting their children. However, if the housing estates are segregated, local school populations will also generally be monocultural and parental engagement will be on the same basis. In turn, this may also lead to monocultural inter-associational forms of civic engagement through single-identity school governors and ward councillors.

Intra-associational forms are where cross-cultural engagement develops naturally from the day to day co-operation – and disputes – that arise from any participative process. For example, in a local chamber of commerce business people of all backgrounds will share ideas and best practice, as well as agree on collective actions and make representations to statutory agencies on an ongoing basis. Similarly, in the local council chamber, politicians from different parties will establish budget priorities and agree on a range of local policies, and similar processes will be conducted in the governing bodies of schools, hospitals, colleges, police authorities and the like. In some areas the community is well represented by a range of people who reflect the diversity of the area that they serve. However, despite the apparent openness of these institutions, and that they are intended to be 'representative', they rarely achieve such a composition. In fact, most fail to either attract, or allow, anything like a true reflection of local society and most remain dominated by men rather than women, older people rather than the younger generation and the white host community rather than people from minorities.

Many attempts have been made to address the balance of representation in these institutions and as many are connected with governance of communities, they are clearly a priority for action. However, the measures to redress the imbalance have largely been developed because of the evident inequality and unfairness and to ensure that each section of the community is represented in the decision-making process. This is clearly an essential aim, but little thought has been given to the role that such bodies might play in building understanding and trust between each community and developing deeper links between communities at all levels. Renewed priority must therefore be given to positive action measures to encourage wider representation and to ensure that all representatives become 'gateways' to the wide range of interests – and diversity – within their communities.

However, the whole ethos of these institutions may need to change as there is an assumption that broadening the representation is sufficient in itself. This appears to be based, first, on the thesis that the white community is represented by the majority of committee members who are white, and that the white members will speak for the whole white community – and from a white perspective – whereas, the BME community members are invited to regard themselves as advocates for a particular section of the community. This generalisation will, of course, not be appropriate in all cases, but this view of the leadership role of BME leaders is stereotypical and marginalising and, further, has also led to an under-investment in white leadership and in some cases to an under-representation of poorer white communities, especially where institutional membership is aligned with social class and dominated by middle class interests.

Second, the BME representation is often on the basis of advocacy for BME groups as a whole and fails to recognise the differences and subtleties within and between them. Again, communication between the institutional leaders and the communities, and a 'gatekeeper' mentality is likely to be a problem. There is a much more general problem about what exactly a 'community leader' is and how representative he or she can really be. Ouseley (2001, p. 10), for example, noted that,

> so-called community leaders are self styled, in league with the establish-
> ment key people ... retain their power base by maintaining the segregated
> status quo ... people at street level are rarely told what is really going on
> by politicians or leaders.

Without wishing to repeat the point about the nature of community lead-ers and community leadership (see earlier discussion), the issue here is how the associational forms of cross-cultural contact assist, or inhibit, the development of communication which can help resolve conflicts and develop understanding between different groups. In other words, it is not sufficient that the institutional links are simply forged on the basis of 'rep-resentativeness' in general terms and thought must be given as to how these bodies develop links with each community so that genuine engage-ment takes place and communication within and between each commu-nity is facilitated.

Inter-associational forms are likely to have more difficulties. In this case, institutions are based upon a separation of interests, but networked through umbrella bodies. They often do little to encourage cross-cultural integration, as their primary purpose is to build a coalition of interests in order to become a more effective advocacy and lobbying group. As with intra-associational groups, the leaders of the separate bodies will have an opportunity to meet together and in so doing, develop an understanding of other cultural issues, but there is less chance that this will extend to meaningful relationships between the different groups at any other level.

It is ironic, that because many of the statutory agencies failed to accom-modate minority views and provide equal access, many separate interest groups were set up to develop special provision and have consequently allowed those institutions to continue in the same way as before – that is, without accommodating diverse interests. For example, to represent minor-ity business interests, chambers of commerce often have separate BME sec-tions within them, or independent bodies have been created. The same is often true of 'black environmental networks', black sections within political parties and trade unions and black-led housing associations. These may well have legitimacy from the point of view of representation, but they often institutionalise the lack of representation within mainstream services. Governance will require 're-engineering' to develop cross-cultural civic life but there seems to be a lack of clarity about how to develop into the mainstream, once the groups have been 'capacity built' and established themselves as sectional interests. Do black-led housing associations, for example, simply continue as separate bodies or seek to enter the mainstream movement from their new found position of strength and thereby change the mainstream institutions themselves? This debate has recently been revisited by the Commission on Integration and Cohesion, which believes that 'single group funding should be the exception rather than the rule' (CIC, 2007, p. 160). This recommendation has not been fully accepted by Government, but they have now agreed to prioritise creating interaction (Blears 2007).

The inter-associational model can, to a limited extent at least, foster the growth of cross-cultural development, where it is part of that group's objectives and activities. The Inter-Faith Network's *Directory of Inter Faith Organisations in the UK* (2004), for example, lists around 180 local groups and whilst many include amongst their activities the role of 'advising public bodies' or 'sending representatives to strategic meetings', most describe their main aims as to 'sustain good relations between religious and ethnic communities' (Milton Keynes) or their activities as 'multi faith dialogue ... promoting good community relations' (Peterborough). In other words, aiming to be both representative and building broad-based understanding within and between the communities served, is perfectly possible and more conducive to good community relations.

Associational engagement is not limited to government bodies, nor to the 'establishment' bodies, like faith organisations. Part of civic life is to be found in the hundreds of other non-governmental bodies, which are constituted on a voluntary basis and though they may not have any particular aim to promote community relations and are simply based upon a particular interest, they nevertheless, can draw people together, across boundaries, and facilitate cross-cultural understanding. Varshney (2002, p. 299) draws upon the work of Darby in Northern Ireland (1986) to suggest the beneficial effect of the Lions Clubs, Rotary Clubs and integrated clubs and societies in respect of many sporting activities as well as other social organisational forms (see below), like single-parent clubs, to explain the lack of inter-ethnic conflict in one area in contrast to others.

Similarly, Varshney (ibid.) highlights the work of Horowitz (1983) and Lieberson and Silverman (1965) who studied racial violence in the United States in the 1960s and suggests that the pre-existence of African-American integration in local associational structures is a possible explanation of the local variation in inter-ethnic conflict. Further, he points out that the Kerner

Commission, which investigated cities where riots took place in the 1960s only considered the factors in those cities and did not compare them with peaceful cities. To his knowledge, no study has yet taken place which could validate his view that 'civic associations – labour unions, churches, PTAs and so on – were on the whole racially better integrated in the peaceful cities'.

The review of the riots in the northern towns and cities of England in 2001 (Cantle, 2001) did compare those areas with other towns and cities elsewhere in the country that did not experience riots. The Review pointed to the differences in the extent of segregation, the lack of contact between the different ethnic groups and the variation in civic and political leadership, but it did not specifically draw out the ways in which either everyday, or associational, forms of cross-cultural contact had contributed to cohesiveness. This there fore tends to support the thesis that mutual trust can be established through cross-cultural contact but it remains an area to be fully evidenced.

Social incidental forms of cross-cultural contact are beginning to be quantified, generally under the ambit of 'social capital' and it is beginning to be easier to demonstrate the contribution that they make in breaking down barriers between communities and establishing mutual trust. For example, the London Borough of Camden (Khan and Muir, eds, 2006) produced *Sticking Together*, a report which examined social capital within their area. It is possible that without a particular stimulus, or engineered social contact, there will be no meaningful exchange between people of different backgrounds. This may especially be the case where they are preconceived notions by one group about 'others'. However, there is the potential at least for near neighbours to meet in the street, or in local shops, for parents to meet at the school gate, or for people to talk to each other when exercising, or walking the dog. There is some evidence to suggest that, in heavily segregated societies, or where divisions have been manifest this will not happen naturally, or will even be prevented. For example, in Oldham following the riots in 2001, a series of 'banal encounters' had to be engineered in order to allow different groups to engage for the first time. These banal encounters included:

- White women inviting Asian women to help them cook pancakes and the Asian women reciprocating with chapatti cookery lessons.
- Asian young people inviting a group of white youngsters to their community to see where they lived and how they relaxed. The white youngsters again reciprocated and brought the Asian youngsters to their estate.
- White primary schools twinned with BME schools with interaction facilitated by visits and other joint activities.

These may seem like rather basic measures, but in each case, it was the first time that the two groups had had any contact with the other and whilst very rewarding in the end, was controversial at the start and not without its problems. (The Asian young people and their white young hosts were stoned by white elders during the estate visit; and many parents refused to allow their children to participate in the twinning initially.)

Varshney (2002, p. 292), also supported what he called 'the utility of small steps' and gave details of two encounters between working class women from the Hindu and Muslim communities. In both Saharanpur and Ahmedabad, the contact between these working women had helped to keep the peace and stop communal violence in the neighbourhoods where such contact had been established.

There is a tendency, however, to focus upon those towns and cities where relationships between communities have broken down, or where violence has taken place. In fact, even in progressive multi-ethnic communities like the City of Leicester, considerable barriers between communities can exist and preclude incidental cross-cultural contact. In Leicester, they too have developed school twinning and other measures as a means of allowing communities to engage for the first time. The lack of knowledge of different communities, the absence of trust between people of different backgrounds also appears to be a much more general problem across modern multicultural societies as a whole. Certainly, the failure to interact with people from other communities, as evidenced by a recent public survey (CRE, 2004b) which indicated that 94 per cent of white people only had friends who were mostly, or all, from the white community, indicates a wider problem. Some of this can be attributable to the segregation, at different levels, within communities, but highlights that, even in apparently mixed communities, 'visual' contact does not guarantee any meaningful exchange.

In Northern Ireland, even social incidental contact has actually been prevented by the enmity and low-level violence between the two communities. For example, a new supermarket recently built between a Catholic and Protestant estate was used by Protestants and Catholics only for a short period of time before one community systematically harassed and intimidated the other to prevent 'mixed shopping'.

Social organisational forms may also require some from of external assistance to ensure that effective cross-cultural contact actually takes place. This again is highly variable, with, for example, many drama societies, sports clubs, orchestras, film societies and the like, having mixed membership – and will be a fertile ground for the development of cross-cultural friendships. However, many such groups are also formed on a single identity basis, partly for historic reasons, or because of cultural traditions, but may also have been more recently created specifically as a means of preserving a separate culture, or because people feel more comfortable and safe with such arrangements. Certainly, there are many such bodies which are mono-cultural in form and, as NICVA (2004, ev 200) and others have pointed out, some of the funding bodies have actually promoted and institutionalised separate development. This is often on the basis of building the capacity of a particular group, generally disadvantaged and under-represented, to enable them to move into more mainstream activities. Unfortunately, the ethos and funding of such groups have been maintained on a single identity basis with no further development initiated.

Sports clubs and facilities have also been singled out for criticism, for example, low levels of Asian participation in football has received attention. But many sports not only fail to attract a representative membership, but more importantly, they have also failed to even begin to develop representative coaching and management structures, or include minorities in the governance arrangements. Again, the response to these deficiencies has often been to set up separate structures, such as 'Asian football initiatives' to promote greater involvement, though often on a single identity, with a separate Asian football club or league, rather than integrated structures. Yet, sport often provides both a safe ground and a universal language in which the rules of the game are understood on the same basis across communities. This has been presented as *The Power of Sport* to develop community cohesion (iCoCo, 2006) and contains a number of case studies to promote integration and understanding through the medium of sport.

Structural arrangements are also crucial in promoting – or undermining – cross-cultural contact. Unless schools, housing estates and workplaces are mixed, cross-cultural contact will not occur naturally and it will be difficult to facilitate. Again, this is another area where the equalities agenda is not only important in terms of ensuring equal access, especially to the better schools, housing areas and jobs, but also facilitates cohesion by allowing bridges to be built between communities.

Aldridge and Halpern (2002, para 165) explain the benefits in terms of social capital and upward mobility:

> Large physical agglomerations of social housing make it more difficult for disadvantaged communities to form and maintain bridging social capital. More dispersed provision of social housing avoids this shortcoming ... The benefits of such dispersal policies would not be immediate and might take decades to realise. The benefits appear to be contingent on the dispersal of individual households rather than smaller estates or blocks of dwellings. Even then, social renters who get to live in more affluent areas do not immediately take on better jobs nor see their incomes double. The greatest beneficiaries may be their children and teenagers who grow up with the benefit of more diverse social networks, and access to the aspirations and facilities of the middle classes around them.

Whilst it is encouraging to see Aldridge and Halpern extolling the virtue of more mixed neighbourhoods, they do not appear to advocate more mixed schooling, the corollary of integrated residential areas. This is not surprising since it has been a blindspot for the government in recent years, who are fearful that more integrated schooling may undermine their 'attainment agenda' and their policy of 'parental choice' to drive improvement. The omission is in contrast to the work of Varshney (2002, p. 150) who indicates that the 'communal segregation in the education system' in one of the riot prone areas of India has greatly inhibited inter-communal contact and trust. It is also in contrast to the reports of Ouseley (2001) and Cantle (2001), who both commented on the extent of segregated schooling in the riot towns of Northern England. The role of education in promoting cross-cultural contact is discussed elsewhere in this chapter. Educational segregation was also discussed earlier (in Chapter 3), when it was suggested that integration has not improved in recent years and may be moving in the wrong direction in some geographic areas.

In the Northern Ireland context, McCandless commented:

> We have a system of faith schools which has failed entirely to promote any form of social cohesion. We have almost entirely separate housing. Our workplaces have become increasingly segregated, so it is impossible to meet in neutral venues and to live any kind of lives which are integrated in any way. I suppose we have made this structural. (McCandless, 2004, ev 95)

Drawing upon their international experience, the Minority Rights Group International, warn against:

> separate schools for minorities which do not help to promote understanding between communities and should be avoided unless they are essential for pupils' security. (MRGI, 2007)

McGlynn *et al.* (2004) also support the development of integrated schooling as a means of promoting cohesion and promoting forgiveness and reconciliation, based upon contact theory and the development of positive out-group interaction. Relatively little is published about the dynamics of segregation in Britain and the extent to which residential environments and schools are becoming more, or less, segregated, but recent information collected by the Department for Children, School and Families has recently been made available. This does indicates some further worrying trends towards segregation (Johnson *et al.*, 2006) and may prove to be of crucial importance to the development of cross-cultural contact, tolerance and trust – and to the wider growth and development of social capital.

Social capital and civil society

Following a literature search, Aldridge and Halpern (2002) found that whilst the term Social Capital had been deployed since the 1920s, it has become much more widely used following Putnam's work in the 1990s, culminating in his book *Bowling Alone: The Collapse and Revival of American Community* (2000). This work has therefore had a major impact on recent thinking, even though there is far from universal agreement over the extent and nature of social capital.

For Putnam, social capital is simply about the connections among individuals – social networks and the norms of reciprocity and trustworthiness that arise from them (Putnam, 2000, p. 19). For the most part, Putnam is content to describe 'social capital' in terms of low-level collaboration, between neighbours and local groups of people, sharing tools and working collectively when it is in their interest to do so. This co-operation extends to social activities, like bowling, where groups of people made their own entertainment by developing clubs and societies and hence Putnam's earlier conclusion that the decline in social capital has a lot to do with the growth in the use of television as home entertainment:

> There is reason to believe that deep-seated technological trends are radically 'privatising' or 'individualizing' our use of leisure time and thus disrupting many opportunities for social capital formulation. The most obvious and probably the most powerful instrument of this revolution is television. Time-budget studies in the 1960s showed that growth in time spent watching television dwarfed all other changes in the way Americans passed their days and nights. (Putnam, 1995)

There is a tendency for the debate about social capital to be rather backward looking, focussing on the loss of a sense of 'community', based on an apparent decline in collective action and 'neighbourliness', since the supposed halcyon days of strong communities, clustered around single employers, where people walked to work, took part in activities which were organised by the trades association or local church, with children at the local school, whilst their mothers met in the laundry or at the nearby shops. And older people can still remember communities in which the front door was always 'off the latch' in case a neighbour wanted to pop in and borrow a cup of sugar.

But Putnam advises us to guard against nostalgia:

> Is life in communities as we enter the twenty-first century really so different after all from the reality of American communities in the 1950s and 1960s ... are club meetings really less crowded than yesterday ... do we really know our neighbours less well than our parents did, or is our childhood recollection of neighbourhood barbecues suffused with a golden glow of wishful reminiscence. Are friendly poker games less common now, or is it that we have outgrown poker? (Putnam, 2000, p. 25)

Despite his words of warning, perhaps Putnam is guilty of trying to establish and measure associations as they were and not recognise the more diffuse nature of societal connections. Neighbourhoods were certainly more stable in the past with many more people living and working in the same area and with travel on a much more limited basis. Car ownership was lower and other forms of communications much less developed. Peoples' associations were necessarily more limited to particular areas and are difficult to compare with the way in which people associate and communicate today. There is far less reason to confine associations to any local area and it is much easier to communicate across greater distances and even across national and continental boundaries. Does this mean that social capital is weaker, or simply that it is less intensely focussed in localised areas? A more worrying and recent conclusion from Putnam, is that social solidarity and social capital tend to decline, at least in the short term, as diversity increases and that residents of all races tend to 'hunker down' (Putnam, 2007).

Giddens (2004) points out that there may be a new form of solidarity, which goes along with new forms of individualism, rather than the decline of social capital itself. And, in any event, Aldridge and Halpern (2002) suggest that social capital has not declined universally, with the level declining in two countries (the United States and Australia); stable patterns in two (the United Kingdom and France); and increasing in four (Germany and (probably) Japan from a low base; Sweden and the Netherlands from a high base).

The role of women also needs to be carefully considered as social capital is often conceptualised in terms of men's networks (Molyneux, 2004). Social capital may lean too heavily on the formal associations which are led by men, rather than the more informal social networks where women are more active, in voluntary self-help schemes, church activities and extended kinship ties. The roles played by women may have been expected to have excited more interest as their networks will form a significant part of the glue that binds communities together (and especially as women have been less involved in the conflict and violence that has scarred many communities). However, this has not been the case, with little recognition of the potential that women could play in the 'bridging' of communities, through cross-cultural contact. Similarly, it is difficult to judge whether different forms of association, along ethnic and kinship lines, or in subcultural terms, for example, through youth gang culture, have been recognised as part of 'social capital'.

From a community cohesion perspective, social capital is vital. Without a strong base from which people can develop relationships, whether through associations or as individuals, the barriers are unlikely to be broken down and tolerance and mutual trust are unlikely to be built. These may not necessarily take traditional forms, but what matters, is how well they are used by different sections of society. They may be localised, or even regional or global in character, but all are potentially capable of creating links which promote understanding and trust between people of different backgrounds. It seems likely that local forms, however, will allow for collective problems to be resolved more easily and especially those that relate to particular areas and places. Regular contact and incidental meetings and information exchanges will also help to create the social fabric or glue that trust and reciprocity depend upon. For the concept of social capital to be of any value in community cohesion terms, however, it is essential that it is better understood, not simply seen in conventional terms and that the means by which it can be influenced are developed.

Putnam's work was also helpful in that it distinguished different forms of social capital and, in particular, established *bonding* social capital (among family members or like ethnic groups), from *bridging* social capital (across ethnic groups). The concept of 'bridging' social capital closely coincides with the community cohesion notion of 'cross-cultural contact' and whilst Putnam did not advance this as a means of promoting community cohesion as such, the development of understanding, reciprocity and trust are clearly aligned to it. The impact of different forms of social capital may also be interlinked, in that a high level of 'bonding' social capital may inhibit 'bridging' between different groups. However, there is again a level of simplicity about Putnam's work which is a little disturbing and the assumption that people are divided into 'people like us' and 'people not like us' depends on a view about natural affinities which is not sustainable. We may not consider people of the same skin colour, or faith, to be 'like us' at all. By the same token, we may have such a strong sense of association within a kinship, ethnic or faith group, which may create a high level of intra-associational identification, reinforcing the in-group by excluding the out-group – what Rogers (2003) describes as the 'wrong' sort of social capital; 'tight networks of mutual support among the upper middle class or "own group" ethnic solidarity in areas of high ethnic mix'. Rogers goes on to suggest that highly localised engagement, through the use of volunteering projects, team sports, local church engagement and other face to face contact is not a 'cure for all ills', even if it is easier for cross-cultural (and intra-cultural) contact to be developed at a local level in some instances. Faith organisations are also sometimes seen as reinforcing in-group associations and 'bonding' and are beginning to address the issue of how strong social capital can also 'enable them to cross boundaries and build bridges with others in civil society' (Furbey *et al.*, 2006, p. 3).

Fukuyama (1999) supports the view that social capital can, in some circumstances, produce 'bad results' where it favours exclusive groups by achieving internal cohesion at the expense of outsiders, but also suggests that it can help to promote virtues, such as honesty, the keeping of commitments, the reliable performance of duties, reciprocity and the like. In other words, a set of shared and desirable norms, which will lead to a greater likelihood of co-operation between people. Baumann (1995, p. 221) also distinguishes 'bad' social capital, or what he terms 'mixophobia', in which in-group loyalty can lead to out-group antagonism and contrasts this with 'mixophilia', which broadens identities and favours 'bridging' between communities.

Fukuyama (1999) also emphasises the religious and cultural underpinnings that promote voluntary associations and co-operation. People working co-operatively together inevitably develop a shared agenda, a common understanding and mutual trust. However, the common sense of purpose and the shared norms and values that develop may be secondary to the selfish needs that people seek to satisfy: people will tend to combine into groups and associations when it is their interest to do so. Were people in the same area and neighbourhood really so much like each other and with so much in common, or did they simply have a shared interest in collectivism and became associated out of self-interest?

The current level of analysis of social capital does not allow us to be definitive. In terms of building trust and co-operation between people and in terms of developing understanding and tolerance of 'difference', some level of interaction is vital and the study of social capital attempts, at least, to help us to understand how that interaction is formed. Given the variety of local, regional and national patterns of interaction and the variety of configurations based on class, kinship, ethnicity, faith and many other factors, however, generalising seems somewhat dangerous. There is also a suggestion that social capital develops trust, not simply between people involved in the interaction, but more widely between individuals and state institutions by building 'civil society'. Aldridge and Halpern (2002) appear to see a continuum from the building of trust between people, to improved civic responsibility and crime reduction and to higher levels of trust in public and political institutions. The dynamics of these trends may not, in reality, however, be so entwined, for example, the target of those taking part in many of the race riots in the past has not been other ethnic communities, but the organs of government themselves, particularly the police service.

If the science of social capital is, as yet, underdeveloped then there is little by way of established practice, nor any clear responsibility for engineering improvement. Few, if any, statutory agencies see it as their role to even map and understand the complexities and subtleties involved, let alone develop 'remedial' programmes. At least one local authority has attempted a mapping exercise (Khan and Muir, 2006). One or two voluntary organisations have begun to put their toe into the water with elementary pilot schemes, often described in terms of 'capacity building' – although the capacity of whom and what the capacity will be used for, is often very uncertain. It may only serve to reinforce separation and fail to build bridges between communities or even to establish a greater degree of civil society. Often, it has simply been conceived as a means of retrospectively helping to defuse conflicts between different groups. Nevertheless, the emerging practice of community cohesion is beginning to draw upon some elements of social capital, both in general terms and in relation to specific areas, for example, within education and inter-faith work.

The emerging practice of cross-cultural contact

The post-2001 reports into the 'race riots' in England have spawned a wide variety of approaches and initiatives to build better relations between communities and to try to reduce the 'fear of difference'. A number of individual schemes have been developed, but perhaps the most important early body of work was developed under the 'Pathfinder Programme' – a joint initiative by the Home Office and the Office of the Deputy Prime Minister's (ODPM) Neighbourhood Renewal Unit (NRU), the results of which began to emerge after six months (Home Office and Vantagepoint, 2003). The Pathfinder Programme involved some 14 local partnerships and a further 14 unfunded shadow designated areas, covering a very wide range of towns, cities and rural areas across England, tackling different aspects of diversity. These were chosen from 75 applicant areas, as a result of a two-day selection process.

In each case the 'Pathfinders' and their 'shadows' developed schemes which resonated with local people and fitted the circumstances on the ground. For example, in the London Borough of Tower Hamlets, an area with just under half of the local community from minority ethnic backgrounds and principally (30 per cent) of Bangladeshi origin, the aim was to bring people together who would normally have little reason to communicate. However, the work has also had some interesting spin-off benefits, with the older Bangladeshi people now using a Catholic Centre in one area for evening prayers, during Ramadan. Similarly, the Catholic Centre is 'reaching out' to those people from Eastern Europe who are less familiar with the predominantly Muslim local culture (ibid.).

In Mansfield, a predominantly white working class town in the Midlands, where the ethnic minority population is very low, at around 2 per cent, the aim of their 'Healing History' project was to focus on the now lost culture of the mining industry and to recognise the impact that this has had on the inter-generational conflict and race-related issues in a town dominated by a white, male culture. In Sandwell, a metropolitan borough adjacent to Birmingham, they have chosen to promote the concept of community cohesion and to develop a communication strategy which is based on existing networks, such as those representing the voluntary sector (ibid.).

The government also established a showcase for good practice on community cohesion under the 'Beacon Council' scheme. This scheme is intended to highlight best practice, so that other local authorities can emulate and develop schemes for their own areas. Again, variety was represented in the six chosen areas in 2003, to reflect a diversity of experiences. Tewkesbury is a small town in a rural part of the south west, which had developed positive initiatives in respect of inter-generational conflict and in respect of the divisions between the host and travelling communities. The London Borough of Barnet, a multicultural area with a significant Jewish population, developed a 'Gold Strategy Group' to further cross-cultural liaison between Jewish and Muslim communities. They also developed inter-generational projects and ensured that their diversity was celebrated in at least 25 local communities. Rochdale Borough in Greater Manchester worked through its 'township committees' to build trust between local communities and to break down mono-cultural areas. The Council even sent a teabag to local residents and suggested to them, that by sharing a pot of tea with neighbours, a better sense of community could be developed.

The Neighbourhood Renewal Unit (NRU) established a Community Facilitation Programme (CFP) aimed at those areas which have experienced community conflict or have relatively high levels of tension. This includes Oldham, a borough adjacent to Manchester, which experienced the riots in 2001 (officially described as 'disturbances'). Oldham has an ethnic minority population of about 9 per cent, the national average for England, but the BME communities are largely concentrated in just three wards, which are amongst the most deprived in the country. Schools are also divided along ethnic lines. A charitable company 'Mediation Northern Ireland' (MNI) was brought in to develop conflict resolution techniques and it ran a series of workshops for community leaders, providing a safe, mediated space in which participants could explore the issues that lay at the heart of the conflict in the town. The workshops were held in neutral venue away from normal working and living areas and employed a range of techniques to develop a shared understanding – apparently with very good results. However, MNI stressed the need to take time and to be patient in both establishing the mediation and in carrying out the work. They also stressed the need for consistent and visible support from civic and community leaders (details from www.renewal.net).

The CFP also built local capacity in conflict resolution in Burnley, a town not dissimilar to Oldham in terms of socio-economic and ethnic minority composition and which was also the scene of riots in 2001. Racism was deep seated in the town and a number of far right councillors have been elected in recent years. Local people were trained in mediation and conflict resolution, so that they would not be dependent on outside assistance in the future. The programme was not fully utilised, however, due to the relatively low level of resources deployed, although it does claim some modest successes (ibid.).

A further CFP area was that of Tower Hamlets in London, where the focus of the 'RESOLVE' project was to create a rapid response team, which could work with young people in particular. This included working with gangs and 'hard-to-reach' groups and providing a real presence 'on the street'. The work was received positively and whilst people joining the project were in some cases motivated by self-interest, they have also acted more responsibly in relation to tense and potentially violent situations (ibid.).

Many more initiatives have taken place in local areas, with the support of national and local statutory agencies. These include an alliance of local authorities, public bodies and community-based organisations in East Lancashire; the development of a community cohesion charter in Stoke-upon-Trent; the work of the London Borough of Hounslow and five neigh-bouring boroughs in the West London Alliance to build better community relations; the development of greater contact between different communi-ties by the partnership 'Bradford Vision'; Tameside's (another borough in Greater Manchester) use of 'everyday role models' to challenge bigotry and promote cohesion; Southampton's outreach team which aimed to solve problems through dialogue and to focus on the integration of newcomer communities; the 'train the trainers' cohesion programme in Kirklees (West Yorkshire); the use of young people trained to resolve conflict in Slough; and many more detailed in the Community Cohesion Action Guide provided by local government agencies and central government departments (Local Government Association (LGA *et al.*, 2004)).

Further details of the work of some of the above programmes were given at the 'Community Cohesion Pathfinder Programme: Action Learning Summit' to launch the above Guide. This included a presentation by Oldham Metropolitan Borough which demonstrated the wide variety of work which it had undertaken in respect of community cohesion, since the riots in the town three years earlier and, more crucially, how that needed to be on a comprehensive and all-encompassing basis. This included:

- The partnership basis and cross-sectoral support for the work.
- The construction of a shared vision based on mutual respect, equality and integration.
- Opposition to discrimination and divisive views, statements and activities.
- Equality of opportunity.
- Strong cross-party and cross-sectoral leadership.
- Community empowerment and engagement at all levels.
- A special focus on womens' networks.
- Support to refugees and asylum seekers and the wider communities.
- Inter-faith collaboration.
- Action planning and measurement of progress towards objectives. (Oldham Metropolitan Borough, 2004, presentation to Community Cohesion Action Learning Summit)

Oldham has also provided details of specific service orientated community cohesion work to a House of Commons Select Committee (Oldham, 2004a).

This details the work in respect of,

- primary, secondary and further education, particularly in respect of twinning mono-cultural schools and encouraging mixed intakes,
- youth and community work, including sports development,
- segregated residential areas in social and private housing,
- regeneration and renewal practice,
- tackling racist incidents,
- health, in primary and acute settings,
- employment opportunities in the public sector,
- policing and community safety,
- private enterprise.

Oldham's latest report *Forward Together: Building Community Cohesion in Oldham* (2004b) provides a commentary and list of actions, covering all of the above issues and a range of other initiatives and runs to 111 pages. A review of Oldham's community cohesion programme in 2006 (iCoCo, 2006a) found that few towns or cities had done as much as Oldham to promote community cohesion and documented all aspects of their work, including a number of additional schemes from elsewhere.

Similarly the London Borough of Tower Hamlet's Community Cohesion Strategy (2003) provides an action plan of around 150 initiatives to comprehensively tackle the range of activities required to address the present problem.

This again serves to demonstrate that there are no 'quick fixes' or simplistic solutions to areas affected by community tensions and that a wide range of political and practical measures, undertaken by public, private and voluntary sector agencies and on a range of themes, such as the 67 recommended areas suggested by the Community Cohesion Review Team (Cantle, 2001), will be necessary. Oldham's report (2004b) warned that, in particular, changing its 'highly residentially segregated' areas would 'inevitably be a long term process' and this was reinforced by the subsequent review, which also suggested a step up in the pace of change (iCoCo, 2006a).

Community cohesion is not yet an established practice in all areas and, like the earlier work on the 'equalities agenda', may have difficulty in developing into mainstream programmes. However, the 'equalities agenda' has had some twenty to thirty years of commitment, especially within the public sector and can now boast established practitioners in many of the larger public and private sector bodies. A similar infrastructure is beginning to grow in respect of community cohesion, with around 100 local authorities having dedicated community cohesion officers and, in a number of cases, the staff promoting equalities have been subsumed within these new and broader teams.

There is a lack of clarity as to which agencies are expected to take the lead at national and local levels. Within national government, the Home Office began as the lead department, having established a Community Cohesion Unit in 2002 and with clear ministerial responsibility. Responsibility subsequently changed ministerial hands and is now settled within the Department of Communities and Local Government (DCLG). Doubts were expressed in the past by the Independent Advisory Panel about the ability of government to 'join up' the various programmes vested with different ministries and whether there was a real commitment on the part of other government departments (Cantle, 2004). This has changed simply as a consequence of the re-location to the new department and appears to now have wider acceptance, especially in respect of education. Within local government, there appears to have been a gradual acceptance of their leadership role, and this has been strongly reinforced by the Local Government White Paper, *Strong and Prosperous Communities*, in 2006:

> local authorities, as leaders of their communities, are best placed to understand the particular challenges their city, town or neighbourhood face, and working with communities and other local partners, to decide how to respond. It is only at a local level that the underlying drivers of tensions between different groups – such as access to social housing, crime, disorder and anti-social behaviour problems or deep-rooted deprivation – can be understood and addressed. Only local authorities have the democratic mandate to offer and develop a shared vision, through the Sustainable Community Strategy, for the area. No one else has the mandate to co-ordinate different interests, reconcile diverse views and provide the space for open debate and dialogue. (DCLG, 2006a, p. 156)

This is a demanding and sophisticated task for local government and very far removed from the service delivery model, in which councils simply had to worry about the provision of fairly basic, though often, essential services. The element of partnership is also crucial as local authorities are only responsible for about 50 per cent of public expenditure in their area, with, for example, health, policing, training and skills, regional development, higher and further education and other services outside their control. Many of these services are susceptible to their influence, under the 'community leadership' role but, the task is not straightforward and requires a strong sense of community governance if it is to succeed. The government has previously affirmed its support for the leadership role for local authorities in *Community Cohesion – An Action Guide*, which was supported by local government leaders themselves (LGA *et al.*, 2004). However, there has been more ambivalence about giving the local authorities direct powers to 'manage settlement' as recommended in *The End of Parallel Lives?* (Cantle, 2004). This recommendation was not agreed upon by government, with no real clarity about 'where the buck stops'. The Commission for Integration and Cohesion has proposed a new national agency for this task (CIC, 2007) and it is not clear how this would interface with local government. Meanwhile, local government is concerned about the lack of resources to assist the process of settlement and it believes that new funding mechanisms should be developed to enable financial support to be directed to those areas with higher levels of migration and for the financial mechanisms to be more responsive (iCoCo, 2007).

At the same time, whilst local authorities are being urged by government 'to develop and offer a shared vision' the responsibility for understanding and responding to the social and psychological needs of communities, impacted by changing community dynamics and inward migration may well require more specific powers. Local authorities do have a duty to 'promote good race relations' but this role has remained at a very ill-defined level for many years. At the same time, the role of local Racial Equality Councils (RECs) has become less clear. Despite some pressure to become more involved in promoting more positive relationships (CRE, 2002b), RECs are not established in all areas of the country and have, in any event, little by way of a track record in community cohesion or even in the 'promotion of good race relations', despite the statutory responsibility of the CRE, since 1976. With the creation of the new Equality and Human Rights Commission and the demise of the CRE in 2007, the support for a regional structure is yet to be determined. In the absence of a clear mandate and commitment in the statutory sector, voluntary organisations have often been seen as the most appropriate vehicle for engaging with communities at a neighbourhood level and to build social capital and interpersonal relationships. They have also traditionally provided much of the means by which ethnic minority and faith bodies are supported.

As a result a significant proportion of the development work on community cohesion has been undertaken by voluntary bodies, often with limited budgets and on a short-term basis, although there are now signs that this is beginning to change. A key aim is therefore to 'mainstream' the emerging work and to avoid a situation in which it becomes marginalised within the voluntary sector, thereby underpinning the continuation of existing practice within the statutory agencies. This is, perhaps, nowhere presently more evident than in the education sector, where imaginative 'swapping cultures' programmes have been developed by the charity 'The Minorities of Europe' (2003) and a variety of school twinning schemes have been supported by voluntary effort rather than statutory agencies and without the benefit of any sort of government-backed programme. One of the Ministers responsible for education, in giving evidence to the House of Commons Select Committee extolled the virtues of twinning schemes, whilst admitting that his department had not provided the funding and that 'finance was a problem' (House of Commons, 2004, ev 115). Again, however, there are now signs that the statutory sector is beginning to invest in community cohesion and develop it into a mainstream programme.

The vital work of building relations between different groups of young people in the community has also often been left to poorly funded voluntary bodies, such as the 'Peacemaker Project' in Oldham. 'Peacemaker' is an anti-racist youth development organisation, set up in 1997, as a result of what they saw as the failure of the youth service to engage with young people in a manner that promoted and developed integrated youth provision. It regarded mono-ethnic provision as detrimental to the development of young people especially in a multicultural town (House of Commons, 2004a, p. 34).

Despite the potential, youth work, in both the statutory and voluntary sector, is generally poorly funded and, according to Pinto and Green (2004):

> young people can play a strong role in creating integrated communi-ties ... community cohesion remains a struggle to deliver and the adop-tion of community cohesion as a policy measure has not been met with sufficient change in local youth service provision or practice ... youth workers aren't sure of the meaning of the term and aren't receiving suffi-cient training.

A number of national charities have also been responsible for developing cross-cultural and inter-faith dialogue. For example, the Maimonides Foundation is a joint Jewish–Muslim interfaith organisation, which fosters understanding, dialogue, and co-operation between Jews and Muslims through cultural, academic and educational programmes based on mutual respect and trust. They create forums where the two communities can share their commonalties and discuss their differences through dialogue. The Foundation has used both art and football as 'universal languages' to begin develop fraternal relations between Britain's 275,000 Jews and 1.5 million Muslims, bringing together people form those communities, some of whom have never previously met anyone from the other community (Rocker, 2004). As faith has become an increasingly obvious divide which needs to be bridged, particularly as a result of the focus on the Muslim community, so the number of inter-faith schemes has increased. Initially, these tended to revolve around inter-faith leaders, but have gradually begun to offer contact to the wider community. For example, in Middlesbrough, the 'Festival of Faith' included a series of visits to various places of worship (Middlesbrough BME Network, 2007).

There has also been relatively little by way of properly funded and evalu-ated action-based research, at least by the statutory agencies. Fortunately, some has been funded by charitable bodies, the most significant of which is *Understanding the Stranger*, financed by the Paul Hamlyn Foundation, com-missioned and published by the independent Information Centre about Asylum and Refugees in the United Kingdom (ICAR, 2004). The research examined ways to manage the arrival of asylum seekers, with a view to developing practical steps which would prevent tension from developing in local areas. The research was carried out in six areas in England, including a southern coastal town, a rural area and midlands and northern cities.

The Report used 'contact theory' as an approach and concludes, amongst other things, that,

> one of the most effective ways of encouraging understanding between local people and asylum seekers is for them to meet each other ... arrangements need to be made for local residents and asylum seekers to meet as neighbours. This need not be through specially convened meetings – existing cultural, sporting or community activities can provide good opportunities. (ICAR, 2004, pp. 6, 7)

The research also supports other key aspects of community cohesion work, such as the need to provide balanced and reliable information to communities about newcomers, and seeking to ensure that the press and media act responsibly in the way in which they portray migrants and ethnic minorities. Other research has highlighted the need to tackle the ignorance of the resident population (Allender and Quigley, 2005, p. iv) as a means of reducing hate crime and the necessity of interaction between young people to improve tolerance and reduce conflict (Lemos, 2004, 2004a).

The 'mainstreaming' of community cohesion is gradually being extended with its inclusion in principal government programmes, though often with little by way of a robust research and analytical framework. For example, the Department of Media, Culture and Sport (DCMS) produced *Bringing Communities Together Through Sport and Culture in 2004*. This was little more than a 'stream of consciousness', resulting from a seminar and involving an array of government agencies, which reported that they had managed to help participants in their various programmes to feel differently about people of other cultures and backgrounds and to break down the barriers between them. DCMS is, however, beginning to play a more active part, with the spur of the European Year of Intercultural Dialogue (EYID) in 2008. All European governments are expected to support the Year and the EU are making substantial sums of money available to nation states to develop suitable schemes, much of which is focussed on the arts and cultural activities.

The government and the its agencies have gradually placed more and more pressure upon local authorities and statutory bodies to ensure that community cohesion is taken seriously. Proposals were made by the Scarman Trust (Pike, 2004) to create 'community service agreements' between government agencies and community-based organisations which would formalise the development of specific outcomes, such as the building of 'bonding' and 'bridging' social capital. Adam Fineberg (2004) has also proposed that the existing 'local area agreements' which presently provide funding to local authorities as part of a formal arrangement between them and central government, be extended to incentivise the development of community cohesion as part of an over-arching local strategy. Councils have been subject to a 'comprehensive performance assessment' on a regular basis and the 2005 round placed a much greater emphasis on their community leadership role, including cohesion. The 'Action Guide' published by the LGA and others (LGA *et al.*, 2004) maintains a strong focus on community cohesion and this was complemented by new 'strategic guidance' aimed at the leadership of councils in 2005 (LGA, 2005). A new performance framework for local authorities, based upon Comprehensive Area Assessments (CAAs) and Local Area Agreements (LAAs) has recently been established and community cohesion is a stronger feature of both.

The special funding available for community cohesion work had been limited, hopefully as part of a deliberate strategy to ensure that activity is not restricted to a few special initiatives and that changes are subsequently 'mainstreamed'. This certainly reflected the concern of the Community Cohesion Review Team who were themselves critical of the plethora of previous community-based initiatives and did not want to see yet another set of short life special measures (Cantle, 2001). The focus has therefore been on creating a permanent place for community cohesion in all principal services, building ownership and commitment, improving the knowledge of practitioners and developing models of good practice. Some finance has, however, been made available for capacity building in high-risk areas, for developing 'Pathfinders' to trial new approaches and by assisting with specific projects to pump prime change programmes. But, the challenge of 'mainstreaming' these changes still remains. A lot more needs to be done to systematically embed community cohesion and to ensure that longer-term change is effective. The principles of community cohesion are increasingly understood and accepted but new approaches are still being developed. If it is to be sustained, the commitment of local and national agencies must develop and be maintained in the medium term, at least.

More recently, the influx of EU migrants into the UK has generated concern about the lack of support for managing the settlement of newcomers and has spawned a range of approaches to keep up to date with the dynamics and change within local communities (iCoCo, 2006c; 2007) and to understand emerging tensions (iCoCo, 2007a). In addition, good practice guides have emerged to promote integration of newcomers, to provide them with guidance and assistance and to support the 'host' community through a period of rapid and substantial change (Audit Commission, 2007; iCoCo, 2007c).

In other countries, there may well be a wealth of similar experience upon which to build. For example, Sandercock (2004) provides details of what she describes as 'intercultural' work, for example, in Frankfurt to reduce the host community's fear of the 'other' (ibid., 260); in Rotterdam to develop intercultural activities (ibid., p. 262); and in Vancouver, to promote inter-cultural decision-making and other activities (ibid., p. 268). It may therefore be possible to develop a greater level of understanding of 'what works' through more international collaboration. The British Council which works in over 100 countries 'to build mutually beneficial relationships to increase the appreciation of the UK's creativity and achievements' and in 'thinking big about intercultural dialogue' intends that 'By 2010, 10,000 influential young people in the UK and a range of other countries will have the skills and relationships to take the world community into a new era of intercultural exchange and understanding' (British Council, 2006, pp. 5 and 14).

The European Parliament and Council decided in 2006 to establish the European Year of Intercultural Dialogue in 2008. This was partly in response to the growth in the number of EU countries and the need to promote understanding between them, but also has much wider implications:

> At the heart of the European project, it is important to provide the means for intercultural dialogue and dialogue between citizens to strengthen respect for cultural diversity and deal with the complex reality in our societies and the coexistence of different cultural identities and beliefs. Furthermore, it is important to highlight the contribution of different cultures to the Member States' heritage and way of life and to recognise that culture and intercultural dialogue are essential for learning to live together in harmony. (OJEU, 2006, L412/44)

The EU decision went on to indicate its support for 'shared values', 'respecting and promoting diversity' and 'ensuring equal opportunities' – in total, a very similar approach to that expounded in the UK's formal definition of community cohesion (see Figure 2.1). The EU has set aside 10 million Euros for promoting intercultural work and expects member states to contribute 50 per cent of the cost of schemes, which will boost the overall budget very substantially. The extensive nature of the programme will undoubtedly increase the experience and expertise in this field, though the early indications of the proposals suggest an over-reliance on arts based programmes.

Key public services and policy areas

There are a number of key components of public policy which have a profound impact upon the shape of local communities and the day to day relationships between people.

Regeneration

Many regeneration initiatives, based on distinct areas, have been developed over the years and with a range of complementary objectives, including housing and environmental improvements, reduced levels of crime and anti-social behaviour, better employment opportunities and improved business prospects. The area basis of these initiatives has always been a laudable one – to deal with all or most of the area's difficulties on a comprehensive basis and to ensure that the regeneration is sustained. Further, poor and deprived neighbourhoods have always been at greater risk of inter-communal conflict (Lemos, 2004, p. 63). Area Based Initiatives (ABIs) as they became known, however, were rarely, if ever, developed with the expectation that the cohesion of communities would be improved, although it may have been supposed that the tackling of disadvantage would improve the pride in the area, raise aspirations and opportunities and thereby reduce the possibility of divisions and disaffection. The success of such areas was, nevertheless, generally overestimated, simply because of the very high levels of population turnover in many of the targeted communities and the consequent dynamic nature of the areas.

The introduction of competition between areas in the early 1990s for the allocation of resources, had profound and unintended consequences in respect of cohesion. The 'City Challenge' scheme introduced by the Conservative Government allowed a small number of local authorities to spend an extra £37.5 million in a defined area, if they could demonstrate innovation and a clear strategy which was capable of delivering long-term improvement. The successful schemes did, in fact, unlock some new approaches, and the 'challenge' and competitive nature of this round of funding was soon followed by more schemes and then extended by the Labour Government elected in 1997. The new approach was soon widely hailed as a success. The allocation of resources, based on the competition between communities became accepted practice. However, the Community Cohesion Review Team set up in 2001 to review the riots in a number of northern towns, found that the competitive nature of regeneration programmes was one of the most significant factors which had undermined community cohesion:

> The most consistent and vocal concern was expressed about the damaging impact of different communities bidding against each other and the difficulty about having to convince them of the present approach. (Cantle, 2001)

Whilst many of the initiatives were based on geographic areas, the nature of the assessment of 'need' had in many cases, created a coincidence with distinct communities which were heavily dominated by, either the white community on the one hand, or by a BME community on the other. This fostered a strong perception of unfairness, particularly as the bidding regime often pitted several communities in the same town or area against each other and emphasised differences and promoted competition rather than co-operation:

> area based regeneration initiatives ... reinforced the separation of communities and we saw few attempts to tackle problems on a thematic basis which could have served to unite different groups. The development of cross-cultural contact and the promotion of community cohesion was not valued as an end in itself. (Ibid.)

This should not have been a surprise, given that over 70 per cent of the BME community live in the 88 most deprived areas in the country (SEU, 2004, p. 5) and are amongst the country's most deprived section and are heavily concentrated in the worst housing in the inner cities. Deprived white areas, which were also the target of some of the additional funding, were also often to be found in physically distinct and isolated communities, commonly on council estates on the edge of towns and cities. This meant that it was inevitable that an area-based approach, focussed on tackling deprived areas would almost certainly be highly coincidental with black or white communities and, further, that remedial work would then be conducted on the basis of separate development.

The government initially struggled to come to terms with the Review Team's findings. Despite recognition of the need to change its approach in the official response to the Review Team (Denham, 2001), it rather appeared that a flagship policy had suddenly been torpedoed. Special initiatives, based on competition and targeting were growing at that stage and the government made greater use of them to exercise more control of local government by allocating funds according to national rather than local priorities and by controlling the way in which local government would actually deliver the schemes (these often involved the transfer of responsibility to other agencies, breaking the domination of local government). In short, local government had 'to dance to the government's tune' to receive funding. The government had also invested heavily in a new centralised agency for the development of all aspects of regeneration – The Neighbourhood Renewal Unit (NRU). Nevertheless, a year later the government endorsed new national Community Cohesion Guidance (LGA *et al.*, 2002) which largely put the onus on local authorities and their partners to prioritise and target expenditure and to develop better communication strategies. At the same time, however, area-based initiatives were quietly downgraded and the funding streams began to dry up, partly for other reasons, such as the change in the priorities of the European Union (an important source of additional resources and match-funding in some regions). The government had also been forced to recognise that the plethora of initiatives they had spawned, often unrelated to each other and by different departments and agencies on different timescales and against different criteria and objectives, were causing confusion. Criticism by a Select Committee in 2003 (House of Commons, 2003) was particularly strident and recognised the problem for community cohesion caused by the present approach and despite government assurances to the Select Committee that its Regional Coordination Unit (RCU) was addressing the problem, the Select Committee urged stronger action.

However, regeneration activity was continuing, even if at a lower level, and it soon became necessary to develop new approaches, which would be compatible with the community cohesion agenda, rather than simply warn against the consequences of ill-conceived schemes. The task of drawing up new guidelines fell to a 'regeneration practitioner group' set up under the auspices of the Independent Community Cohesion Panel. This developed a new 'how to do it guide' in 2003 (Home Office and Office Deputy Prime Minister, 2003a) which suggested a number of practical ideas to address the problem, including changing the basis upon which 'need' is defined, as well as proposing the concept of 'area focus' so that regeneration could be undertaken on a more flexible basis, using 'thematic' programmes which could span different areas and communities to eliminate competition between them and allow for cross-cultural contact and co-operation. The Guidance also proposed the 'twinning' of the governance arrangements to ensure shared development. Fuller guidance was issued a year later (Home Office and Office Deputy Prime Minister, 2004b), which developed the same themes, stressed the need to fully understand community dynamics and emphasised cross-cultural contact and the integration and support for newcomers. It also included case examples.

The government's attention was beginning to shift away from community-based regeneration schemes and towards much more ambitious 'transformational' programmes. In 2003 it produced plans for the building of hundreds of thousands of homes in the South East and the Midlands (Office of the Deputy Prime Minister, 2003a), which it justified by describing it as 'building sustainable communities'. This was followed by a further programme (Office of the Deputy Prime Minister, 2004) under the title of *The Northern Way*, which would provide a mixture of renewal and new building in the Midlands and north of England. However, the government again showed a remarkable ability to ignore previous lessons and did not 'join up' its policies. Neither policy document even referred to 'community cohesion' (and there was little comfort for those expecting to see how, in any other terms, these communities might legitimately be described as 'sustainable'). The danger that we might simply be building yet more segregated communities, or exacerbating divisions in existing communities never occurred to the ODPM – it was simply not their primary departmental responsibility.

Guidance on community cohesion and 'transformational regeneration' schemes has not been produced, despite its obvious importance, although some very good pointers are given in an excellent 'good practice guide', *Community Cohesion and Housing* (Blackaby, 2004), since updated and expanded (Perry and Blackaby, 2007). However, a recent formal investigation by the CRE (CRE, 2007a) has shown that regeneration practice has not developed in line with previous guidance and that the impact of regeneration programmes, either in terms of racial equality, or cohesion, were given insufficient attention. Such considerations were not built in from the outset and neither mainstreamed nor adequately reflected in the performance framework. The potential to create tensions between areas over the distribution of funding still remained (ibid., p. 24) and the CRE even 'found no evidence that consultation events were bringing people together' (ibid., p. 45). More worryingly still, was that regeneration processes seemed to lack real connection to the sustainable communities agenda, a point echoed in another recent report (iCoCo, 2007b).

Much more emphasis now needs to be placed on the ways in which new housing schemes and large-scale renewal take account of community cohesion and, in particular, they should ensure that:

- a community cohesion baseline is established with an impact study prepared in each case providing in-depth consideration of the likely community dynamics;
- the processes of consultation and engagement, deciding upon priorities and decision taking and governance are designed in such a way to develop intercultural dialogue and build trust between communities in the longer term
- through the mix of housing tenures and types and through estate layout and design, the new developments are accessible by all communities, by 'engineering' the housing market and social housing requirements; and that integrated, rather than segregated areas are created;
- 'white flight', as a result of institutional pressures, false perceptions and prejudices from existing mixed areas is avoided;
- community facilities, social and cultural requirements are addressed, especially so that minorities feel that these new places are 'for them'. For example, will all sections of the community feel safe and will the type of shops, places of worship, schools and, most of all, the available jobs – make it a place that everyone wants to live?
- the design of new housing areas and spaces in the public realm maximise the opportunities for social contact at both the informal level of interaction and in formal facilities and venues.

Housing

Provision of new developments and renewal activity is therefore of critical importance, as it shapes so much of our formal and informal social interaction. It is particularly closely related to the education agenda, as housing patterns will often determine school catchment areas and, therefore, the social interaction beyond the school gate. Housing patterns will also determine other aspects of social interaction and access to services, such as health and sporting and leisure activities.

But the extent to which housing is integrated or segregated depends on a range of factors including the preferences and choices of the communities themselves. These preferences may, however, be constrained by affordability and social class, by fear and insecurity, or may be the result of a positive desire to live in an area which has a sufficient critical mass of any one community to support the shops, social, religious and cultural activities of that community. Whether segregation is the result of a positive or negative choice, what matters in terms of community cohesion is whether those areas become so exclusive as to deny the opportunity for cross-cultural contact, allowing ignorance and fear to develop. Some degree of concentration of particular communities in given areas is, however, desirable, so that a critical mass of one community can support a range of community-specific facilities. Once this tips over into an exclusive, or mono-cultural, environment based upon 'parallel lives', the opportunities for cross-cultural contact are diminished and the potential for the demonisation of those communities appears to be greatly increased.

The difficulties for the housing agenda should not, however, be underestimated. In social housing, mono-cultural estates are difficult to break down without strong and consistent support for inward minority communities and with a programme to tackle the prejudice in the host community at the same time. Blackaby (ibid.) provides some useful guidance as to how the social housing sector can support people who move into areas which are dominated by other cultures, including asylum seekers and refugees. This includes providing culturally sensitive services, ensuring that families are not isolated and have group support, effectively tackling discrimination and harassment and – of particular importance – working with the host community to promote understanding and tolerance and encourage 'welcoming' activities.

In the private sector, public and statutory agencies clearly have fewer levers to pull and the agencies concerned are not under a duty to positively promote good race relations. Further, there is some, though limited, evidence of prejudice and discrimination amongst estate agencies and other advisers and that they may also, on occasion, create or exacerbate the 'white flight' from some neighbourhoods, and attempt to restrict inward movement from minority communities. Other institutional problems include access to house purchase finance, which in its present form, is not culturally acceptable to some communities. There is also clearly a link to social class, with the more deprived communities least able to exercise real choice. Local authorities have generally had a limited impact in this area and have tended to focus more on their housing provider role. However, as Blackaby (ibid.) again points out there are a range of measures that they can take, including creating accreditation schemes for professional services, making referrals to professional bodies in cases of unacceptable performance, placing conditions through land sales and planning powers and tougher regulation of private landlords. The private sector is beginning to adjust its approach with, for example, a number of banks developing 'Islamic friendly' mortgages and other Sharia-compliant financial products. The Chartered Institute of Housing and the Housing Corporation have recently updated Blackaby's work and the new *Community Cohesion and Good Practice Guide* (Perry and Blackaby, 2007) now includes a range of good practice examples and proposes a range of measures to create positive relationships in communities and to create more mixed neighbourhoods.

The Housing 'equality agenda' has therefore moved on significantly from its preoccupation with lettings and access issues, but this remains very important, even though social housing now only accounts for around 20 per cent of total housing stock (ODPM, 2003b). The need to measure access to social housing in terms of both the quantity and quality of choices made available to different sections of the community has long been recognised and forms a fundamental part of ethnic monitoring schemes. However, links to the community cohesion agenda now also reflect the concern about whether the exercise of choice can reinforce, or break down, patterns of segregation (Chartered Institute of Housing, 2003). This is to some extent at least, a threat to the government's new 'choice agenda' (which has similar potential problems to 'parents choice' in the education sector), in that a 'market' in housing might simply reflect existing market conditions rather than deal with the underlying structural problems. The government's Choice Based Lettings scheme, or CBL, initially did little to recognise the reality of tenants' choices, but the government is now attempting to respond to the research evidence which suggested that the choices of BME communities was 'circumscribed' in some cases (Deputy Prime Minister, 2004, p. 24). The assumption behind the 'choice agenda', that a free market does, or ever can, exist on the basis that those exercising choices are in an equal position and the supply offered is also equally balanced, is as unlikely as the assumption that 'perfect competition' exists in the private sector.

It is therefore essential that housing providers and agencies re-examine their systems and processes, not only to address the race equality agenda particularly in respect of access, but also to positively address the more difficult barriers in both the social and private housing markets and how they can be shaped to promote good race relations and harmonious communities.

Education

The education system is another very significant factor in community cohesion, not simply in respect of schools, but also embracing preschool provision, supplementary schools and further and higher education. Provision is clearly linked to housing areas and therefore to the extent of segregation of local communities which generally determine catchment areas, particularly in preschool and primary provision. Schools have, in some areas, been moving towards more mono-cultural intakes, or, at least, failing to break them down, and are either more dominated by BME or white communities (school and neighbourhood segregation was discussed in Chapter 3) and there is some evidence that this has been given added impetus by the introduction of 'parental choice'.

Oonagh King MP, revealed her sense of 'shock' at finding segregated schools in her London constituency:

> I have mentioned before in Parliament my shock at visiting two schools next door to each other soon after I was elected in 1997. They shared a playground with a fence down the middle. On one side of the fence there were white children playing with a smattering of Afro-Caribbeans and on the other there were brown, Muslim and Bangladeshi children. Perhaps it is because my father was brought up in the segregated south that I was horrified by that; I could not believe it. We read about such things, but when we see them in Britain, we must think that something is seriously wrong. (King, 2004)

School segregation reflects, to some extent, the polarisation of neighbourhood catchment areas, which in turn, have been the product of social housing letting arrangements and the movement of population in owner-occupied areas. It is not confined to any particular part of the country, nor to any form of urban or rural environment – white and black schools are both 'mono-cultural'. However, the phenomenon of 'white flight' seems to have been fuelled by prejudice and racist views in some urban neighbourhoods. This can also be a function of social class to some extent, as the house prices in catchment areas of high performing schools tend to be significantly higher than others and, in general, BME communities are at the lower end of the income scale. Predominantly white neighbourhoods may be less attractive to minority households where there are concerns about safety and security in the neighbourhood or reflect a desire to live in an area in which a minority culture predominates.

Not all schools relate to the catchment of the neighbourhood in which they are situated. Specialist schools, the new academies and, of course, faith schools tend to have different admissions criteria. Faith schools, however, are often both single faith and mono-cultural, as faiths in Britain are generally closely aligned with race and ethnicity (see, for example, Brimicombe, 2007, in respect of London). Christian schools will often have a white intake, more so in the case of Roman Catholic schools than Church of England. However, some Church of England schools have also become mono-cultural and cater predominantly for either for white children or, where they are placed in inner city areas serving a high Asian population, almost exclusively for Asian children. Muslim parents have also favoured such schools for their faith ethos, in the absence of any designated state Muslim schools. In other areas, despite a high BME population, faith schools have rigorously enforced their faith criteria, with white children taking all, or nearly all, of the places, and remaining mono-cultural. However, faith schools are not responsible for all mono-cultural schools, as these have also developed in greater number outside the faith sector. It must also be said that some faith schools, particularly in large cities, are also amongst the most ethnically mixed schools in the country. Schools are therefore a product of parental choice and also a reflection of catchment areas. However, these two factors are entwined, as the poorer areas in which many BME communities live have poorer attainment levels and are therefore less favoured by those households in a position to exercise an alternative choice.

Despite concerns about faith schools, both in terms of whether they promote separateness and whether any faith organisations should be providing state backed education and directly or indirectly supporting their own beliefs, the number of faith schools seems set to grow. Ministers have recently announced that Muslim and Jewish faith schools which are presently outside the state system and privately funded are now to be encouraged to become state aided. The Government has, firstly, been obliged to recognise that state support for Christian schools means that the demands for parity by schools supported by other faiths is almost impossible to resist. However, the Government, in keeping with its concern to 'prevent violent extremism' in the Muslim community (DCLG, 2007a) is in any event, anxious to ensure that the 100 or so non-state aided Muslim schools are brought within the state regulatory system, subject to the national curriculum and the new 'duty to promote community cohesion'. More generally, the Government has promoted a number of means by which moderate Muslim voices should be heard and that young people, in particular, might be turned away from the appeal of 'violent extremism' (see for example DCLG, 2007b).

The particular focus on faith schools has tended to mask the fact that schools in both faith and non-faith sectors have tended to reinforce the segregation of communities and thereby deny children the opportunity to build their direct knowledge and understanding of other faiths and cultures. Further, educational attainment remains, to some extent at least, culturally determined and reinforces separation in further and higher education and the sphere of employment. It is not easy, however, to break down the mono-cultural nature of schools, nor even to reverse the evident trend towards them. But the process must be commenced, and some success has been achieved by gradualist approaches to redefining catchment areas or changing admissions criteria. This has worked particularly well for popular schools. Other schools have managed to change the way in which they are perceived by different communities and, perhaps by outreach work, have convinced under-represented communities that the school 'is for them' – in other words, it is capable of responding sensitively to a broader range of diverse needs.

The problem of mono-cultural schools is often seen as an inner city phenomenon, but this is far from the case and the white mono-cultural schools in suburban and rural areas pose more difficult problems, simply because of the lack of a multicultural population in those areas. A substantial number of white children are therefore growing up in a multicultural country without any direct experience of other cultures, perhaps until they attend university (although university provision remains at well below 50 per cent and itself can be 'colour coded' (Phillips, 2005)). Some further education colleges also offer the possibility of a multicultural intake, and tend to be less clearly related to distinct geographic areas. However, attitudes are often formed at an earlier age and even where colleges offer a mixed intake cross-cultural social patterns can be hard to develop.

The prospect of enforced integration of schools has not been an appetising one and no recent proposals have been put forward to 'bus' children, as in some of the American models. This would be counterproductive and fuel resentment on either side. However, some schools are now responding to the challenge by developing twinning arrangements between schools of different cultures, either within the same city or area, or even between different parts of the country. Many local authorities now have some school twinning arrangements in place, generally at primary level, though presently limited to a handful of schemes. However, Oldham has now twinned over 50 schools (iCoCo, 2006a) and is attempting to extend the arrangement to parental networks to try to ensure that the objectives are supported and that the good work done at school to build cross-cultural understanding and friendships is not undone at home. Bradford has evaluated its 'school linking' programme (Raw, 2006), which is also extensive and has demonstrated how successful such schemes can be. Ministers recently responded positively to the recommendation for a national school twinning programme from the Commission on Integration and Cohesion (CIC, 2007, p. 115) though, as yet, there seems to have been little appreciation of the resource requirements and the need to ensure that such programmes are given real prominence alongside so many other pressing requirements, particularly in respect of the target focussed attainment agenda faced by schools. To be successful, twinning programmes also have to be complemented, in some cases at least, by the introduction of joint teaching programmes and shared extra-curricular activities, and especially by cross-community parental links, in the hope that the boundaries are gradually broken down and the confidence to integrate is developed over time.

The educational community in Britain has a relatively good record in relation to inclusion generally. They have been particularly active in breaking down segregated education on the grounds of disability and learning difficulty and recognise, in this respect, that,

> segregated education is a major cause of society's widespread prejudice ... desegregating special education is therefore a crucial first step in helping to change discriminatory attitudes. (Centre for Studies on Inclusive Education, 2004)

However, they have been slow to recognise the continuing and, in some cases, worsening, nature of segregation along ethnic lines in British schools and to apply the same principles.

The government has responded in small ways by encouraging Admissions Forums to consider cohesion, requesting Local Education Authorities (LEAs) to relate school-building programmes to wider objectives and by requiring faith schools to consider more inclusive intakes and admit children from other faiths and of no faith (Deputy Prime Minister, 2004). From 2002, the national curriculum was amended to include citizenship education, and was intended to broaden children's horizons, and promote wider understanding and respect for others. Although some schools rose enthusiastically to the new challenge, it appeared to have had a limited impact. The Government therefore set up a Review under Sir Keith Ajegbo and his report *Diversity and Citizenship* (Ajegbo, 2007) appears to provide a new way forward and signal a new determination to tackle the problem. The Ajegbo Report made a wide range of recommendations, most of which were practically based. This included reviewing the curriculum, building links with local communities to explore the local context, developing teacher training and providing new resources. The Report also recommended the development of the 'Who Do We Think We Are' project to 'excite schools to get involved' and 'a focus on a whole school exploration of identities, diversity and citizenship' (ibid., p. 13).

More general advice on community cohesion was also slow to emerge – and to get the full backing of the relevant Department of State. In the absence of this, the Independent Community Cohesion Panel's Education Practitioner Group developed more detailed guidance on the problems of mono-cultural schools and prepared a 'community cohesion standard' (Home Office, 2004c), which covered intake and school composition; the ways in which the schools can foster cross-cultural contact in the wider community and; the representativeness of staff, their multicultural skills and their ability to act as role models. It was adopted by government, albeit with relatively weak support and with little by way of real exposure and promulgation. However, the Government has now introduced a 'duty to promote community cohesion' on all state maintained schools with effect from September 2007, as part of the Education and Inspections Act 2006 and guidance has been issued by the Department of Children, Schools and Families (DCFS, 2007) to support practice. The Guidance set out an approach based upon three principal strands:

Teaching, learning and curriculum – helping children and young people to learn to understand others, to value diversity whilst also promoting shared values, to promote awareness of human rights and to apply and defend them, and to develop the skills of participation and responsible action – for example through the new 'Identity and Diversity: living together in the UK' strand within citizenship education.

Equity and excellence – to ensure equal opportunities for all to succeed at the highest level possible, striving to remove barriers to access and participation in learning and wider activities and working to eliminate variations in outcomes for different groups.

Engagement and extended services – to provide reasonable means for children, young people, their friends and families to interact with people from different backgrounds and build positive relations, including: links with different schools and communities; the provision of extended services; and opportunities for pupils, families and the wider community to take part in activities and receive services which build positive interaction and achievement for all groups.

However, the Guidance also draws attention to the nature of the school's population and whether it serves multicultural or monocultural communities and the impact of local community tensions and wider societal impacts and states:

all children and young people can benefit from meaningful interaction, schools will need to consider how to give their pupils the opportunity to mix with and learn with, from and about those from different backgrounds. (DCFS, 2007, p. 1)

In the light of the earlier discussion about growing school segregation (see Chapter 3) this perhaps remains the biggest challenge – and whether to engineer intercultural dialogue through twinning and other special arrangements, or to facilitate natural integration in schools and communities. The CIC hints at the need 'to mainstream integration and cohesion' (CIC, 2007, p. 115) through the plans to re-build all schools, but did not attempt to spell out the implications of this policy and local areas are left to develop their own approaches.

Support to voluntary and community organisations

There has been increasing recognition that the way in which different sections of the community are supported can sometimes inadvertently reinforce, rather than reduce, ethnic, faith and cultural divisions. 'Single Group Funding' was first questioned in *The End of Parallel Lives?* (Cantle, 2004) in which some benefits were also recognised. It had been justified largely on the basis of providing resources to disadvantaged groups, to ensure that they have leadership and advocacy acting on their behalf; that they had access to public services on a more equal basis, as they were better able to identify and fill in any gaps in mainstream provision; and that they could protect their own heritage. The special provision policy – one which has existed for many years – appeared to become an end in itself and has now come to be regarded as somewhat counterproductive as it tends to create an acceptance that the mainstream provision can remain inflexible and insensitive to minority needs. Others have argued that single group funding (also called single identity funding) was partly responsible for a model of multiculturalism which reinforced separation and militated against bridge building between communities (Hussain *et al.*, 2007).

Certainly, the provision of resources to distinct communities has helped to create a group of community leaders who feel obliged to cling to separate funding in order to safeguard their position as much as to protect their community's interests. 'Capacity building' resources are often provided to new communities for the very necessary reason of ensuring that, as a group, they can fully participate in the political process and advance their particular interests, though it may also institutionalise the idea of 'special needs'. Nevertheless, single-group funding has helped to build the confidence of minority groups and, particularly, through the housing association movement, enabled individuals from those minorities to acquire management and organisational skills, which has contributed to leadership competence. The problems and potential of present voluntary organisation approaches and funding is recognised by those involved – for example, 'PeaceMaker' an anti-racist youth development organisation suggests that:

> Often organisations do not know where to begin and in some instances do not see mono-ethnic provision as a hindrance to the development of community cohesion. Parallel Service Provision or Single Group Funding is in most instances detrimental to the development of cohesive communities. It is usually BME groups who view this as an attack on their organisations. (House of Commons, 2004a, p. 34)

and

> single group funding should not simply be seen from a defensive point of view, in essence from black and minority groups, but should be seen as an opportunity for mainstream service providers who had previously failed these communities to change the way they service these communities ... their aim should not simply be to service their own communities it should be to capacity build their communities to access mainstream service provision. (Miah, 2004, ev 90)

The funding of voluntary organisations is beginning to change and, as the impact of mono-ethnic provision is becoming better understood, either in terms of community cohesion, or in terms of the more general role of 'bridging' social capital, so cross-cultural incentive funding is emerging. For example, in Leicester, a Beacon Council for community cohesion, a new 'community cohesion fund' has been set up which will only provide finance on the basis of cross-cultural engagement (Green, 2004). Similarly, the

Northern Ireland Community Relations Council has established a 'cultural diversity grant scheme' which provides support to organisations who develop opportunities 'to extend knowledge and understanding of other cultures', to 'challenge stereotypes of other communities', to 'develop networks of communication, trust and co-operation between divided communities' and to 'increase the ability and confidence of groups to identify and address those issues that divide them' (Community Relations Council, 2004). The government has also begun to recognise the extent of separation inherent in the arrangements and now wants community centres to 'cater for a range of cultural groups rather than separate centres for different groups' (Deputy Prime Minister, 2004, p. 17). In addition, for the very practical and pragmatic reasons of having several hundred identifiable communities in London and over 100 in other major cities, the cost of supporting and catering for separate representation from so many different communities is creating real pressure for more sharing of resources. Many local authorities, other agencies and the voluntary and community organisations themselves are carrying out reviews of existing provision with a view to developing a much greater degree of shared provision and collaboration.

The recent CIC Report *Our Shared Future* (CIC, 2007) has strongly supported the current direction of this debate and declared that 'funding to community groups should be re-balanced towards those that promote integration and cohesion' and believe that 'Single Group Funding' should be the exception rather than the rule for both government and external funders (ibid., p. 160). The CIC believe that in those exceptional cases where single group funding continues, the reasons for it have to be explicit and whenever funding is renewed the organisation has to be able to 'clearly demonstrate the progress the organization has made in becoming more outward-facing' (ibid., p. 163). They also recommend that guidance is drawn up for grant-making bodies to guide future decisions on a consistent basis. This recommendation has been largely accepted by government (Blears, 2007).

The future role of voluntary organisations should be central to the development of community cohesion, for a number of reasons. First, the statutory agencies have had less experience of working with communities at an informal level and have traditionally seen their role as one of service provider, rather than addressing psychological needs of communities. The statutory sector may also be more likely to encounter resistance to 'state interference' in the personal realm and their interventions may also be viewed with concern about motivation, which may be seen as 'political'. However, politicians are also unlikely to rush into this area, seeing it as unimportant and 'dismissing activists in civil society as naive or unwilling to get involved in the messy compromises of real politics' (McCartney, C., 1999, p. 47). Politicians also seemed reluctant to recognise the potential of such work and to invest in anything more than short-term initiatives. The voluntary sector has often had to provide the innovation and drive to get schemes off the ground and has only been supported in certain areas such as those which attempt to develop integration in schools in Northern Ireland (ibid.) and in the area of youth work more generally (Miah, 2004, ev 90).

The statutory sector has in any event been complicit in the separate funding streams and also actively encouraged it on occasion, sometimes as part of local political negotiations, in which support from one community or another has been solicited in exchange for the provision of specific services or funding of particular facilities. Further, the statutory sector appears to have no better record of cross-cultural engagement with regard to those services which are concerned with community development, for example, in youth work and cultural programmes.

There is a sense, then, in which the statutory sector finds it convenient to support a particular style of leadership in the voluntary and community sector. It is simply very much more convenient to work through a small number of leaders, who can speak on behalf of their community and to channel all communications through one point. Some community leaders also, it has to be said, favour a controlling 'gatekeeper' style, with most of the power and authority vested in themselves, effectively making decisions on behalf of their community. This is even more the case where their community has a deferential respect for community leaders and elders and where the organisation's finances, including their salaries, depend upon their position being maintained. Other community leaders have a much more democratic and open style and offer themselves as 'gateways' to their community, attempting to empower community members, encouraging them to become autonomous and able to represent their own interests. In this model, community leaders, earn respect and are open to re-selection, constantly keeping in touch with their community and welcoming accountability. In addition, 'gateway' leaders are much more likely to get beyond the 'usual suspects' and encourage women and younger people to develop their own representative voices and structures. Cohesion programmes, therefore, also need to consider the impact on intra-community leadership and association and to encourage and incentivise more democratic and open styles.

Other public services and policy areas

These include health and social care, sports, leisure and cultural programmes, employment and community safety and policing. Advice and guidance has been provided by the LGA, with the support of government departments and the CRE in respect of all these areas, on two occasions (LGA *et al.*, 2002, 2004) and it generally stresses the need to tackle inequalities, improve cross-cultural work and develop better communications and trust with all sections of the community.

The development of a consistent standard of neighbourhood policing to build points of contact and mutual trust has been seen as of particular importance (Cantle, 2001; ACPO/Centrex, 2005). The role of sports and arts, as both a relatively safe place to explore notions of difference and to use the 'universal language' that sports programmes in particular provide is beginning to be recognised. *The Power of Sport* (iCoCo, 2006) for example provides both a clear policy direction and a number of practical examples of the way in which sport initiatives can be used to build bridges between communities. The Department of Culture, Media and Sport has also been developing a number of 'pathfinder' programmes which again indicate the way in which cultural and sporting programmes can foster intercultural dialogue (DCMS, 2007).

In some areas, other agencies have taken the lead and developed innovative new schemes. For example, in respect of employment, Blackburn with Darwen Strategic Partnership has created the concept of 'Investor in Cohesion', a toolkit for employers to achieve cohesion in the workplace (Blackburn with Darwen Strategic Partnership, 2004). This emphasises the need for the employer to understand the make-up of the workforce in terms of language, faith and background and urges them to consider their different needs. Training and development, the tackling of inequalities and cross-cultural programmes are also encouraged. There has been little by way of national initiatives, as yet, to help break down the pattern of stereotypical patterns of employment and to use the workplace as a means of developing 'bridging' social capital and cross-cultural contact in the workplace and in the wider community. This may take time to develop and is likely to follow on from the more widespread use of local initiatives like Blackburn's.

The recent influx of Eastern European migrants into the UK has, however, focussed attention on employers in several respects and with regard to cohesion, one in particular – the use of the English language. Employers are attracting many seasonal workers, for example in the 'picking, plucking and packing' areas of harvesting soft fruit and processing of other foods. They have also attracted many longer-term workers such as residential and care home workers, bus drivers, hotel and catering staff and many other service industry workers, even by advertising or recruiting directly in countries like Poland. However, the language skills of such staff have often been lacking, with a consequent inability to understand health and safety instructions, give customers appropriate information and understand their own employment rights (with many suggestions that minimum wage levels being undercut). The cost of providing English language lessons has then fallen upon the state, or upon the individual themselves. The CIC has now recommended that 'employers should offer English classes for new migrants' (CIC, 2007, p. 72). This is closely connected to the development of the citizenship agenda and the CIC also emphasised the need for English to become much more widely accepted as a common language to ensure wider participation in democratic debate and participation and therefore, as 'fundamental to integration and cohesion' (ibid.). However, they also suggested a much wider and more pro-active role for employers and that they should 'promote understanding of different cultures and groups by providing cultural training in the workplace' (ibid.)

Positive communications and the role of the press and media

The failure of the press and media to understand the issues and to develop a supportive approach to multiculturalism has been identified as a component of both local and national misconceptions of the 'other', particularly by focussing on negative pictures of asylum seekers and black and ethnic minority communities (Cantle, 2001; Ouseley, 2004). That is not to say that all sections of the press and media have a poor understanding of the issues, nor lack commitment to multiculturalism, as the editor of the Leicester Mercury and the Head of Regional Affairs of Carlton Television have demonstrated, in their evidence to a House of Commons Select Committee (House of Commons, 2004). Guidance is again available and the LGA's *Community Cohesion – An Action Guide* refers to several toolkits and case studies (LGA *et al.*, 2004). The approaches set out in these guides attempt to preserve the freedom of the press whilst ensuring that extremist views do not dominate reporting; that there is a positive view of diversity and that rumours and myths are not perpetuated. More proactively, the press and media can play a role in dispelling such myths, and by improving their communication channels with all sections of the community can widen their networks and develop a strong business case for promoting a more positive and inclusive portrayal of black and ethnic minorities.

Local authorities and other statutory agencies are beginning to develop much more pro-active strategies and are better able to respond to rumours and misinformation, which in the past, have given rise to community tensions, disorder and riots. A communications 'toolkit' has been developed (iCoCo, 2006b) with a range of techniques and good practice ideas to develop a wider 'sense of belonging', provide positive messages about diversity in the local community, in a spirit of openness and transparency about the key challenges and, with the help of a separate but related document, how to counter myths and misinformation (LGIU, 2006). Good communications, based upon up to date intelligence about community concerns, is clearly essential if tensions and conflicts are to be prevented (see below).

The far right and those other groups, including religious extremists, that spread hatred and seek to undermine community harmony need to be countered – they are communicating all the time, through their own networks and undermining the positive messages that seek to bring communities together and promote respect and understanding. Clearly this is easier to undertake where there is a political consensus (see below) and where there is a broad moral climate of opinion which is supported by a range of local partners, including employers, faith leaders, sports stars, celebrities and all parts of local civil society, who see it as their role to communicate through their own channels and spheres of influence.

The role of leaders

A great deal has already been said about the failure of leadership at all levels and the ambivalence of leaders in the run up to the riots in 2001. The political vacuum meant that it was relatively easy for the extreme right wing organisations to dominate the debate, to demonise minorities, to spread myths and misinformation and to undermine the value of multiculturalism in the area.

Cross-party protocols have now been established by mainstream political leaders in many local areas, with agreement to defend multiculturalism and the minority communities against ill-informed and prejudiced views. However, more needs to be done to improve understanding and to build the capacity of political leaders, through an ongoing training and development programmes. This could also be applied to the political parties themselves, even before candidates are selected. Indeed, it should perhaps be a requirement to undertake such training before seeking public office, to improve the chances that political representatives are much more familiar with multicultural communities. The same requirement could be made in respect of senior officials in central and local government and the various agencies supported directly and indirectly by them. It is also possible to argue that, given the general and specific legislative requirements of public bodies in respect of pursuing equal opportunities, preventing discrimination and promoting good race and community relations, membership of an extreme political organisation which is not committed to such aims is incompatible with public service.

The role of leaders, particularly in the present context of governance, where 'influence' is regarded as being as important as direct power, must be to work through partnerships and alliances. Certainly, it will be essential for such alliances to help create an over-arching vision, which is capable of uniting different communities and ensuring that tolerance and respect for difference is at the heart of that vision. This commitment should also translate into more formalised requirements for the preparation and implementation of local community cohesion strategies for all areas (within a broader-based local community plan) under which performance is clearly managed. The lack of a clear steer from government, as to whether local authorities, or some other local agency or combination of them, is expected to 'manage settlement' of newcomers and address the social and psychological needs of the host community should not prevent local authorities from attempting to assume this role – it can only be in the interest of the local area to do so. However, the report of the Commission on Integration and Cohesion in mid-2007 recommended a new national agency to oversee this role and it is possible that the Government will accept this recommendation or at least, develop a more proactive national function in this regard.

However, the expertise and skills of the leaders and the various agencies for which they are responsible are not yet fully developed and much of the expertise in this area resides in the equal opportunities dimension of cohesion, rather than in the rest of the agenda. There are signs that these agencies are now able and willing to adapt and take on a very much enlarged and more proactive role in respect of cohesion. Also, at a local level, the 'champions of change' are beginning to be established, with many Local Strategic Partnerships (LSPs) in which all principal agencies work together to develop a strategy for the local area. They have become action orientated establishing cohesion sub-groups, with clear programmes and plans led by appointed 'champions'. Racial Equality Councils (where they exist) are also increasingly helping to promote community cohesion, though none have clear responsibilities and accountabilities and their future is less than certain following the demise of the CRE. Local authorities have increasingly accepted a 'community leadership' role but there is little by way of an agreed meaning behind the concept and still a real question about whether this should include programmes which are intended to change attitudes and shape values. They will certainly need support and encouragement – and practical help – to take forward the values debate and ensure that cross-cultural work is the norm in schools, in the workplace and in social and recreational spheres. Cross-cultural contact is essential, for changing attitudes and values to ensure that positive interaction between different communities takes place, but requires a reasonable level of new skills and has to be carefully 'engineered'. And because it is still new, the local and national institutions and the various professional bodies that underpin them will have a tendency to revert to more familiar and established patterns of work, based on single cultures. However, as barriers are broken down and our institutions increasingly reflect multicultural patterns, it will become easier and more natural to create change and take bolder decisions.

Monitoring and review

The scope and coverage of community cohesion has gradually been exemplified by both subsequent guidance and proposals for measurement and monitoring. Objective indicators form part of the proposals put forward in the Home Office publication, *Building a Picture of Community Cohesion* (Home Office *et al.*, 2004). These include the number of racist incidents or attacks in the local area and levels of deprivation of different communities. The proposals, however, also include subjective indicators, based on the perception of local residents, gained by survey techniques, for example 'the percentage of people who feel that local ethnic differences are respected'; 'the percentage of people who feel that their local area is a place where people from different backgrounds can get on well together'; and 'the percentage of people from different backgrounds who get on well with people from other backgrounds'. It was intended that these be measured over time to enable trends to be established, and, indeed, the perceptions of people themselves about the state of community relations has become increasingly significant with the CIC basing its positive conclusion on the state of community cohesion on this indicator:

> The national picture is a positive one – perceptions of cohesion are good in most areas – on average 79% of people agreed that people of different backgrounds got on well in their local area and the level of agreement fell below 60% in only ten out of 387 local areas. (CIC, 2007, p. 8)

This perception is encouraging though as it is drawn at a local authority level it can mask some very real difficulties within the smaller constituent parts of an authority's area and different perceptions by minority communities. Local authorities are of course able to develop a finer grained picture for themselves, monitor trends and use other information to augment this indicator. They are also able to track changes in response to community cohesion programmes which they develop and establish a clearer idea of 'what works'.

The Government recently indicated that it is to extend the number and range of 'perception indicators' (HMG, 2007), by establishing a new Public Service Agreement (PSA), which is intended to condition the work of a number of central government departments, as well as local government and other agencies, upon a wider range of cohesion targets. In addition to the indicator 'how well people think they get on with others from different backgrounds' two more will be added: the extent of 'meaningful interaction with people of different backgrounds' and whether people feel that they 'belong to their neighbourhood'.

The number and range of indicators could and should be extended to provide a much finer grained analysis. Wood *et al.* (2006) proposes a wider view of 'openness and interculturalism' based upon how well and often different communities mix; how easy it is for people to move between different communities and institutional networks; and the extent of co-operation and collaboration between people from different cultural and ethnic backgrounds. Their indicators include broader notions of societal cultural mixing, including diversity in the 'retail offer', the extent of public art that draws upon different cultural traditions, as well as more straightforward – and perhaps obvious, though far from agreed measures – such as intermarriage.

A citizenship survey in 2005 (DCLG, 2005) hinted at an additional set of indicators, in which social relationships would be taken into account, especially in relation to cross-cultural mixing. The survey gave details of the number of people who had friends from different backgrounds to themselves (which was 50 per cent in overall terms, though 90 per cent of black people had such friendships compared to 47 per cent for whites). The survey also gave details of the extent and nature of social capital and the perceptions of rights and responsibilities, which would have to be included in the revised definition of community cohesion recently proposed by the Commission on Integration and Cohesion (CIC, 2007).

At a broader level, community dynamics need to be better understood and mapped. There is little by way of monitoring trends in segregation and integration in the residential environment and school population, for example, and the government has shown little inclination to monitor these and similar trends, as recommended in the report of the Community Cohesion Panel (Cantle, 2004). Nevertheless, this can be done at a local level, with benchmarks established so that comparisons with other areas can be made.

The challenge of monitoring and reviewing the state of cohesion and anticipating trends is severely hampered by the lack of up to date and reliable population data. Keeping track of the size and diversity of local populations is clearly key to understanding the variety of needs, being able to respond appropriately with resources, as well as ensuring that potential disputes and conflicts are managed. Practice has been developing since the Institute of Community Cohesion developed its COHDMAP project in 2005, which was developed into proposals to assist local agencies to better estimate their local populations in-between the decennial census dates, using a number of local sources from schools, health agencies, social housing providers and other sources (iCoCo, 2006c). However, the problem appeared to become more urgent as the wave of EU migration developed and a number of local authorities and other local service providers became concerned about coping with increasing and unquantified demands and a mismatch between the resources which they had been allocated by central government and the amount that they would have received if the population estimates provided by central government agencies had more accurately reflected the demands upon them. A second iCoCo report provided an assessment of the scale of the difference between actual and estimated local populations and the impacts upon local services (iCoCo, 2007) and noted, in particular

> ... our governmental and administrative processes have not kept pace with the change. Our data sources are inadequate at both the national and local level and we are unable to respond to increased demands for public services and to anticipate trends and developments. Further, whilst the economic gains at the national level are significant, the mechanisms to identify and allocate resources to the local level are clearly insufficient, perhaps leading to unnecessary tensions and conflicts. (iCoCo, 2007, p. 12)

A key feature of population mapping has been the link with local perceptions about community relations and the ability of local agencies, often led by the police service, to monitor and anticipate community tensions for which iCoCo has developed a 'toolkit' in conjunction with the Metropolitan Police (iCoCo, 2007a).

A local authority performance framework will have a number of dimensions. One of these is that of 'scrutiny' by backbench councillors. A guide has also been provided (LGIU, 2005) to underpin the scrutiny function and to provide a level of challenge to help ensure that each local authority has a realistic vision in place, with an action plan capable of supporting it.

However, it is unfortunately the case that external agencies – particularly inspectorates are more often responsible for engendering change in local authorities and raising performance levels. Councils are subject to a Comprehensive Performance Assessment, or CPA, which rates them from 'excellent' to 'poor' and this includes a key number of performance measures. This is soon to be replaced by the Comprehensive Area Assessment, or CAA, which whilst providing for more locally determined priorities will remain a significant 'test' for local authorities. The introduction of community cohesion within the performance framework is already beginning to further concentrate the minds of local authorities. The Audit Commission is the lead body for inspections but a number of other agencies are also involved and from 2008, the OFSTED inspectorate will have a particularly important role in assessing the new school 'duty to promote community cohesion'. Local Authority Agreements (or LAAs) are also driving change and represent an agreement, generally over three years, between central and local government as to local priorities. The framework now includes the possible introduction of community cohesion and, like other areas, is essentially target driven. Councils and local partners are also increasingly recognising the importance of the agenda. The need to promote harmonious community relations is self-evident. But the damage done by a riot or disturbance goes well beyond the cost of physical repairs and severely tarnishes the reputation of a whole town or city and can deter investment and visitors. Economic self-interest is, therefore, a key driver of the cohesion agenda.

Conflict prevention, resolution and reconciliation

Much of the initial investment in community cohesion to date has followed on from localised conflicts, or has been developed in order to prevent similar conflicts in other towns and cities. As the local and central government strategy has become clearer, however, cohesion has become more widely used as a new approach to improving tolerance and acceptance of diverse groups and promoting equalities and integration. This will allow more investment to be put into prevention rather than remediation and will enable communities to develop more positive relations from the start, instead of the more difficult task of re-building them after they break down. A new tension monitoring 'toolkit' (iCoCo, 2007a) is designed to enable local agencies to 'get upstream' and prevent tensions building up and developing into conflicts and general disorder.

Much of the work done to resolve conflicts and re-build relations tends to reinforce the tenets of community cohesion and is based upon breaking down barriers by promoting interaction and removing structural inequalities and injustices. The United States Department of Justice Community Relations Service, for example, advocates the setting up of local 'human relations commissions' as a means of helping communities to resolve disputes and conflict based on racial discrimination and denial of equal rights (U.S. Department of Justice, 1998). The Community Relations Service (CRS), which was set up in 1964 as the Federal Government's 'Peacemaker' for community conflicts and tensions claims to have successfully dealt with hundreds of conflicts each year in all of the US states and territories (U.S. Department of Justice, 2003).

The conflicts generally arise from 'hate crimes' involving acts of violence and intimidation against individuals and small groups of people which escalate into community-wide tensions. The CRS advocate a range of actions to resolve the conflict and improve community relations:

- establishing a clear commitment by the local government of the area to tackle 'hate crime', through the passing of an ordinance;
- creating local coalitions from business, civic, religious and voluntary organisations to create a positive climate and encourage dialogue;
- encouraging responsible reporting by the press and media;
- mediation and conciliation programmes, including work in schools;
- communication and interaction between majority and minority groups ('often a key factor in preventing tensions and restoring harmony');

(U.S. Department of Justice, 2001).

The involvement of third party *mediation* is often crucial to the process of resolving conflicts. Whilst it has been used extensively by the CRS, it has had only limited use in England as part of the programme of community cohesion, generally with funding from the government's Neighbourhood Renewal Unit (NRU). In Oldham, it has been developed as a key part of their 'Building Good Relations' project (Oldham MBC, 2004b, p. 25) using the charity MNI to facilitate the work. The work of the mediator is also, it seems, to retrospectively apply the principles of community cohesion. It involves enabling the two parties to get into a relationship, (using a neutral space and a neutral mediator), which can develop to the point that they can transcend their own position and think creatively about new relationships, even if this only amounts to reaching an accommodation about how order is maintained and further violence prevented, in the first instance (O'Reilly, 2004).

Coleman and Deutsch (1998) emphasise the skill of the mediator in creating an effective working relationship between both sides and its ability to create a problem-solving attitude in parties to school-based conflict. They also emphasise the need for the mediator to have a good understanding of the conflict and be tuned to the misunderstandings, ethnocentrism, the stereotypes and real cultural distinctions embodied in both groups. However, the quality of the mediator and the mediation process may not, in itself, be sufficient. The pre-existing notions of the 'other', the power relationship and the willingness to engage in a peacemaking arrangement are also fundamental (see 'inter-ethnic conflict' below).

The concept of *truth and forgiveness* has gradually gained credibility and been developed as a possible instrument of reconciliation in those areas facing the most deep-seated and long-term inter-ethnic conflicts. Fourteen countries have established Truth Commissions, or similar bodies (Chapman, 2002, p. 257), the most notable of which is in South Africa. Truth-finding may be regarded, by some, as a means of coming to terms with the past and paving the way to reconciliation, even though it may be painful and divisive in the short term; it can promote unity and understanding and transcend the conflict and divisions of the past (Ibid.).

The 'truth and forgiveness' methodology may not be transportable and may have limited relevance to relatively small-scale conflicts based on ethnic or faith differences in modern democracies. However, it does emphasise the need to address the social–psychological needs of communities:

The immediacy of hatred and prejudice, of racism and xenophobia, as primary factors and motivators of the conflict require approaches that are rooted in the social-psychological and spiritual dimensions that traditionally have been seen as either irrelevant to or outside the competency of international diplomacy. (Leaderach, J.P., 1993, p. 12)

The methodology is also founded on the principles of openness and honesty and the creation of real dialogue across the wider community with a view to establishing new values, based on understanding and consensus. The concept of 'forgiveness' is tied very closely to religious thought and to Christianity in particular and this may well limit the applicability of this approach, with aggrieved groups, or nations, preferring simply to 'forget' rather than to attempt to forgive. However, it may also be that the failure of peacemaking attempts and to create more collaborative partnerships and change behaviour of those involved, is simply due to inability of the various agencies to deal with 'the wounds, feelings and deeply rooted perceptions of the victimized sides' (Botcharova, 2002). A wider acceptance of the value of addressing these needs in some form or another also seems to be emerging through the use of the formal public apology. This has been used in a range of circumstances, for example, in Oregon a 'Day of Acknowledgement' was held in 1999 to mark the 150th anniversary of legislation excluding blacks from the State; the City of Liverpool in England expressed regret for its role in the slave trade in the same year; and in Richmond, Virginia a history project drew attention to its racial past and recognised historic sites that had previously been denied or ignored (Henderson, 2002, p. 267).

Many of the acts of forgiveness, however, are at the interpersonal level, often in the private realm and dependent upon some form of contact between victim and perpetrator. They may also be dependent upon personal beliefs about justice and morality, and, whilst they do not condone what has been done, they may facilitate a sense of healing for those involved (The Forgiveness Project, 2004). There are potentially wider benefits from 'socio-political forgiveness', when a whole group engages in the forgiveness process. This takes place in the domain of a conflictual inter-group relationship, rather than an interpersonal one and may contribute to improving relationships simply by acknowledging the past wrongs and, ostensibly, making a commitment to building new relationships based on a new sense of honesty and trust (Montiel, 2002, p. 271).

Just as community cohesion depends upon wider engagement of the population, Botcharova (2002, p. 283) points out that successful peacemaking goes beyond traditional concepts of ceasefire and top-level negotiations. Sustainable transformation of conflict requires inter-community relationships to change through the 'reconciliation of the common people'. Building those relations may, however, take many years, and Leaderach (1997) has emphasised the need for 'decade thinking', especially where the conflict has festered over many years.

The 'truth and forgiveness movement', however, tends to focus on inter-personal relationships and 'justice' and is often conceived in terms of individual wrongdoing, atonement and reparation – often with immunity from prosecution. Community cohesion, whilst also seeking to build cross-cultural relationships, emphasises the different levels of association (in the workplace, in schools, in neighbourhoods) and the sense of belonging for all communities and it also seeks to address basic inequalities. As Chapman (2002, p. 275) points out, the South African experience does not appear to have prompted the white community into coming to terms with the injustice of the apartheid system and has not yet resulted in a significant redistribution of resources from whites to blacks and a more equitable social and economic system.

The emerging practice of tackling deep-seated and violent *inter-ethnic conflict* in a range of countries, mostly other than modern western democracies, also has some useful analogies with community cohesion, even though the scale of the more recent tragedies like the Balkans, Rwanda and Sudan is completely different.

In the first place, conflict and divisions may have become so institutionalised that the power and position of leaders and stakeholders may actually depend upon the continuation of the conflict. Varshney (2002, p. 150) compares two areas, in the history of Hindu–Muslim politics in India, one with an 'institutionalised riot system' and the other with an 'institutionalised peace system'. Varshney also points out that even the press and media can be part of the institutionalised problem, as riots and conflicts make 'hot news' and good copy, whereas the quiet continuation of everyday life does not (ibid., p. 297).

Further, if each community has a demonised view of the other, it is possible that this will be reinforced by contact, rather than diminished. Initial encounters will be prejudiced by the misinformation and myths that will inevitably be the only 'known' information about the other. This may be broken down over time, but only if a more balanced picture of each other is allowed to emerge. However, the demonisation of each other's communities may not be such a big obstacle as it first appears, if it has no real ownership in either community and has been fuelled by extremists and general propaganda generated externally to both groups. The 'race riots' in Bradford, Burnley and Oldham in 2001 and some of the earlier race riots in Britain, were certainly fed by the extreme right and were not based on any enduring antagonisms and conflicts between the different groups. Whilst each group was wary of the other and suspicious about contact, it has not proved to be difficult to create opportunities for face to face contact and to explode some of the earlier myths and misconceptions. By contrast, in Northern Ireland, where divisions between the two communities have been based on deep-seated enmity and where enduring and bitter struggles on an everyday basis have persisted over many years, the opportunities are more limited. It has not proved possible to bring the two communities together to discuss and resolve differences in the same way, but common ground has been found by using environment improvement schemes as a neutral activity to get communities working together in a limited way (Groundwork, 2003, ev 60).

The context in which cross-cultural contact takes place will, in any event, always be important and few communities can isolate themselves from the external environment in which good community relations may be either fostered or undermined. This may include the reported statements of civic and community leaders, the balance between local celebrations of culture and inter-cultural distance and the general climate created by formal and informal communications, such as rumours and banter at local football matches.

The general level of education, again both formal and informal, and the extent to which people from either community are able to 'imagine the other person' may also be important (Scarry, 1998, p. 40). This will depend upon whether each community has a homogenised view of the world, in which the 'other' is seen as a foreigner. Scarry suggests that 'generous imaginings', for example, because of exposure to different conceptions of people through literature, would greatly assist the elimination of 'inherently aversive structural positions'.

At a more immediate and practical level, Amir (1998) suggests a number of principles that seem to evolve from the studies of contact between ethnic groups, which he has reviewed. Whilst noting that there is increasing evidence to support the contention that contact does change attitudes, he is cautious about the validity of some of the findings and whether the same results will always be found in real social situations. He concludes, however, that prejudice is likely to be reduced where both groups have a similar status, or the status of the minority group is higher and where the contact is pleasant

LIBRARY UNIVERSITY OF CHESTER

and rewarding. He also confirms that where the general climate is in favour of promoting inter-group relations and that the interaction is in respect of functionally important activities, or in support of the development of over-arching goals, success is more likely. When these conditions are not met he believes prejudice could be strengthened. Amir's pragmatism and caution is sensible although the handbook in which it was published suggests that, in overall terms, the case for 'ethnic coexistence work' is sufficiently strong to advocate its professionalisation.

This is proposed on the basis that:

> Co-existence work thus tends to concentrate neither on the deep psychological level nor on the macro-societal, political, and economic levels. It does not pretend to resolve either deep-seated, long-lasting hatreds or fundamental, structural injustice. Co-existence work goes on where ethnic enemies actually interact: in the street, in neighbourhoods, in institutions of higher learning, in hospitals, in sports clubs, in business enterprises, in community groups, in religious organizations … . Thus, co-existence work is activist, pragmatic, incremental – and hopeful.

And, perhaps, more tellingly, that:

> Helping people to see the human face of others is an indispensable prelude to humane action. (Weiner, E., 1998, pp. 13 and 15)

Community cohesion programmes are 'helping people to see the human face of others'. But they also aim to tackle injustices, to ensure that everyone has a stake in society and to build a real sense of belonging based upon a new model of multiculturalism, in which difference is valued within a strong framework of inter-connectedness and commonality.

LIBRARY, UNIVERSITY OF CHESTER

Bibliography

Adorno, T.W., et al. (1950) The Authoritarian Personality (New York: Harper and Row).

Ajegbo, Sir K. (2007) Diversity and Citizenship (London: Department for Education and Skills).

Age Concern (2004) House of Commons Select Committee on Social Cohesion. Sixth Report of Session, Vol. 2 (London: The Stationery Office).

Aldridge, D. and Halpern, S. (2002) Social Capital: A Discussion Paper (London: Performance and Innovation Unit, Cabinet Office).

Algerant, R. (2004) letter to The Times 3 February 2004.

Alibhai-Brown, Y. (2000) Beyond Multiculturalism (London: Foreign Policy Centre).

Alibhai-Brown, Y. (2004) in the Evening Standard 1 September, 2004.

Allender, P., and Quigley, A. (2005) Challenging Hate Crime in Coventry (Coventry: Coventry University).

Allport, G.W. (1954) The Nature of Prejudice (Cambridge, MA: Addison-Wesley).

Amir, Y. (1998) 'Contact Hypothesis in Ethnic Relations', in The Handbook of Interethnic Co-existence, Weiner, E. ed. (New York: The Continuum Publishing Company).

Ansari, H. (2004) 'The Infidel Within', Muslims in Britain Since 1800 (London: Hurst & Co).

Association of Chief Police Officers (ACPO)/Centre for Policing Excellence (Centrex) (2005) Professionalising the Business of Neighbourhood Policing (ACPO/Centrex).

Association of Metropolitan Authorities (1985) Housing and Race: Policy and Practice in Local Authorities (London: AMA).

Association of Metropolitan Authorities (AMA) (1987) Contract Compliance the Fair Deal, Report of National Conference 9 December 1986 (London: AMA).

Audit Commission (2007) Crossing Borders, Responding to the Challenges of Migrant Workers (London: Audit Commission).

Back, L. and Solomos, J. (1996) Racism and Society (London: Macmillan).

Baldwin, C., Chapman, C and Gray, Z. (2007) Minority Rights: The Key to Conflict Prevention (London: Minority Rights Group International).

Banton, M. (1977) The Idea of Race (London: Tavistock Publications).

Barry, B. (2001) Culture and Equality: An Egalitarian Critique of Multiculturalism (Cambridge MA: Harvard University Press).

Baubock, R. (2002) 'Liberal Pluralism Under Attack', in Cohesion, Community and Citizenship (London: The Runnymede Trust).

Baubock, R. (2003) 'Farewell to Multiculturalism? Sharing Values and Identities in Societies of Immigration', Equal Voices, Issue 12, May 2003 (Vienna: EUMC).

Baumann, Z. (1995) Life in Fragments (Oxford: Blackwells).

Bertossi, C. (2002) 'Republican Citizenship, Equality and the French Dilemma', in Cohesion, Community and Citizenship (London: The Runnymede Trust).

Billig, M. (1995) Banal Nationalism (London: Sage).

Billig, M., Deacon, D., Downney, J and Richardson, J. (2006) 'Chilly Brittania?' in Catalyst Magazine May–June 2006.

Blackaby, B. (2004) Community Cohesion and Housing. A Good Practice Guide (Coventry: Chartered Institute of Housing and the Housing Corporation).

Blackburn with Darwen Strategic Partnership (2004) Investor in Cohesion (Blackburn: Strategic Partnership).

Blair, T. (2004) Speech to the Confederation of British Industry, 27 April 2004, London.

Blair, T. (2004a) Speech to Business and the Environment Programme, September 2004, London.

Blears, H. (2007) Letter from Hazel Blears, Secretary of State for Communities and Local Government to Darra Singh, 5 October 2007.

Bloomfield, J. and Bianchini, F. (2004) *Planning For The Intercultural City* (Stroud: Comedia).

Blunkett, D. (2001) *Politics and Progress: Renewing Democracy and Civil Society* (London: Politico's Publishing).

Blunkett, D. (2003) *Civil Renewal: A New Agenda* (London: Home Office).

Blunkett, D. (2004) *New Challenges for the Race Equality and Community Cohesion* in the 21 Century, Speech to the Institute of Public Policy Research, 7 July 2004 (Home Office).

Blunkett, D. (2005) *A New England: An English Identity Within Britain*, speech on the 14 March 2005 (London: Institute of Public Policy and Research).

Bodi, F. (2002) in *The Guardian*, 1 July 2002.

Bonney, R. *et al.* (2003) *Integrated Cities: Exploring the Cultural Development of Leicester* (Leicester: University of Leicester).

Botcharova, O. (2002) 'Implementation of Track Two Diplomacy', in *Forgiveness and Reconciliation*, Helmick, S.J. and Petersen, R.L. eds (Philadelphia and London: Templeton Foundation Press).

Bourne, J. (2007) *In Defence of Multiculturalism*. IRR Briefing Paper No. 2 (London: Institute of Race Relations).

Bragg, M. (2003) *The Adventure of English* (London: Hodder and Stoughton).

Brimicombe, A. (2007) Ethnicity, Religion and Residential Segregation in London: Evidence From A Computational Typology of Minority Communities. Environment and Planning, Vol 34, pp. 884–204 (London: Environment and Planning).

British Council (2006) *Making a World of Difference* (London: British Council).

Brown, G. (2004) Speech to the British Council, 7 July 2004.

Brown, R. (1995) *Prejudice* (Oxford: Blackwell).

Brubaker, R. (2005) 'The "Diaspora" Diaspora', in *Ethnic and Racial Studies*, Vol. 28, No. 1 (London: Routledge).

Burgess, S. Wilson, D. and Lupton, R. (2004) *Parallel Lives and Ethnic Segregation in the Playground and the Neighbourhood*, CMPO Working Paper No 04/094 (Bristol: CMPO).

Burnett, J. (2004) 'Community Cohesion and the State', in *Race and Class*; Vol. 45, No. 3 (London: Institute of Race Relations/Sage Publications).

Burnett, J and Whyte, D., (2004) 'New Labour's New Racism'. IRR News, 10 October 2004.

Cantle, T. (2001) *Community Cohesion: A Report of the independent Review Team* (London: Home Office).

Cantle, T. (2004) *The End of Parallel Lives?: Final Report of the Community Cohesion Panel* (London: Home Office).

Cantle, T. (2007) ' "Race" and Community Cohesion' in *Sociology Review*, Vol. 16, No. 3, February 2007.

Carling, A. (2006) *What Myth? Racial and Ethnic Segregation, the Index Wars and the Future of Bradford* (Bradford).

Cashin, S. (2004) *(The Failures of) Integration: How Race and Class are Undermining the American Dream* (New York: Public Affairs).

Castles, S. and Miller, M. (1993) *The Age of Migration* (Basingstoke: MacMillan).

Castles, S. (1997) 'Multicultural Citizenship: The Australian Experience', in *Citizenship and Exclusion*, Bader, V. ed. (England: MacMillan Press).

Central Statistical Service (1974) *Social Trends No. 5* (London: HMSO).

Centre for Studies on Inclusive Education (2004) *The Inclusion Charter* (Bristol: University of West of England).

Children and Young Persons Unit (CYPU) (2002) *Colour Blind: What it Means to be British in the 21st Century* (London: CYPU).

Chapman, A.R. (2002) 'Truth Commissions as Instruments of Forgiveness and Reconciliation', in *Forgiveness and Reconciliation*, Helmick, S.J. and Petersen, R.I.. eds (Philadelphia and London: Templeton Foundation Press).

Chartered Institute of Housing (2003) *Offering Communities Real Choice—Lettings and Community Cohesion* (Coventry: CioH).

Cheshire, P. (2007) *Segregated Neighbourhoods and Mixed Communities* (York: JRF).

Clarke, T. (2001) *Burnley Speaks, Who Listens?* (Burnley: Burnley Borough Council).

Coleman, P.T. and Deutsch, M. (1998) 'The Mediation of Interethnic Conflict in Schools', in *The Handbook of Interethnic Co-existence*, Weiner, E. ed. (New York: The Continuum Publishing Company).

Coles, M.I. (2004) *Education and Islam: A New Strategic Approach* (Leicester: SDSA).

Commission on Integration and Cohesion (CIC) (2007) *Our Shared Future* (London: CIC).

Commission on Integration and Cohesion (CIC) (2007a) *'What Works' in Community Cohesion* (London: CIC).

Commission on Integration and Cohesion (CIC) (2007b) *Integration and Cohesion Case Studies* (London: CIC).

Commission for Racial Equality (CRE) (2002) *The Voice of Britain* (London: CRE).

Commission for Racial Equality (CRE) (2002a) *A Place For Us All* (Manchester: CRE).

Commission for Racial Equality (CRE) (2002b) *Getting Results: A New Approach to Funding Local Racial Equality Work* (London: CRE).

Commission for Racial Equality (CRE) (2004) *Strength in Diversity: Towards a Community Cohesion and Race Equality Strategy. A Response* (London: CRE).

Commission for Racial Equality (CRE) (2004a) *Connections* (CRE: Spring 2004).

Commission for Racial Equality (CRE) (2004b) reported in *The Guardian* 19 July 2004.

Commission for Racial Equality (CRE) (2005) *Promoting Good Race Relations—A Guide For Public Authorities* (London: CRE).

Commission for Racial Equality (CRE) (2007) *A Lot Done, A Lot to Do; Our Vision for an Integrated Britain* (London: CRE).

Commission for Racial Equality (CRE) (2007a) *Regeneration and the Race Equality Duty: Report of a Formal Investigation in England, Scotland and Wales* (London: CRE).

Community Relations Council (CRC) (2004) *Community Relations and Cultural Diversity Grant Scheme* (Belfast CRC).

Community Services Volunteers (2004) *'Citizenship in the Curriculum Two Years On'*, in *The Guardian*, 14 September 2004.

Cornell, S. and Hartmann, D. (1998) *Ethnicity and Race: Making Identities in a Changing World* (London: Pine Forge Press).

Crick, B. ed. (2001) *Citizens: Towards a Citizenship Culture* (Oxford: Blackwell).

Crick, B. (2003) 'The New and the Old', *The Report of the Life in the United Kingdom Working Party* (London: Home Office).

Daniel, W.W. (1968) *Racial Discrimination in England* (England: Penguin Books).

Daniels, J. and Houghton, V. (1972) 'Jensen, Eysenck and the Eclipse of the Galton Paradigm', in *Race, Culture and Intelligence* (Middlesex: Penguin).

Darby, J. (1986) *Intimidation and the Control of Conflict in Northern Ireland* (Dublin: Gill and MacMillan).

Denham, J. (2001) *Building Cohesive Communities: A Report of the Ministerial Group on Public Order and Community Cohesion* (London: Home Office).

Department of Canadian Heritage (2003) *Annual Report on the Operation of the Canadian Multiculturalism Act 2001–2002* (Ontario: Department of Canadian Heritage).

Department for Children, Schools and Families (2007) *Guidance on the Duty to Promote Community Cohesion* (London: DCSF).

Department for Communities and Local Government (DCLG) (2005) *2005 Citizenship Survey: Community Cohesion Topic Report* (London: DCLG).

Department for Communities and Local Government (DCLG) (2006) *Improving Opportunity, Strengthening Society—One Year On* (London: DCLG).

Department for Communities and Local Government (DCLG) (2006a) *Local Government White Paper Strong and Properous Communities. Cmnd 6939–1* (London: DCLG).

Department for Communities and Local Government (DCLG) (2007) *Improving Opportunity, Strengthening Society—Two Years On* (London: DCLG).

Department for Communities and Local Government (DCLG) (2007a) *Preventing Violent Extremism—Winning Hearts and Minds* (London: DCLG).

Department for Communities and Local Government (DCLG) (2007b) *Preventing Violent Extremism, Pathfinder Fund 2007–08: Case Studies* (London: DCLG).

Department for, Culture, Media and Sport (DCMS) (2004) *Bringing Communities Together Through Sport and Culture* (London: DCMS).

Department for Culture, Media and Sport (DCMS) (2007) *Changing Lives and Places, Lessons for Cultural Pathfinders* (London: DCMS).

Deputy Prime Minister and First Secretary of State (2004) *Government Response to the ODPM Select Committee Report on Social Cohesion*, Cm 6284 (London: The Stationery Office Ltd).

Dorling, D. and Rees, P. (2003) *A Nation Still Dividing: The British Census and Social Polarisation 1971–2001* (Leeds: University of Leeds).

Dozier, R.W. (2002) *Why We Hate* (New York: Contemporary Books).

Entzinger, H. (1994) 'A Future for the Dutch "Ethnic Minorities" Model?', in *Muslims in Europe* (London: Pinter Publishers).

European Monitoring Centre on Racism and Xenophobia (EUMC) (2002) *Racism and Xenophobia in the EU Member States: Trends, Developments and Good Practice* (London: EUMC).

European Monitoring Centre on Racism and Xenophobia (EUMC) (2003) *Equal Voices*, August, Issue 13 (Vienna, EUMC).

Ferlander, S. and Timms, D. (1999) *Social Cohesion and On-Line Community* (Luxembourg and Brussels: European Commission and Centre for Research and Development in Learning Technology, Stirling University).

Fineberg, A. (2004) *Growth Coalitions and Community Cohesion*, www.growthcoalitions. org.uk.

Foot, P. (1969) *The Rise of Enoch Powell* (Middlesex: Penguin Books Ltd).

Foreign Policy Centre (2005) European Civic Citizenship and Inclusion Index (Begium: British Council).

Forrest, R. and Kearns, A. (2000) *Social Cohesion, Social Capital and the Neighbourhood*. Paper presented to ESRC Cities Programme Neighbourhoods Colloquium, Liverpool, 5–6 June.

Fukuyama F. (1999) *Social Capital and Civil Society*, Seminar paper prepared for the IMF Conference as Second Generation Reforms, October 1999.

Furbey, R., Dinham, A., Farnell, R., Finneron, D. and Wilkinson, G. (with others) (2006) *Faith as Social Capital, Connecting or Dividing?* (York: JRF).

Gagnon, F. and Pagé, M. (1999) *Conceptual Framework for an Analysis of Citizenship in the Liberal Democracies: Volume 1: Conceptual Framework and Analysis* (Ontario: Department of Canadian Heritage).

Glazer, N. (1997) *We Are All Multiculturalists Now* (Harvard: Harvard University Press).

Giddens, A. (2002) *Runaway World: How Globalisation is Reshaping our Lives* (London: Profile Books Ltd).

Giddens, A. (2004) *Challenging Social Capital*, conference report of The Global Exchange Forum (London: Barrow Cadbury Trust and The Foreign Policy Centre).

Gilroy, P. (1992) *There Ain't No Black in the Union Jack* (London: Routledge).

Glover, S. *et al.* (2001) *Migration: An Economic and Social Analysis*, RDS Occasional Paper No. 67 (London: Home Office).

Goodhart, D (2004) 'Too Diverse?', in *Prospect* magazine, February 2004 (London).

Goodhart, D. (2004a) 'Diversity Divide', in *Prospect* magazine, April 2004 (London).

Goodhart, D. (2006) *Progressive Nationalism: Citizenship and the Left* (London: Demos).

Goulbourne, H. (1998) *Race Relations in Britain Since 1945* (Basingstoke: Palgrave MacMillan).

Green, R. (2004) 'Have Faith in Diversity', *Local Government Chronicle*, September 2004.

Griffith, P. and Leonard, M. (eds) (2002) *Reclaiming Britishness: Living together after 11 September and the rise of the Right* (London: The Foreign Policy Centre).

Grigg, M. (1967) *The White Question* (London: Secker & Warburg).

Groundwork (2003) *Evidence to the House of Commons Select Committee on Social Cohesion ODPM: Housing, Planning, Local Government and the Regions Committee, Social Cohesion: Written Evidence* (London: The Stationery Office Ltd).

Hansen, R. (2003) 'Migration to Europe since 1945: Its History and its Lessons', in *The Politics of Migration*, Spencer, S. ed. (Oxford: Blackwell).

Harrison, H. (2005) 'From Community Cohesion to an Inclusion and Co-operation Agenda' in *Housing, Race and Community Cohesion*, Harrison *et al.* (Oxford: Chartered Institute of Housing).

Harsman, B. (2006) 'Ethnic Diversity and Spatial Segregation in the Stockholm Region', *Urban Studies* Vol. 43, No. 8.

Henderson, M. (2002) 'Acknowledging History as a Prelude to Forgiveness', in *Peace Review*, Vol. 14, No. 3, Sept. 2002.

Hewstone, M., Cairns, E., Voci, A. Hamberger, J. and Neins, U. (2006) 'Intergroup Contact, Forgiveness and Experience of the Troubles in Northern Ireland', *Journal of Social Issues* 62 (1), 99–120

Hewstone, M., Paolini, S., Cairns, E., Voci, A. and Harwood, J. (2006a) 'Intergroup Contact and the Promotion of Intergroup Harmony', in *Social Identities: Motivational, Emotional, Cultural Influences*, Brown R. J. and Capozza, D. eds (Hove, England: Psychology Press).

HM Government (HMG) (2007) Public Service Agreement 21, *Building Cohesive, Empowered and Active Communities* (London: HMG).

Home office (1975) *Racial Discrimination*, Government White Paper cm 6234 (London: HMSO).

Home Office (2002) *Secure Borders, Safe Haven: Integration With Diversity in Modern Britain*, Government White Paper Cm 5387 (London: The Stationery Office Ltd).

Home Office and Vantagepoint (2003) *The Pathfinder Programme* (London: Home Office).

Home Office and Office Deputy Prime Minister (2003a) *Community Cohesion Advice for Those Designing, Developing and Delivering Area Based Initiatives (ABIs)* (London: Home Office).

Home Office (2003b) *2001 Home Office Citizenship Survey: People, Families and Communities* (London: Home Office).

Home Office (2004) *Strength in Diversity: Towards a Community Cohesion Strategy* (London: Home Office).

Home Office *et al.* (2004a) *Building a Picture of Community Cohesion* (London: Home Office).

Home Office and Office Deputy Prime Minister (2004b) *Building Community Cohesion into Area Based Initiatives* (London: Home Office).

Home Office (2004c) *Community Cohesion Standards for Schools* (London: Home Office).

Home Office (2005) *Improving Opportunity, Strengthening Society: The Government's strategy to increase race equality and community cohesion* (London: Home Office).

Horowitz, D. (1983) 'Racial Violence in the United States', in *Ethnic Pluralism and Public Policy*, eds Glazer and Young (Lexington: Lexington Books).

House of Commons (1981) Fifth Report of the Home Affairs Select Committee 1980–81 Vol. 1, *Racial Disadvantage* (London: HMSO).

House of Commons Select Committee (1975) *The Organisation of Race Relations Administration* (London: HMSO).

House of Commons (2003) ODPM: Housing, Planning, Local Government and the Regions Committee, *The Effectiveness of Government Regeneration Initiatives*, Vol. 2 (London: The Stationery Office Ltd).

House of Commons (2004) ODPM: Housing, Planning, Local Government and the Regions Committee *Social Cohesion, Sixth Report of Session 2003–04, Vol. 2* (London: The Stationery Office Limited).

House of Commons (2004a) ODPM: Housing, Planning, Local Government and the Regions Committee, *Social Cohesion, Sixth Report of Session, Vol. 1* (London: The Stationery Office Ltd).

House of Commons (2005) Home Affairs Committee *Terrorism and Community Relations* Sixth Report of Session 2004–05, Vol. 1 (London: The Stationery Office Limited).

Howe, D. (2004) 'Turning on Each Other', in *The Guardian*, 5 August 2004.

Hudson, L. (1972) 'The Context of the Debate', in *Race, Culture and Intelligence* (Middlesex: Penguin).

Huntingdon, S.P. (2002) *The Clash of Civilisations and the Making of the World Order*, (London: Simon & Schuster).

Husband, C. (1994) 'The Political Context of Muslim Communities' Participation in British Society', in *Muslims in Europe* (London: Pinter Publishers).

Hussain, A., Law, B. and Haq, T. (2007) *The Intercultural State: Citizenship and National Security* (Leicester: East Midlands Economic Network).

Hussain, D. (2004) 'British Muslim Identity' in *British Muslims Between Assimilation and Segregation*, Seddon M.S., Hussain, D. and Malik, N. eds (Leicester: The Islamic Foundation).

Hutchinson, J. (2000) 'Ethnicity and Modern Nations', in *Ethnic and Racial Studies* Vol. 28, No. 4 (London: Routledge Journals).

Iceland, J. (2002) *Beyond Black and White: Metropolitan Residential Segregation in Multi-ethnic America* (Washington DC: US Census Bureau).

Improvement and Development Agency for Local Government (IDeA) (2002) *Taking Forward Community Cohesion in Leicester* (London: IDeA).

Improvement and Development Agency for Local Government (IDeA) (2003) *The Councillor's Guide 2003/4* (London: IDeA).

Information Centre about Asylum and Refugees in the UK (ICAR) (2004) *Understanding the Stranger* (London: ICAR).

Institute of Community Cohesion (iCoCo) (2006) *The Power of Sport—Policy and Practice: Sport and Cohesion* (Coventry: iCoCo).

Institute of Community Cohesion (iCoCo) (2006a) *Challenging Communities to Change: A Review of Community Cohesion in Oldham* (Coventry: iCoCo).

Institute of Community Cohesion (iCoCo) (2006b) *A Sense of Belonging, The Communications Toolkit* (Coventry: iCoCo).

Institute of Community Cohesion (iCoCo) (2006c) *Cohesion Mapping of Community Dynamics (COHDMAP)*(Coventry: iCoCo).

Institute of Community Cohesion (iCoCo) (2007) *Estimating the Scale and Impacts of Migration at the Local Level* (London: Local Government Association).

Institute of Community Cohesion (iCoCo) (2007a) *Understanding and Monitoring Tension in Local Communities* (London: Local Government Association).

Institute of Community Cohesion (iCoCo) (2007b) *Promoting Sustainable Communities and Community Cohesion* (Leeds: ASC).

Institute of Community Cohesion (iCoCo) (2007c) *New European Migration, A Good Practice Guide for Local Authorities* (London: Improvement and Development Agency for Local Government).

Jenkins, R. Speech to the meeting of Voluntary Liaison Committees, London, 23 May 1966.

Johnson, R., Burgess, S., Wilson, D. and Harris, R. (2006) *School and Residential Ethnic Segregation: An Analysis of Variations Across England's Local Education Authorities* CMPO paper 06/145 (Bristol: Bristol University).

Joshua, H., Wallace T. with Booth, H. (1983) *To Ride the Storm—The 1980 Bristol Riot and the State* (London: Heinemann).

Karim, K.H. (1996) *The Definition of Visible Minority: A Historical Analysis* (Ontario: Department of Canadian Heritage).

Keane, J. (1998) *Civil Society: Old Images, New Visions* (Cambridge: Polity).

Khan, H., and Muir, R. eds (2006) *Sticking Together, Social Capital and Local Government* (London: The London Borough of Camden and IPPR).

King, O. (2004) House of Commons debate on social cohesion 21 October 2004, *Hansard* (London: House of Commons).

Kundnami, A. (2002) *An Unholy Alliance? Racism, Religion and Communalism* (London: IRR).

Kymlicka, W. (1995) *Multicultural Citizenship, A Liberal Theory of Minority Rights* (Oxford: Clarendon Press).

Kymlicka, W. (2003) 'Immigration and the Politics of National Opinion', in *The Politics of Migration*, Spencer, S. ed. (Oxford: Blackwell).

Leaderach, J.P. (1993) *Pacifism in Contemporary Conflict: A Christian Perspective*, Paper to the U.S. Institute of Peace, 1993.

Leaderach, J.P. (1997) *Building Peace: Sustainable Reconciliation in Divided Societies* (Washington, DC: Institute of Peace).

Leith, B. (2002) *What Makes a Society Cohesive?* Speech to a Colloquium 7 May 2002 (London: Institute of Social Cohesion).

Lemos, G. (2004) *Community Conflict: Causes and Action* (London: Lemos and Crane).

Lemos, G. (2004a) *The Search for Tolerance: Challenging and Changing Racist Attitudes and Behaviour Among Young People* (York: Joseph Rowntree Foundation).

Leonard, M. and Griffith, P. (2003) *The European Inclusion Index: Is Europe Really Ready for the Globalisation of People?* (London: The Foreign Policy Centre and British Council).

Lewis, B. and Schnapper, D. (eds) (1994) *Muslims In Europe* (London: Pinter Publishers).

Lewis, G. (2005) 'Welcome to the Margins: Diversity, Tolerance and Policies of Exclusion', in *Ethnic and Racial Studies*, Vol. 28, No. 3 (London: Routledge).

Lieberson, S. and Silverman, A. (1965) 'The Precipitants and Underlying Conditions of Race Riots', *American Sociological Review*, 31, No. 2, December 1965.

Lloyd, J. (2003) 'The Closing of the European Gates? The New Populist Parties of Europe', in *The Politics of Migration* (London: Blackwell).

Local Government Association (LGA), Office of the Deputy Prime Minister, Home Office, Commission for Racial Equality and the Inter Faith Network (2002) *Guidance on Community Cohesion* (London: LGA Publications).

Local Government Association (LGA), Home Office, ODPM, CRE, The Audit Commission, The IDeA, The Inter-Faith Network (2004) *Community Cohesion— An Action Guide* (London: LGA Publications).

Local Government Association (LGA) and Improvement and Development Agency (IDeA) (2005) *Leading Cohesive Communities: A Guide for Local Authority Leaders and Chief Executives* (London: LGA).

Local Government Information Unit (LGIU) (2005) *Scrutiny of Community Cohesion Issues* (London: LGIU).

Local Government Information Unit (LGIU) (2006) *Countering Myths and Misinformation During Election Periods* (London: LGIU).

London Borough of Hounslow (2003) *Community Cohesion in Hounslow: Meeting the Challenge* (London: LBH).

London Borough of Tower Hamlets (2003) *Community Cohesion in Tower Hamlets* (London: LBTH).

Lynch, R. (2001) 'An Analysis of the Concept of Community Cohesion', in *Community Cohesion: A Report of the Independent Review Team* (London: Home Office).

Macmaster, N. (2001) *Racism in Europe* (Hampshire: Palgrave).

Malik, K. (1998) *Hate Thy Neighbour: The Dividing Lines of Race and Culture, Mindfield*, No. 1 (London: Camden Press).

Malik, K. (2001) 'The Changing Meaning of Race', paper to dayschool on *The Reinvention of Race*, Oxford University Department of Continuing Education, 22 September 2001.

Malik, K. (2002) 'The Real Value of Diversity', in *Connections*, Winter 2002 (London: CRE).

Malik, K. (2002a) 'Against Multiculturalism', in *New Humanist*, Summer 2002 (London: Rationalist Press Association).

Marquand, D. (1991) 'Civic Republicans and Liberal Individualists: The Case for Britain', in *The European Journal of Sociology* XXXII, No. 2 (Cambridge: Cambridge University Press).

Marshall, T.H. (1950) *Citizenship and Social Class and Other Essays* (Cambridge: Cambridge University Press).

Martin, S. (2003) 'The Politics of US Immigration Reform', in *The Politics of Migration*, Spencer, S. ed. (Oxford: Blackwell).

McCandless, F. (2004) Evidence to the House of Commons Select Committee on Social Cohesion, p. EV 94–97 (London: The Stationery Office Ltd).

McCartney, C. 'The Role of Civil Society', in *Accord*, Issue 8, 1999.

McGlade, J. (2007) interviewed in *Prospect* magazine, September 2007.

McGlynn, C., Neins, U., Cairns, E. and Hewstone, M. (2004) 'Moving Out Of Conflict: The contribution of integrated schools in Northern Ireland to identity, attitudes, forgiveness and reconciliation', *Journal of Peace Education*, Vol. 1, No. 2, September 2004.

Mc Ghee, D. (2003) 'Moving to our common ground—a critical examination of community cohesion discourses in twenty-first century Britain', in *The Sociological Review*, Vol. 51, No. 3.

Meyer, T. (2001) *Identity Mania: Fundamentalism and the Politicization of Cultural Differences* (London: Zed Books).

Miah, R. (2004) in evidence to the House of Commons Select Committee on Social Cohesion, *Sixth Report of Session 2003–04, Vol. 2* (London: The Stationery Office Limited).

Micklethwait, J. and Wooldrige, A. (2004) *The Right Nation: Why America is Different* (Allen Lane: London).

Middlesbrough BME Network (2007) *Vital Connections*, Issue 5, Summer 2007 (Middlesbrough: Middlesbrough Network, 2007).

Ministry of Housing and Local Government, Welsh Office (1969) *Council Housing Purposes, Procedures and Priorities* (London: Her Majesty's Stationery Office).

Ministry of Public Works and Government Services Canada (2001) *Canadian Citizenship*, Information Pack (Ottawa: MPWGS).

Minority Rights Group International (MRGI) (2007) *Minority Rights: The Key to Conflict Prevention* (London: MRGI).

Modood, T. (1988) ' "Black", Racial Equality and Asian Identity', *New Community*, XIV 3.

Modood, T. (2003) 'Muslims and the Politics of Difference', in *The Politics of Migration* (Oxford: Blackwell Publishing).

Modood, T., Beishon, S. and Virdee, S. (1994) *Changing Ethnic Identities* (London: Policy Studies Institute).

Molyneux, M. (2004) *Gender and the Silences of Social Capital*, Conference Report of The Global Exchange Forum (London: Barrow Cadbury Trust and The Foreign Policy Centre).

Montiel, C.J. (2002) 'Sociopolitical Forgiveness', in *Peace Review*, Vol. 14, No. 3 September 2002.

National Statistics (2004) *Social Trends No. 34* (London: The Stationery Office Ltd).

Nesdale, D. and Flesser, D. (2001) 'Social Identity and the Development of Children's Group Attitudes', in *Child Development 72*.

Northern Ireland Council for Voluntary Action (NICVA) (2004) House of Commons Select Committee on Social Cohesion, *Sixth Report of Session 2003–04, Vol. 2* (London: The Stationery Office Ltd).

Oakley, R. (2005) *Promoting Roma Integration at the Local Level* (London: European Dialogue).

Office of the Deputy Prime Minister (ODPM) and Improvement and Development Agency (IDeA) (2003) *Service Improvement Through Beacons, Round Four Annual Report* (London: ODPM and IDeA).

Office of the Deputy Prime Minister (2003a) *Sustainable Communities: Building for the Future* (London: ODPM).

Office of the Deputy Prime Minister (2003b) *Housing Signpost: A Guide to Research and Statistics*, Issue 17 (London: ODPM).

Office of the Deputy Prime Minister (2004) *Making it Happen: The Northern Way* (London: ODPM).

Office of the Deputy Prime Minister (2006) *The State of English Cities, A Research Study, Volume 2*, (London: ODPM).

Office of National Statistics (ONS) (2003) *Census 2001* (London: ONS).

Office of National Statistics (ONS) (2004) *Focus on Ethnicity and Identity* (London: ONS).

Office of National Statistics (ONS) (2006) Report of the Inter-departmental Task Force on Migration Statistics (London: ONS).

Official Journal of the European Union (OJEU) (2006) L412/44 30 December 2006 (Brussels: EU).

Oldham Metropolitan Borough (2004) presentation to Community Cohesion Action Learning Summit, London, 2 November 2004.

Oldham Metropolitan Borough (2004a) House of Commons, ODPM; Housing, Planning, Local Government and the Regions Committee on Social Cohesion, *Sixth Report of Session 2003–04, Vol. 2* (London: The Stationery Office Limited).

Oldham Metropolitan Borough Council (2004b) *Forward Together: Building Community Cohesion in Oldham, Impact and Outcomes* (Oldham: Oldham MBC).

Optimum Population Trust (OPT) (2004) *OPT Population Projections and Policy* (Manchester: OPT).

O'Reilly, P. (2004) Mediation Northern Ireland, presentation to the *Community Cohesion: Action Learning Summit*, 2 November 2004.

Orwell, G. (1957) 'England Your England', in *Selected Essays* (Middlesex: Penguin Books).

Ouseley, H. (2001) *Community Pride not Prejudice* (Bradford: Bradford Vision).

Ouseley, H. (2004) in *The Guardian*, 10 April 2004.

Page B. (2004) 'The Death of Liberal England?', *Local Government Chronicle*, 9 September 2004.

Pahl, R.E. (1995), 'The Search for Social Cohesion: From Durkheim to the European Commission', in *The European Journal of Sociology*, XXXII, No. 2 (Cambridge: Cambridge University Press).

Pannell, N. and Brockway, F. (1965) *Immigration: What is the Answer?* (London: Routledge & Kegan Paul).

Parekh, B. (2000) *The Future Of Multi-Ethnic Britain* (London: Profile Books) revised edition 2002.

Parekh, B. (2002) 'Common Belonging', in *Cohesion, Community and Citizenship* (London: The Runnymede Trust).

Patterson, S. (1969) *Immigration and Race Relations in Britain 1960–67* (London: Oxford University Press).

Pattie, C., Seyd, P., and Whiteley, P. (2004) *Citizenship in Britain* (Cambridge: Cambridge University Press).

Peach, C., Robinson, V. and Smith, S. (eds) (1981) *Ethnic Segregation in Cities* (London: Croom Helm Ltd).

Perry, J. and Blackaby, B. (2007) *Community and Cohesion and Housing, A Good Practice Guide* (Coventry: CIoH and Housing Corporation).

Pettigrew, T.F. (1998) 'Intergroup Contact Theory', in *Annual Review of Psychology*, Vol. 49.

Phillips, D. (2005) 'Housing Achievements, Diversity and Constraints' in *Housing, Race and Community Cohesion*, Harrison *et al.* (Oxford: Chartered Institute of Housing).

Phillips, T. (2004a) Interview in *The Times*, 3 April 2004.

Phillips, T. (2004b) Quoted in *The Times*, 10 April 2004.

Phillips, T. (2004c) Annual Martin Luther King Memorial Lecture, 17 January 2004, London.

Phillips, T. (2005) Speech to the Manchester Community Relations Council, 22 September 2005.

Pike, M. (2004) *Community Service Agreements: A New Approach to Public Service Delivery* (London: The Scarman Trust).

Pilkington, A. (2003) *Racial Disadvantage and Ethnic Diversity in Britain* (Basingstoke: Palgrave MacMillan).

Pinto and Green (2004) 'Community Cohesion: What's That?', in *Young People Now*, 27 October–2 November.

Poppe, E. and Linssen, H. (1999) 'In-group Favouritism and the Reflection of Realistic Differences ... etc.', *British Journal of Psychology* 38.

Poulsen, M. (2005) *The 'New Geography' of Ethnicity in Britain?* Paper to the Royal Geographic Society in London, 31 August 2005.

Proceedings of a Runnymede Conference (2002) *Cohesion, Community and Citizenship* (London: The Runnymede Trust).

Putnam, R.D. (1995) *Journal of Democracy*, Vol. 6, No. 1, January 1995.

Putnam, R.D. (2000) *Bowling Alone: the Collapse and Revival of American Community* (New York: Simon & Schuster).

Putnam, R.D. (2007) 'E Pluribus Unum: Diversity and Community in the Twenty First Century'. The 2006 Johan Skytte Prize Lecture, *Scandinavian Political Studies Journal* 30 (2) 137–74.

Rachedi, N. (1994) 'Elites of Maghrebin Extraction in France', in *Muslims in Europe* (London: Pinter Publishers).

Ratcliffe, P. (2001) *Breaking Down the Barriers: Improving Access to Social Rented Housing* (London: Chartered Institute of Housing).

Ratcliffe, P. (2004) *'Race', Ethnicity and Difference* (Berkshire: OUP).

Rattansi, A. (2002) 'Who's British—*Prospect* and the New Assimilationism', in *Cohesion, Community and Citizenship* (London: Runnymede).

Raw, A. (2006) *Schools Linking Project 2005–06: Full Final Evaluation Report* (Bradford: Bradford LEA).

Regional Coordination Unit (2004) *ABI Guidance to Departments* (London: Office of the Deputy Prime Minister).

Rex, J. (1961) *Key Problems Of Sociological Theory* (London: Routledge & Kegan Paul Ltd).

Rex, J. (1972) 'Nature versus Nurture: The Significance of the Revived Debate' in *Race, Culture and Intelligence* (Middlesex: Penguin).

Rex, J. and Moore, R. (1967) *Race, Community and Conflict* (Oxford: Institute of Race Relations).

Richards, M., Richardson, K. and Spears, D. (1972) 'Intelligence and Society', in *Race, Culture and Intelligence* (Middlesex: Penguin).

Ritchie, D. (2001) *Oldham Independent Review: One Oldham, One Future* (Manchester: Government Office for the North West).

Rocker, S. (2004) 'Fraternity Eases the Religious and Political Divide', *The Times*, 11 September 2004.

Rogers B. 'Explaining Apathy' in *Prospect*, October 2003.

Rose, E.J.B. and Associates (1969) *Colour and Citizenship: A Report on British Race Relations* (London: Oxford University Press).

Royal Town Planning Institute/Commission for Racial Equality (1983) *Planning for a Multi-Racial Britain* (London: CRE).

Runciman, W.G. (1995) 'Are There Any Irrational Beliefs?', in *European Journal of Sociology* XXXII (Cambridge: Cambridge University Press).

Saggar, S. (2002), 'Ethnic Minorities and the Labour Market', in *Reclaiming Britishness* (London: Foreign Policy Centre).

Sandercock, L. (2004) 'Integrating Immigrants: the challenge for cities, city governments and the city-building professionals', in *Intercultural City Reader* (Stroud: Comedia).

Sandercock, L. (2004a) 'Reconsidering Multiculturalism: towards an intercultural project', in *Intercultural City Reader* (Stroud: Comedia).

Sardar, Z. (2004) 'Can Islam Change?' *New Statesman*, 13 September 2004.

Scarman, Lord (1981) *The Scarman Report* (London, HMSO).

Scarry, E. (1998) 'The Difficulty of Imagining Other Persons', in *The Handbook of Interethnic Co-existence*, Weiner, E. ed. (New York: The Continuum Publishing Company).

Scottish Centre for Research on Social Justice (SCRSJ) (2004) *Building Bridges: Local Responses to the Resettlement of Asylum Seekers in Glasgow* (Glasgow: University of Glasgow).

Secretary of State for the Home Department (1975) *Racial Discrimination*, White Paper Cmnd 6234 (London: HMSO).

Secretary of State for Justice and Lord Chancellor (SoSJLC) (2007) *The Governance of Britain* CM 7170 (London: HMSO).

Simpson, L. (2003) *Statistics of Racial Segregation: Measures, Evidence and Policy*, Occasional Paper No. 24 (Manchester: University of Manchester).

Simpson, L., Ahmed, S. and Phillips, D. (2007) *Oldham and Rochdale: Race, Housing and Community Cohesion* (Manchester: University of Manchester).

Smith, L. (2006) 'Absent Voices' in *The Guardian*, 6 September 2006.

Social Exclusion Unit (SEU) (2004) *Tackling Social Exclusion: Taking Stock and Looking to the Future* (London: ODPM).

Solomos, J. (2003) *Race and Racism in Britain* (Hampshire: Palgrave Macmillan).

Solomos, J. and Back, L. (1996) *Racism and Society* (Hampshire: Macmillan Press Ltd).

Soysal, Y.N. (2000) 'Citizenship and Identity: living diasporas in post-war Europe', in *Ethnic and Racial Studies*, Vol. 23, No. 1 (London: Routledge).

Spencer, S. ed. (2003) The *Politics of Migration: Managing Opportunity, Conflict and Change* (Oxford: Blackwell).

Spencer, S., Ruhs, M., Anderson, B. and Rogaly, B. (2007) *Migrants Lives Beyond the Workplace. The experiences of Central and Eastern Europeans in the UK* (York: Joseph Rowntree Foundation).

Sriskandarajah, D. (2004) 'Migration Targets' in *Prospect* Magazine, October 2004.

Stalker, P. (2001) *International Migration* (London: New Internationalist Publications Ltd and Verso Books).

Strategy Unit (2003), *Ethnic Minorities in the Labour Market* (London: Cabinet Office).

Tajfel, H. (1970) 'Experiments in Intergroup Discrimination', in *Scientific American 223*.

Taylor, A.J.P. (1965) *English History 1914–1945* (Middlesex: Penguin Books).

Taylor, D. (2004) 'The Ripple Effect' in *The Guardian*, 6 April 2004.

The Communitarian Network (2002) *Diversity Within Unity: A Communitarian Network Position Paper* (Washington, DC: The Communitarian Network).

The Forgiveness Project (2004) *The F Word: Images of Forgiveness* www.theforgiveness project.com.

The Guardian (2004) 26 February 2004.

The Inter-Faith Network for the UK (2004) *Inter Faith Organisations in the UK— A Directory* (London: Inter-Faith Network).

The Minorities of Europe (MoE) (2003) *The Swapping Cultures Initiative* (Coventry: MoE).

The Prime Minister (1965) White Paper *Immigration from the Commonwealth*, Cmnd 2739 (London: HMSO).

The Times (2004) 14 September 2004.

The Times (2004) 27 September 2004.

Tyler, C. (2004) *The Guardian*, 23 March 2004.

United Nations Development Programme (2004) *Human Development Report, Cultural Liberty in Today's Diverse World* (New York: UNDP).

United Nations Population Division (UNDP) (2002) *International Migration Report 2002* (New York).

United Nations Population Division (2002a) International Migration 2002, Wallchart (New York).

University of Newcastle *et al.* (2002) *The Development of a Migration Model* (London: ODPM).

U.S. Department of Justice Community Relations Service (1998) *Guidelines for Effective Human Relations Commissions*. Revised edition, September 1998 (Washington DC: U.S. Dept. of Justice)

U.S. Department of Justice (2001) Hate Crime the Violence of Intolerance in *CRS Bulletin* (Washington DC: US Dept. of Justice).

U.S. Department of Justice (2003) *About the Community Relations Service*, www.usdoj.gov.

Varshney, A. (2002) *Ethnic Conflict and Civic Life: Hindus and Muslims in India* (New Haven & London: Yale University).

Vidal-Hall, J. (2003) 'Leicester: City of Migration' in *Index on Censorship: Migration Now*, Owen, U. ed. (UK: Thanet Press).

Weiner, E. ed. (1998) 'Co-Existence Work; A New Profession', in *The Handbook of Interethnic Co-existence*, Weiner, E. ed. (New York: The Continuum Publishing Company).

Wolfe, A. (2002) 'The Costs of Citizenship: Assimilation and Multiculturalism in Modern Democracies', in *Cohesion, Community and Citizenship* (London: The Runnymede Trust).

Williams, R. (1981) *Culture* (Glasgow: Fontana).

Wilmore, N. (2005) 'Engaging With Young People', *Local Government Chronicle*, 14 April 2005.

Winder, R. (2004) *Bloody Foreigners, The Story of Immigration to Britain* (London: Little Brown).

Wood, P., Landry, C. and Bloomfield, J. (2006) *Diversity in Britain, A Toolkit for Cross-cultural Co-operation* (York: JRF).

Wrench, J. *et al.* (2003) 'Migrants, Minorities and Employment in 15 EU Member States' in *Equal Voices* November 2003 (Vienna: EUMC).

Yeboah, S.K. (1988) *The Ideology of Racism* (London: Hansib Publishing Ltd).

Younge, G. 'Bitter White Whine', in *The Guardian* (26 February 2004).

Zuckerman, P. (2003) *Invitation to the Sociology of Religion* (New York: Routledge).

Index